IN THE SHADOW OF THE CIVIL WAR

Other Books by Nat Brandt

The Man Who Tried to Burn New York

The Town That Started the Civil War

The Congressman Who Got Away with Murder

Con Brio: Four Russians Called the Budapest String Quartet

Massacre in Shansi

Harlem at War: The Black Experience in WWII

Mr. Tubbs' Civil War

When Oberlin Was King of the Gridiron: The Heisman Years

Chicago Death Trap: The Iroquois Theatre Fire of 1903
with John Sexton

*How Free Are We? What the Constitution
Says We Can and Cannot Do*
with Yanna Kroyt Brandt

Land Kills

A Death in Bulloch Parish

IN THE SHADOW
OF THE CIVIL WAR

Passmore Williamson and the Rescue of Jane Johnson

NAT BRANDT with Yanna Kroyt Brandt

The University of South Carolina Press

Published by the University of South Carolina Press
Columbia, South Carolina 29208

www.sc.edu/uscpress

Manufactured in the United States of America

16 15 14 13 12 11 10 09 08 07   10 9 8 7 6 5 4 3 2 1

Library of Congress Cataloging-in-Publication Data

Brandt, Nat.
  In the shadow of the Civil War : Passmore Williamson and the rescue of Jane
Johnson / Nat Brandt with Yanna Kroyt Brandt.
      p. cm.
  Includes bibliographical references and index.
  ISBN-13: 978-1-57003-687-3 (cloth : alk. paper)
  ISBN-10: 1-57003-687-X (cloth : alk. paper)
  1. Williamson, Passmore. 2. Abolitionists—Pennsylvania—Philadelphia—
Biography. 3. Quakers—Pennsylvania—Philadelphia—Biography. 4. Johnson,
Jane, b. 1820? 5. Fugitive slaves—Pennsylvania—Philadelphia—Biography.
6. Williamson, Passmore—Trials, litigation, etc. 7. Slavery—United States—
Legal status of slaves in free states. 8. United States. Fugitive slave law (1850)
I. Brandt, Yanna. II. Title.
  E450.W727B73 2007
  973.7'115092—dc22
  [B]   2006103022

This book was printed on a Glatfelter recycled stock with a 20 percent
postconsumer waste content.

Dedicated to the memory of a dear family friend,
Ruby Lee Stewart Covington

CONTENTS

ILLUSTRATIONS

PREFACE

In the tumultuous nineteenth century, blacks, free and enslaved, fought slavery in any way they could—from subtle sabotage to outright rebellion. In time, white men and women joined in the fight, not necessarily because they had any particular affection for black people, nor even because they believed blacks to be equal. Rather they believed that the concept of one person owning another was inherently evil. But to convince others of that took more than rhetoric. It took what Philadelphia sailmaker James Forten called "an appeal to the heart."[1] It was critical, his fellow black, physician and scholar James McCune Smith said; whites had to shed their own color and acquire instead a black heart, imagining themselves as black, to understand what it meant to be black.[2] As Forten, Smith and other abolitionists black and white discovered, sympathetic and deeply moving descriptions of the inhumane treatment blacks endured, stories of the courage many displayed in order to seek freedom, made converts more readily than antislavery rhetoric did.

The rescue of Jane Johnson and her children became part of that litany of dramas that drew increasing attention in the North to slavery and its human implications. There were other stories as well. Accounts of kidnappings—such as the experience of Solomon Northup, who was snatched from upstate New York and spent eleven years in brutalized servitude. Accounts of escapes—such as that of the ingenious William "Box" Brown, who had himself shipped from Richmond to Philadelphia in a crate. Accounts of desperate slaves—such as Margaret Garner, a runaway who was recaptured and killed her infant daughter rather than have the child grow up in bondage. Accounts of the successful contravention of the Fugitive Slave Law—such as the Jerry Rescue in Syracuse, New York, and that of John Price in Oberlin, Ohio. Accounts of blood shed as slave and southern owners or agents confronted one another—such as at the Christiana Riot and in

the Wilkes-Barre incident; accounts, as well, of the recapture of runaways and the public outrage against slavery that they engendered—
such as that of Anthony Burns in Boston. All these incidents put a
personal face on the moral abstraction of talking about slavery. They
aroused a growing antagonism against slavery in the North and, concomitantly, bitterness in the South at the manner in which its way of
life was being slandered.

Similarly, the rescue of Jane Johnson was symbolically another nail
in the coffin of slavery. It attracted wide attention. More important, it
dramatized many of the issues that led to the Civil War, pitting a free
state not only against the federal government but also against a law
that slave states considered sacrosanct. It created a heroine out of a
black woman who was willing to risk her newfound freedom to aid the
very persons who had helped her. And it created a hero out of a man
who was willing to defy the law and let his conscience be his guide in
order to help a slave achieve freedom.

ACKNOWLEDGMENTS

We are indebted to a goodly number of individuals at repositories of research material in and around Philadelphia—in particular, the staffs of the American Philosophical Society, the Historical Society of Pennsylvania, The Library Company, the Friends Historical Library at Swarthmore College, and the Chester County Historical Society. Their cooperation, and patience, as well as the assistance provided by others, made possible this book. Several of them bear mention by name:

Mark Harwell, American Philosophical Society
Pat O'Donnell, Friends Historical Library, Swarthmore College
William C. Kashatus, Pamela C. Powell and Diane P. Rofini,
    Chester County Historical Society
Sandy Sudofsky, Arch Street Friends Meeting House
Karen Winner, Central Philadelphia Meeting House
Dorothy Rodgers, Genealogical Society of Pennsylvania
Jefferson M. Moak, National Archives and Record Administration,
    Mid-Atlantic Region
Robert J. Plowman, Delaware County Government Archives, Lima
Paula Heiman, Pennsylvania Historical and Museum Commission,
    Harrisburg

We are especially indebted to several experts in their fields who offered not only encouragement but also suggestions as to ways to better the text. They are Phil Lapsansky of the Library Company of Philadelphia, Christopher Densmore of the Friends Historical Library of Swarthmore College, Roland Baumann, archivist of Oberlin College, and Richard Newman of the Rochester Institute of Technology. Any errors or misinterpretations that remain are, of course, ours.

A special word of thanks goes to Shirley Atwood of Virginia Beach, Virginia, who is Passmore Williamson's great-great-great niece. She provided us with a previously unpublished photograph of Williamson as well as news clippings and legal papers dealing with his later life.

The Philadelphia Municipal Archives, on the other hand, had serious problems. Obviously underfunded and understaffed, it was in need of major attention and support, because it contains many valuable archives that had been neglected and/or vandalized. Entire sections of the Moyamensing prison records, for example, were missing or, if available, contained a number of ripped-out pages. A problem for serious researchers delving into Philadelphia history, many documents in this major archive were mostly inaccessible.

IN THE SHADOW OF THE CIVIL WAR

Prologue

More than forty years now and she still couldn't call the clothes on her back her own. More than forty years now and she was still not her own person. Taught to sweep and mop, to make beds and launder. Taught to wait on table, to wash dishes, to polish silver. Taught to care for someone else's babies. Purchased just like you bought a horse or a bolt of cloth or a bushel of potatoes. There'd been a deed of sale. She couldn't even call her two young boys sitting beside her her own. She looked at them. They had been up since before dawn, excited by the train trip from Washington. Tired now, a bit cranky. But she didn't dare get too attached to them. She had just left an even younger child behind, knowing she would probably never see him again.

Her master—that's what she had to call him—her master was taking her far away so that she could serve his wife. Through Philadelphia, he had explained, by ferry across a river to a train depot on the other side, going to New York City, to a ship that would take them to a country where another language was spoken. She so wanted to be free. She was determined to escape. She'd heard talk about runaways who had followed the North Star, who had found freedom. She had even contrived in secret to patch together a disguise. It was in her trunk, being put on the ferry with her master's baggage. Maybe in New York, maybe before they got on the ship, maybe then she would have the opportunity.

She sat, as her master had bidden her, on a bench in the verandah while he went into the hotel dining room to eat. She didn't dare try to bolt. Not with the two youngsters in tow, into a city she'd never been in before, not where she didn't know anyone, wasn't sure who to trust. She had already taken a chance, telling that hotel servant—a black woman like herself—that she wished to be free. What had the woman answered? "I pity you." And that other hotel worker—the black man—what had he said? He'd try to get help for her when the train reached New York. He would wire ahead. Could she really count on that?

Her master was coming down the hallway now from the dining room. It must be time to board the ferry. Would she ever be free?

1

The Chronicler

I hear the voice of Garrison, of Garrison, of Garrison,
I hear the voice of Garrison, loud pleading for the slave;
Set the captive free, set him free, set him free,
Set the captive free from his chains.

"Song for the Times," *Anti-Slavery Harp,* 13

It was "very warm," William Still thought, "intensely hot" in fact for a mid-July day in Philadelphia. Still was wearing a top hat as a shield against the blazing late-afternoon sun, but otherwise he had chosen to don the jacket of the suit he wore to work. It couldn't have been comfortable in the heat, for Still was striding quickly down Fifth Street, an urgent note in his hand. A "colored boy" he had never seen before had handed him the note at the office of the Pennsylvania Anti-Slavery Society.[1]

Still was the society's clerk, a title that belied his critical duties. He was entrusted with running the storefront operation at the society's headquarters at 31 North Fifth, where he distributed abolitionist literature and sold books, tracts, and subscriptions to newspapers dedicated to the abolitionist cause. But more importantly, he was the society's "receiving agent."[2] He kept in touch by mail with abolitionists in other northern states as well as with sympathizers in the South, becoming widely known in abolition circles as a go-between, forwarder of information, and arranger of escapes. A journalist would describe him as "somewhat tall, neat in figure and person" with, as the journalist added, "a smiling face."[3]

It is doubtful that Still was smiling that day. The note he was carrying demanded immediate attention. Still served as secretary of the society's General Vigilance Committee. One of its functions—a controversial one that brought it into direct conflict with the federal government—was to inform slaves brought by their owners into Pennsylvania, a free state, that they were entitled to their freedom "without another moment's service." The committee would assist them and even provide "counsel without charge" if requested.[4]

Significantly, Still was also chairman of the Vigilance Committee's special Acting Committee. It was responsible not only for telling a slave about his or her opportunity for freedom, but also for providing food, shelter, and transportation north on what was known as the Underground Railroad. The so-called railroad was a conglomeration of literally dozens of undefined "routes"—trails, roads, rivers north, even coastal waterways—leading to states as far-flung as those in New England and to communities such as Toronto, Kingston, and Port Stanley in Canada, as well. The railroad's participants developed their own set of signals. "The wind blows from the South today" alerted sympathizers to the presence of fugitive slaves in a particular area. Its "conductors," "ticket agents," and "station masters"—blacks and whites —numbered in the thousands. A total of 348 "conductors" were said to handle "passengers" throughout Pennsylvania, and as many as nine thousand "passengers" would pass through Philadelphia alone in the years between 1830 and 1860.[5] No complete roster of names exists of those who risked imprisonment to help escaped slaves, and only a few of them—such as Levi Coffin in Cincinnati, Dr. John Rankin in Ripley, Ohio, Thomas Garrett in Wilmington, Delaware, Isaac Hopper in Philadelphia—ever became known publicly. "There was no regular organization, no constitution, no officers, no laws or agreement or rule except the 'Golden Rule,'" said "stationmaster" Isaac Beck, "and every man did what seemed right in his own eyes."[6] Which, of course, was strictly forbidden by the Fugitive Slave Law. For that matter, any assistance whatsoever was forbidden.

The law was one of a crazy quilt of measures that made up the Compromise of 1850. It was an attempt in Congress to keep the continuing dispute between slave states and free states from boiling over. And compromise it was, seesawing between the demands of the North and the South and, as it would turn out, satisfying neither. One bill permitted the admission of California as a free state. That pleased northerners. Another bill, establishing the territories of New Mexico and Utah, left it to the settlers to determine whether they wanted slavery when the territories became states. The measure, embodying a formula known as popular sovereignty, was for the benefit of southerners. Yet another bill outlawed slave trading in the District of Columbia—a source of profound embarrassment to northerners—but it did not make it illegal to own slaves in the nation's capital. Provisions of these laws, whatever their intention, did little to soothe either the fifteen states that permitted slavery or the sixteen states, including newly admitted California, where slavery was illegal.

The Compromise of 1850 was just one more in a series of repeated attempts to resolve the question of slavery, a problem that harked back to the founding of the nation itself. The word "slavery" was never mentioned in the United States Constitution, hammered out in Philadelphia's State House in 1787, but it was the great unspoken word in it. It was clear what was meant by Clause 3, Section 2, Article IV, an acknowledgment that the "peculiar institution" did exist, that it was tolerated, that it would not be abolished: "No Person held to Service or Labour in one State, under the Laws thereof, escaping into another, shall, in Consequence of any Law or Regulation therein, be discharged from such Service or Labour, but shall be delivered up on Claim of the Party to whom such Service or Labour may be due." And it was clear that Clause 3, Section 2, Article I of the Constitution also spoke tacitly of slavery. It read that in the apportionment of representatives to Congress based on population, free individuals but only "three fifths of all other Persons"—meaning, of course, slaves—would be counted as part of a state's entire population. In addition, in order to fortify the constitutional provision regarding the return of escaped slaves, Congress in 1793 passed legislation spelling out what a slave owner could do to get back a slave. This law clearly recognized slaves as property—chattel that could be bought and sold.

In 1797 yet a second law dealing with the recovery of fugitive slaves was fueled in great part by fears of the impact of two major events: the French Revolution, when a subjected populace rose up in bloody revolt against authority, and a successful and bloody slave uprising in Haiti. This second law specified that runaways were not entitled to a legal defense or jury trial. The only restriction on the slave trade was the prohibition against the importation of slaves after 1808. Nothing, however, was done to stem the practice of slavery within the nation, nor the trade in slaves between states. Virginia and Maryland, in particular, became breeding grounds for black men, women, and children who were subsequently sold and shipped to slave owners south and west, to Alabama, the Carolinas, Florida, Georgia, Mississippi, Texas. The District of Columbia, the nation's capital itself, became the center of the domestic traffic, its slave pens flourishing, until 1850, when the trading in human lives there was outlawed. By then, there were well over three million blacks enslaved in the South, most of them treated inhumanly, without any of the "unalienable Rights" or any chance whatsoever for the "Pursuit of Happiness" promised in the Declaration of Independence.[7]

In the North, beginning almost as soon as independence from England was declared, one state after another, Pennsylvania included, legislated against slavery, either abolishing the practice outright or, as in Pennsylvania's case in 1780, establishing a gradual emancipation program. In the South, however, the need for cheap labor to work the cotton, rice, sugar, and tobacco plantations buttressed the institution, and as the new nation expanded westward the issue often grew divisive. So it seemed inevitable that in the first half of the nineteenth century the nation would be torn by battles over the admission of new states to the Union—should they be free or slave? Sectionalism grew more divisive each passing year. Divisions within political parties were reflected in the nation's major religious denominations as well; disputes over slavery and theology divided Baptists, Methodists, and Presbyterians into separate branches, North and South.

Every attempt to resolve the issue seemed doomed. The Missouri Compromise of 1820 drew a territorial line across the continent, barring slavery north of it and including the territories of the Louisiana Purchase from the expansion of slavery. But the issue arose again in 1846 when war with Mexico broke out. Abolitionists interpreted the war as an effort by the South to extend slavery into America's southern neighbor. In fact, many southern politicians favored the annexation of all of Mexico as slave territory. The southerners' advocacy of annexation proved ineffective, but they were able to stymie the so-called Wilmot Proviso, an amendment to an appropriations bill that would have prohibited slavery in any territory that the United States acquired as a result of the war. For their part, anti-slavery speakers fulminated against the war, exploiting the conflict as a freedom-or-bondage issue. John Greenleaf Whittier declared that the plaza "of every conquered Mexican village" was becoming "a market-place for human flesh," while fellow poet James Russell Lowell condemned the war as a "national crime committed in behoof [*sic*] of Slavery, our common sin."[8]

The Compromise of 1850 did little to smooth over the growing division in the nation. And of all its provisions, the Fugitive Slave Law was the most controversial. In actual practice, it incensed both sides—the North when it was enforced, the South when it was ignored. The law was intended to appease southerners who pressured for more stringent legislation to prevent what had become a continual flight of slaves to states in the North. The runaways were not only costly, but their escapes dramatically mocked southern claims of a paternal system of contented slaves unconcerned with freedom. From the time of the law's enactment in the fall of 1850, its provisions only intensified the animosity of abolitionists to slavery and, portending perhaps the final bloody conflict in the years ahead, swayed other northerners who had remained indifferent about the issue to finally take a stand. To them, it was a repugnant law with horrific consequences.

Under the Fugitive Slave Law, federal circuit courts were authorized to appoint commissioners to adjudge the claims of slave owners and grant certificates for the removal of a runaway to the state from which he or she had escaped. However, the kidnapping of free blacks was commonplace at the time; there were gangs that scoured northern states, snaring and carting off free men and women when they could catch them unawares. At one point, for example, a number of young black men, some of an estimated twenty youths aged eight to fifteen who disappeared one year from Philadelphia, were believed to have drowned in the Delaware River. But rumors spread in the black community that they had been kidnapped by bounty hunters.[9] Actually, the Fugitive Slave Law never legalized such abductions, but it eliminated whatever legal recourse a kidnapped slave enjoyed. Even without a warrant, the owner of an alleged slave, or his agent, could seize any person they claimed was a slave and take the individual immediately before a federal judge or one of the commissioners. The alleged slave was denied the benefit of a trial or even the chance to testify in his or her own behalf.

The commissioners, by the way, received ten dollars for every slave they ordered remanded to his or her owner, but only five dollars for every person they decided to free. While it is impossible to determine how much the difference in compensation influenced their decisions, within fifteen months of the law's taking effect, judges and commissioners sent eighty-four alleged runaways back south, while releasing only five. In the ten years between 1850 and 1860, the judges and commissioners released only eleven alleged fugitives; they remanded south a total of 332 blacks.[10]

Another provision of the law gave a slave owner the right to enlist a federal marshal or his deputies to capture an alleged runaway, and if they refused or were derelict in carrying out a warrant, each faced a fine of one thousand dollars, a substantial amount then. Each also faced a thousand-dollar penalty if a fugitive in their custody somehow got away.

What particularly infuriated northerners was the provision in the law that the commissioners appointed to adjudge the claims of slave owners had the power to call upon any citizen for help in capturing a runaway. It didn't matter what that citizen thought about the institution of slavery, whether he or she condoned it or opposed it. He, or she, could be ordered to participate in a fugitive's capture. Failure to do so could result in a fine as high as one thousand dollars and imprisonment for up to six months. By its enactment, the Fugitive Slave Law made slavery a national commitment, forcing northerners to be actively complicit and supportive of the system. It mocked southern idealizations by making it clear that southerners considered slaves in monetary terms rather than as human beings. It was a law that almost begged to be disobeyed. Perhaps no legislation enacted by Congress in the nineteenth century stirred up such heated passion as the Fugitive Slave Law. It was a law based solely on property rights—the rights of the slave owner. It totally disregarded human rights, and its passage spurred a revival of abolitionists' commitment to aiding runaways.

Following the Compromise of 1850 there was another controversial congressional effort to soothe tempers, though it, too, proved futile: the Kansas-Nebraska Act of 1854. It nullified the provisions of the Missouri Compromise and substituted in its stead popular sovereignty, the idea that the citizens of a territory could choose for themselves what kind of state it would become, slave or free, when admitted to the Union. The act divided Kansas from Nebraska with the expectation that its citizens would vote Kansas to be a slave state. Warring factions would turn it into "Bloody Kansas."

It was a time of trouble, and adding to the turmoil was a human element that had been festering for years, attracting increasing attention, adding fuel to the controversy over the issue of the extension of slavery: tragic incidents and stories of brutality told by former slaves or the fate of free blacks such as Solomon Northup who were shanghaied into slavery. Abolitionists were outraged.

Pennsylvania sat on the Mason-Dixon line, which symbolically came to divide North from South, and Philadelphia was within a few days' walk from Maryland, a slave state. Hundreds of runaways, the majority of them from the Chesapeake area, passed through the city each year, attracted to it by Pennsylvania's policy on emancipation. Some even settled in the city. The fugitives often were barefoot, in rags, hungry. They had been passed along from farmplace to farmplace, from village to village, mostly at night, assisted chiefly by other blacks, who were the prime "conductors" of the Underground Railroad. They were active aiders and abettors, spiriting runaways through and out of Philadelphia, though their actions drew little public notice at the time and sparse credit historically for more than a century. In one black neighborhood alone in Philadelphia, all the residents along Paschall's Alley, just south of Coates Street in the Northern Liberties section of the city, were known to open their doors to runaways.[11] The escaped slaves came bearing stories of whippings, of being shackled, forced to work from dawn to dusk. Light-skinned children were mute testimony to the rape of black women. Women, men, children—they all spoke of families torn apart when a spouse was sold or a child parted from parents. They needed help.

If the fugitive was fortunate, he or she came to the attention of William Still. He was in many ways an unusual black man. For one thing, he was one of the few blacks in the city who worked intimately with white abolitionists. Most blacks, whether free men and women or escaped slaves, kept to themselves, as wary of whites as whites were of them.

Still himself was the child of former slaves, the youngest of eighteen children. His father, a Maryland slave, had earned money in his spare time and was able to purchase his freedom and move to New Jersey. Some masters permitted their slaves who had a craft or special talent to work for pay in what little free time they had, and many used the money to buy their way out of bondage. Still's mother, however, was an escaped slave. Her first attempt to flee, with four children in tow, had ended in their capture. But on a second attempt, with only two of her youngsters, she succeeded in getting away and was able to rejoin her husband. The family changed its surname from Steel to Still to forestall further pursuit of the mother. She also changed her given name from Sidney to Charity.

By the time William was born on October 7, 1821, the growing family was living in freedom on a forty-acre farm in a secluded, far-off section of Burlington County, New Jersey, known as the Pines. The farm was outside the town of Medford, an agricultural area populated in the main by Quakers. William worked on the family farm and did odd chores for some of his Quaker neighbors.

The death of his father just before Christmas in 1842 marked a turning point in Still's life. He left home and decided to seek his fortune elsewhere, eventually heading two years later across the Delaware River to Philadelphia, which seemed to promise a range of opportunities for a young black man. Two sisters were living there, so he would not be totally without family connections. He was twenty-two years old at the time.

There are several conflicting accounts of when and how William Still learned to read and write. One story has it that, although he received only a rudimentary schooling (and ran into prejudice in a local school in New Jersey), he was passionate about learning and yearned for an education. He took to reading as he drove the family wagon to and from market. He was particularly interested in history and geography. Another story claims that a wealthy Philadelphia widow who hired him as a servant encouraged his love of books. Within three years, it is said, Still was fluent at reading and writing.[12]

Yet a third story says that it was J. Miller McKim, a former Presbyterian minister, who taught Still to read and write.[13] The truth, however, is that by the time Still met McKim, he was already literate.

McKim, who was from Berks County, Pennsylvania, was a powerful presence and mentor in Still's life. Inspired by the abolitionist writings of William Lloyd Garrison, McKim had abandoned the pulpit to become a dedicated lecturer against slavery. Like many such advocates, McKim was often threatened with violence, so he decided to move to nearby Philadelphia in 1840, believing that the city would provide a more congenial environment for his beliefs. He became the publishing agent for the Pennsylvania Anti-Slavery Society, responsible in great part for the publication of its organ, the *Pennsylvania Freeman*. He later took on the role of the society's corresponding secretary, serving for some twenty-five years as its chief operating officer.

In 1847 McKim needed help at the North Fifth Street office of the society. By this time, Still had been in Philadelphia for almost three years, going from one job to another, frustrated in his attempt to settle down in work that both was meaningful and would provide him with a decent living. He heard about the opportunity at the society's office and made out a written application, saying that even though the salary being offered, $3.75 a week, was small, "I go for liberty and improvement."[14] Impressed, McKim offered Still work as a combination janitor/mail clerk. Before long he also recognized Still's talents and intelligence. The young man was promoted and given greater duties and increased wages. His responsibilities expanded particularly after the passage of the Fugitive Slave Law.

Once the law was passed in 1850, the activities of both men became increasingly focused on aiding escaped slaves. For Still, this brought great personal risk. The same year that he began work at the Anti-Slavery Society, 1847, he married Letita George. The couple made their home on a short, alley-like street that no longer exists, Ronaldson's Row. It was tucked between Ninth and Tenth streets below South Street in the very heart of the city's major black community. [15] Their home became a sanctuary for runaway slaves, a way station before being transported farther north to New York State, New England or Canada, passed along from hiding place to hiding place by the friendly "conductors" of the Underground Railroad. In the decade before the Civil War, it was reported, almost every fugitive fleeing through Philadelphia took shelter in the Stills's "humble" home.[16] And what had begun as a clerk's job at the Anti-Slavery Society became a lifelong passion. Still would devote his life, first to helping runaway slaves and then, after emancipation, to helping fellow blacks to receive an education, work training and other assistance that could better their lives. A contemporary biographer who knew Still wrote that he had "seen his race bowed and broken by slavery."[17]

Still would speak of McKim's "caution, sound judgment, and mental balance" in "periods of excitement."[18] The same might be said of Still. He was involved in helping an extraordinary number of fugitives. The society's General Vigilance Committee—which Still described as being "synonymous with the underground railroad"[19]—would boast, for instance, that in the period alone between December 1852 and February 1857 it had helped nearly five hundred runaways to gain their freedom.[20] Still himself noted that in a single month in 1857, sixty escaped slaves—of all ages and both sexes—were "sent northward on freedom's journey."[21] "Fugitives from southern injustice are coming thick and fast," the abolitionist weekly *Provincial Freeman*, published in Canada, declared in 1854. "The underground railroad never before did so large a business as it is doing now."[22] McKim was ecstatic: "Our road is doing now a smashing business," he declared after several groups made up of thirty-six fugitives reached Philadelphia. "The dividends—of gratification and joy—to the stockholders, are large," he added.[23]

The death of his father in 1842 had been a turning point for Still, propelling him out of the safety and security of the family homestead into an alien and unwelcoming world. Ten years later, an amazing coincidence spurred another turning point in Still's life. An old, white-haired black man named Peter Friedman walked into the Anti-Slavery Society's office. He had bought his freedom in Alabama and had traveled more than a thousand miles to Philadelphia, where he heard that "his people" lived, in hopes of earning enough money to purchase the freedom of his wife and three children, whom he had left behind. Friedman—or Freedman as his name is sometimes spelled—had been roaming the city streets, trying to locate "his people" and thought that someone in the society's office might have a clue as to their whereabouts. Friedman began to describe the members of his family. He told how he and a brother had been left behind with a grandmother when his mother, Sidney, successfully fled from Maryland with two younger sisters. His father Levin, he knew, had died in the early 1840s. He understood that a sister Mary ran a school for black children in Philadelphia. Still could not believe what he was hearing. Friedman was describing the events experienced in his own family. He realized that Friedman was his brother, a brother he had never met. Their mother had been unable to take all her children when she had fled her master a second time. Still had been born free years later in New Jersey, but as a youth he had heard his parents talk about the boys who had been left behind. Suddenly it occurred to Still what he must do: "All over this wide and extended country thousands of mothers and children, separated by slavery, were in a similar way living without the slightest knowledge of each other's whereabouts."[24] From then on, Still took it upon himself to keep a list of the fleeing slaves that came through the Anti-Slavery Society's office, recording not only their names and where they were from, but also the stories of their escapes and whom they had left behind—husbands, wives, mothers, fathers, brothers, sisters, who might someday escape, too, and want to locate kin who had fled before them.

Still kept detailed records of the fugitive slaves who passed through the society's office. It was a dangerous thing to do, because his notebooks were proof that he and others were helping runaway slaves. That was clearly in direct violation of the Fugitive Slave Law. Still, however, persisted, compiling the names and stories of the hundreds of escaped slaves who were ushered into the welcoming hands of the Anti-Slavery Society and sped along on the Underground Railroad to safety and freedom.

Although the message Still was carrying now did not deal with a fugitive slave, it was nevertheless another appeal for help and the reason for his haste. Reaching the corner of Arch Street, Still, the note in hand, turned, heading for the office of another member of the Acting Committee. The time was 4:30 P.M. The day, Wednesday, July 18, 1855. The member's name was Passmore Williamson.

2

The Quaker

I am an Abolitionist!
I glory in the name:
Though now by Slavery's minions hiss'd
And covered o'er with shame.

"I Am an Abolitionist," *Anti-Slavery Harp,* 16
(to be sung to the air "Auld Lang Syne")

Passmore Williamson was at his desk on the ground floor of the house on the southwest corner of Arch and Seventh streets that he and his father used as their office. It had been the family home, but now just his father and his stepmother, Deborah, lived there,[1] using the second floor as their living quarters. Like his father, Thomas, Passmore was a conveyancer and scrivener, dealing in land deeds, estates, and property transfers, fields that would in the future become part of the purview of lawyers. It was a thriving business. Philadelphia and its environs were in the forefront of the Industrial Revolution in America; canals and railroads opened up new areas of the state almost, it seemed, daily. The city could already boast that it was the center of textile manufacturing in the United States, a leader as well in the publishing business. Its medical schools set the standard for the rest of the country; its banks vied with those of New York and Boston as underwriters of the nation's expansion. Indicative of the extensive opportunities, there were scores of conveyance offices in the city.[2] Passmore, a newspaper reporter noted, shared his father's reputation "for urbanity, integrity and philanthropy."[3]

That afternoon Passmore was pouring over papers in preparation for a trip he was scheduled to make that night to Harrisburg. He was to attend a meeting there the next morning of the Atlantic and Ohio Telegraph Company.[4] He was so engrossed in what he was doing that he didn't look up at first when William Still rushed in and dropped the note he was carrying onto Passmore's desk. Williamson's father, who was standing beside him, picked up the scrap of paper. Although at one time a schoolteacher, Thomas found it difficult to decipher the note. It was "illegibly written." So he passed it to his son. Passmore threw down his pen and, irritably it seems, picked up the piece of paper.[5]

"MR. STILL—*Sir*," it read, "Will you come down to Bloodgood's Hotel as soon as possible—as there are three fugitive slaves here and they want liberty. Their master is here with them, on his way to New York."[6]

Looking up, Passmore said he could not leave to go to the hotel. It was situated nearly a mile away at the juncture of Walnut and Delaware streets, just by the Walnut Street wharf. At the foot of the dock, the Camden & Amboy Railroad ran a ferry that crossed the Delaware River to Camden, New Jersey, where the line's rail terminal for its train service north was located. The ferry left the Philadelphia side of the river at regularly scheduled hours; the next one was due to depart at 5:00 P.M. Passmore explained that he was far too busy preparing for the trip to Harrisburg that night. He couldn't take time out to follow up on the message.

Still proposed that they try to obtain a writ of habeas corpus, a legal ploy that abolitionists were increasingly using to compel slave owners or their agents to bring kidnapped men and women into court for a hearing. Use of the writ had already stymied a number of cases involving the shanghaiing of free blacks. If, however, the fugitives were indeed slaves, the writ would at least provide the opportunity for legal maneuvering and block their being immediately spirited out of the state. Any delay provided abolitionists with the chance to question the veracity of the evidence a slave owner or agent presented. Pennsylvania law did not recognize slavery, so there was always a chance that a sympathetic judge might find, or be persuaded to favorably adjudicate, some technical reason to avoid implementation of the Fugitive Slave Law, in effect openly challenging the supremacy of federal law over Pennsylvania law. Moreover, there was the distinct possibility that

15

the state's so-called Liberty Law had been violated. As far as abolitionists were concerned, the Fugitive Slave Law of 1850 had done nothing to invalidate it.

Neither Passmore, Still, or, indeed, Passmore's father had time to debate the finer nuances of the legal issues involved. The situation was urgent. Passmore argued that it was too late in the day to obtain a writ of habeas corpus. It would be "impossible," he said. Courts in Philadelphia ordinarily adjourned by three o'clock in the afternoon. So far as he knew, there was no jurist in the city who had authority to grant the writ, and, anyway, he added, "there was not sufficient time to procure the writ, and to have it served, even if a Judge were at hand to grant it."[7]

Instead, Passmore asked Still to go immediately to Bloodgood's Hotel to try to get the names and a description of the slaves and their master. That would enable him to wire ahead to abolitionist friends in New York City, who could watch out for them when they arrived in that city. There was a good chance they could be intercepted there. Following Pennsylvania's lead, New York had gradually abolished slavery. It, too, was now a free state. In fact, three years earlier, a free black in New York City had successfully obtained a writ of habeas corpus to obtain the freedom of eight slaves ranging in age from two to twenty-three. A Virginia couple had brought them into the city en route to boarding a ship bound for Texas. (A long drawn-out litigation ensued when the State of Virginia contested the release of the slaves. Their freedom was finally upheld in 1860 by New York State's Court of Appeals in a five-to-three decision.)[8]

With time running out, Still started out the door, then suddenly turned on his heel. Was there anything to prevent the slaves leaving their master if they wanted to? he asked. "They have a perfect right to go where they please," Passmore responded, "and they can do so unless forcibly restrained by their master." Still hastened away. The ferry was scheduled to leave in less than half an hour.

Passmore returned to arranging his papers for the trip to Harrisburg. His father went back to his own desk. Then abruptly, just a few minutes later, Thomas said, Passmore "again threw down his pen, left his desk, put on his coat and hat, and, without a word spoken by either of us to the other, he hastily left the office." The father had no doubt where Passmore was headed "or the purpose for which he went."[9]

To look at him, no one would have taken Passmore to be a radical abolitionist. He was, an observer wrote, "a good specimen of the class sometimes called 'genteel' Quakers."[10] But that assessment was far from accurate. Passmore was secretary of the Acting Committee of the General Vigilance Committee, which was comprised of the most active and radical abolitionists in the city, who thought little of defying federal law. That Still had rushed to see him made sense. For one thing, Passmore's office was within a short distance from where Still worked. Then, too, he was the logical member of the Acting Committee for Still to consult.[11] The other two members of the committee were a barber and a tailor, both of whom were black. They had developed critical connections in the colored community to help spirit runaways from house to house as they escaped north. The barber, Jacob C. White Sr., also hid runaways in his home on Old York Road and helped provide transportation for blacks wishing to migrate to Haiti. He was considered "one of the most active and reliable members of the Vigilance Committee."[12] But neither he nor the tailor, Nathaniel W. Depee, were experienced in legal matters.

On the surface, Williamson certainly appeared benign if not, indeed, priggish, though he had a wry sense of humor. He dressed well but conservatively, favored muttonchops, took care to part his wavy hair.[13] He was not given to speeches, was not an orator like Frederick Douglass, Theodore Dwight Weld, Charles Burleigh or Angelina Grimké, who were known for rousing audiences with outbursts of passion. "He is not rash, selfish, or fanatical," said a friend.[14] Passmore, though, shared with them fervency for the abolitionist cause. At thirty-three years of age, Passmore was but a few months younger than Still —"in the prime of life," a reporter wrote, "tall and slender, of a pleasant expression." His "countenance is intelligent, animated and thoughtful, with no marked peculiarity, and his conversation at once suggests a calm firmness of principle and a quickness of benevolent sympathy, as characteristics of the man."[15]

A family man, Passmore and his wife Mercie enjoyed a loving relationship. "My dear dear Husband," Mercie wrote on the occasion of Passmore's twenty-eighth birthday in 1850, when she was away on a trip to Canton, Ohio, "This should properly commence with a good bye kiss should it not? as we parted without it, or one. I saw thy anxious look as thee stood on the platform, but [it] was so crowded that I could not catch thy eye. . . . I wish I was going to be where I could give a birth day [sic] kiss. My spirit will visit thee and give thee an embrace. Now don't deny its having been there because thee did not see it." Mercie signed the letter "most truly and affectionately thy wife."[16] Their first child, named for Passmore's father, Thomas, was born before that year was out; a daughter, Sarah, two years later. Now, in the summer of 1855, Mercie was pregnant again, expecting their third child in the latter part of August, six weeks away.

Both Mercie and Passmore had strong ties to the Society of Friends. On her mother's side, Mercie—née Knowles Taylor—was a great-niece of Samuel Comfort, who was a grandson of the noted Quaker John Woolman, a leading advocate of the abolitionist movement in the eighteenth century.[17]

On his father's side, Passmore could trace his lineage, and his given name, to John and William Passmore, brothers who emigrated from an area on the Thomas River west of London early in the eighteenth century, settling in the colony that William Penn had established in America. They apparently knew Penn, for their home in Ruscombe had been within a short walk from the house where Penn, enfeebled by a stay in debtors' prison, lived in 1710.[18] In England, the family had been in the cloth-making business and had a most peculiar and unofficial coat of arms: three pairs of budgets gules—that is red-dyed leather water bags—suspended from a yoke.[19]

The Passmore connection with the Williamsons occurred in 1789 when a pregnant Phebe Passmore married William Williamson. The couple settled in Chester County, not far from Philadelphia, but both were disowned by the morally strict Society of Friends because of Phebe's premarital pregnancy.[20] The circumstances of their being received back in the Society are unclear, but the couple had seven children, all of whom were raised as Quakers. Passmore was named after one of their sons who had died at the age of twenty-eight a few years before Passmore himself was born on February 23, 1822. The ties between the two families, the Passmores and the Williamsons—both prominent in Chester County—had been further cemented when Passmore's father, Thomas Williamson, married Elizabeth Pyle, the daughter of Ann Passmore and John Pyle.[21] Thomas and Elizabeth had five children, but only Passmore and two younger sisters, Ann and Mary, survived infancy. Their mother Elizabeth died in the spring of 1846 when she was in her early fifties. Passmore's father subsequently married Deborah M. Garrigues, a woman past childbearing age.[22]

Thomas was a member in good standing of the Arch Street Meeting House on Fourth Street and an overseer of the Philadelphia Monthly Meeting of the Society of Friends. Passmore was raised in what was called the Orthodox branch of the society.

At the heart of the Friends religious faith is the belief that every person is capable of attending to God, and that one's behavior is a reflection of submission to God's will. Quakers at that time were per-force especially rigid behaviorists. A member could be "read out" or be "disowned" for blasphemy, not attending meetings, marrying out of religion, excessive drinking, and nonpayment of debts. They banned music or singing of any kind. They were pacifists as well, and could be dropped from membership for participating in matters related to the military (though in practice many of them have participated in the nation's wars). Believing as they do that a person's religious experience, the opportunity to experience God directly, is critical, Friends have no need for a written creed or doctrine, or clergy, or sacraments, or a cross or any other religious symbol in their worship. Their meeting houses were—still are—simple, austere. They sit silently, contemplating, and speak out only when possessed by a personal, spiritual revelation, something they wish to impart to their fellow congregants.

Back then, Friends were different outside their meeting houses, too, purposely setting themselves apart from other people, preferring what they called plainness to ostentation. They wore drab clothing—no ruffles or lace were allowed. Nor was unnecessary ornamentation permitted either; one row of buttons sufficed instead of two on coats, and a standing collar rather than a rolling one was considered sufficient. Quakers also abjured the names of months because of their pagan origin; instead January was the "first" month, February the "second," March the "third," and so forth. They never said "good-bye," preferring instead to say "farewell." And because they did not respect earthly rank—all persons are equal under God—they employed "thee," "thou," "thy," and "thine" in speaking and writing to one another. Similarly, they refused to take off their hats except when, in prayer, they were addressing God. Their refusal to doff their headgear to royalty and nobles caused resentment in class-conscious England, where the Society of Friends was founded. As avowed pacifists, many Quakers not only refused to serve in the army but they also would not pay taxes earmarked for war, practices that prompted the Society in general to be stigmatized both in England and in America.

The resentment in America began at the time of the French and Indian War in the mid-1750s. Quakers withdrew from political power rather than support the conflict. The animosity grew in intensity during the American Revolution, twenty years later, when many of them refused military service or to pay levies in support of the war. Their experience at that time was traumatic. Patriots regarded Quakers as English sympathizers if not outright loyal royalists. They were ostracized, the estates of some were confiscated, a few were forced into exile.

The result of their pacifism was that Quakers became pariahs. It was a fateful transformation, for Friends had set the tone of the colonial Pennsylvania government. They had been among, if not the, leading citizens of the state, had put their stamp especially on Philadelphia, "the City of Brotherly Love." But time and events had conspired against them. Quakers remained wealthy and were able to regain cultural and moral respect after the Revolution, but the animosity left by the war, then the waves of immigrants from Ireland and the Continent that flooded the state in the early decades of the nineteenth century, as well as the Quakers' own inclination for living apart, left the Society of Friends isolated and with little political influence.

To top it all, a revolution within the Society itself worsened matters. The painful division—one that would wrack the Society for the next 125 years and create further schisms—occurred when a Long Island, New York, farmer named Elias Hicks fought against elders in the faith and certain dogmas that had replaced the simplicity of the denomination's earliest years. The bitter separation occurred in 1827 when his supporters, known as Hicksites, broke off from what became known as the Orthodox. A perfectionist in Quaker theological terms, Hicks was concerned that Friends had become too worldly. Orthodox Quakers, most of whom lived in an urban environment, were learning to enjoy the benefits of the new industrial age and felt comfortable relaxing some of the strictures of the past. Hicks did not approve. He personally was against slavery, but he also was against the idea of Quakers mixing with individuals outside their religious community, no matter what the organization was dedicated to.

The slavery issue was contentious, because even Quakers who opposed slavery believed that active involvement in the abolition movement should be shunned. They agreed with Hicks that detachment was reasonable. They believed the issue was not their business, that Quakers should stay "quiet" and, following Hicks's advice, not mix in worldly affairs. As the *Friends' Weekly Intelligencer* put it, "We trust that Friends every where [sic] will be governed by the principles of their forefathers, and while refusing to aid in measures which their consciences condemn, that they will at the same time be preserved from that hasty and overactive opposition which begets violence and thwarts its own purposes."[23] Moreover, other Quakers supported colonization of blacks in Liberia or the West Indies, which a number of other Americans also saw as the solution to slavery. Only a few

Quakers—James and Lucretia Mott were among the most visible in Philadelphia—thought the Society of Friends should once again take an active role in pressing for the complete outlawing of the "peculiar institution."

Despite the internal division within Quaker ranks, the Society had been in the forefront of the movement to eradicate slavery, even though as early as the seventeenth century some Quakers had owned slaves in America and there were Quakers who were partners in their importation. But in 1696, the Philadelphia Yearly Meeting advised its members against importing slaves, and sentiment grew that it was inherently wrong whatsoever to own slaves, that God had created everyone equal. Eventually, by 1758, any Quaker who purchased a slave was prohibited from attending meetings devoted to Society of Friends business and from even contributing to it. Eighteen years later, at the start of the American Revolution, the purchase, sale, or ownership of a slave meant disownment from the Society of Friends. By 1784 all Quakers in Pennsylvania, including Passmore's ancestor Augustine Passmore, who possessed five slaves, had freed their slaves.[24]

After the turn of the century, as new states were added to the Union, slavery became an increasingly divisive force among other denominations, as well. The growing unrest over the issue proved particularly acrimonious among Protestant sects. Wealthy Unitarians, members of the Rev. William H. Furness's church, left his congregation because of Furness's conscience-provoked anti-slavery sermons and activities.[25] Other ministers lost their pulpits as a result of speaking out, too, leaving many clergymen wary of espousing abolitionism. Every Christian denomination should simply "detach itself from all connection with slavery, without saying a word against others," a Presbyterian minister advised. "Not a blow need be struck. Not an unkind word need be uttered. No man's motives need be impugned, no man's property rights invaded."[26] Whether Quaker, Unitarian, Presbyterian, Baptist, or Episcopalian for that matter, most white Americans did not consider blacks equal partners, intellectually or socially. Nor, despite the fact that they opposed the institution, were they uniformly involved in any abolition movement.

Passmore Williamson was an exception to the general rule. When he was twenty years old in 1842, he decided to become an active participant in the abolitionist cause, attending rallies and demonstrations against slavery. "There was so much discussion of the paramount question of the day," he explained, "that naturally my youthful interest was aroused."[27] There was more than discussion. Philadelphia was being rocked by a serious rash of race riots, against blacks, then against the Irish, and he could hardly have failed to witness for himself the enmity and violence. The city at times was on the brink of chaos, and militia troops had to be called out to quell the rioters. The violence reflected the riots and unrest experienced in other parts of the nation, North and South, fed not only by political differences over immigration or tariffs or currency reforms, but also by the increasingly sensitive issue of slavery. As a teenager in 1838, Passmore must have been aware that an unruly mob had burned to the ground the newly opened Pennsylvania Hall—Philadelphia's "temple of freedom"—which had been built as a meeting center by abolitionists.

The burning of Pennsylvania Hall was evidence of a growing antagonism against anti-slavery advocates. The animosity was especially evident in the South, fueled to a great extent by the increasingly bitter denunciations of slavery by abolition proponents, who openly encouraged slaves to flee their masters. Moreover, southerners were already sensitive to the possibility of slave revolts ever since the success of such an uprising in Haiti. Slave rebellions within southern precincts, such as Nat Turner's Insurrection in Virginia in 1831, intensified their worries.

Passmore could not have helped but be influenced by the tremendous forces surging through the land. The nation as a whole was undergoing a vast transformation, in the process of doubling in population before 1860 and, concomitantly, expanding the territory where slavery was permitted. America was gradually changing from a government run by aristocratic white male property owners, men from Virginia and Massachusetts to a large extent, to a society in which any male individual, as long as he was white, could vote, have a say in, and even serve in the government. Not a full-fledged democracy, to be sure, but doors were opening. At the same time, a religious fervor had swept the country. It was a revival reminiscent of the fervor created in the 1700s and was called the Second Great Awakening. Its advocates, Protestant evangelists, promulgated the idea that in God's eyes, all men were equal no matter the color of their skin—a point of view that rang true to Quakers. Such reasoning injected a new spirit into the abolitionist movement and questioned the gradual abolitionism propounded by initial reformers. Those reformers—all men, for only men could join the group—were elitist: all white, predominantly lawyers, but politicians, businessmen, and philanthropists as well. Theirs was a passionless type of abolitionism. It was not intended to appeal to or to stir up the public's emotions. They focused instead on influencing legislative action and providing legal aid to blacks. When their organization—the Pennsylvania Society for the Relief of Free Negroes Unlawfully Held in Bondage—was founded in Philadelphia on the eve of the American Revolution in 1775, its chief function, as its name connoted, was to help free blacks who had been kidnapped into slavery. Even so, it was revolutionary—the first society in the world dedicated to helping blacks. In 1784, after the success of the American Revolution, the organization's focus expanded to the wider issue of slavery as a whole. It was now the Pennsylvania Society for Promoting the Abolition of Slavery and for the Relief of Free Negroes Unlawfully Held in Bondage —better known colloquially then and ever afterwards as the Pennsylvania Abolition Society. At one point, Benjamin Franklin was its president. The society worked within the political and legal systems of the time. It spearheaded the pressure for Pennsylvania's gradual emancipation statute, fostered schools for blacks, provided legal and financial support for both free and enslaved blacks, and was instrumental in passage of the national ban against the importation of slaves.

Passmore matured at a time when the South stiffened its resistance to abolitionism. Increased pressure for emancipation, as well as slave unrest in the mid-1830s, changed a "someday" attitude to a definite "never." At the same time, in the North, silence over slavery, or abolition with its threat of disunion and civil war, no longer seemed a viable alternative.

In 1848, six years after his decision to become involved in "the paramount question of the day," Passmore was elected secretary of the Pennsylvania Abolition Society, a post he was to hold for the next three years.[28] By then, a growing number of abolitionists, Passmore among them, were no longer content to rely on persuasion as a way to end slavery. They felt that the Abolition Society was not aggressive enough in the struggle—too "gradualist," they argued. They also criticized the society as elitist because it limited its membership to white males, who had to be nominated for membership. The Abolition Society's members were, in Lucretia Mott's eyes, "halfway" abolitionists[29] who had lost their fervor. Mott's name would become linked for all time with the most aggressive faction of the movement. She and like-thinkers believed that members of the Abolition Society seemed content only to petition legislatures and the federal government on the question of domestic slavery. Even Edward Needles, who served as the society's thirteenth president for a dozen years after 1840, thought that the

organization had for some time become immersed in a period of lax-
ness and apathy, as a result of which membership had declined and
the society's activities had shrunk.[30]

Dissatisfied with the Abolition Society's approach, Mott, her husband, James, and J. Miller McKim, among others, became founding
members of the society's radical counterpart, the Pennsylvania Anti-
Slavery Society. For one thing, the new society welcomed blacks into
its ranks, an acknowledgment of the leading role that blacks had been
playing for decades in the assistance and guidance of runaway slaves.
Their participation in the society was also an acknowledgment of the
increasing voice blacks themselves were bringing to the abolitionist
cause—poignant appeals to the heart by black writers. James McCune
Smith, who had been born in bondage in New York, believed that
Americans had to realize not only "the eternal equality of the Human
race," but also had to understand what it meant to be black. "The
heart of the whites must be changed, thoroughly, entirely, permanently
changed," Smith, a doctor, declared.[31] Wealthy and prominent black
Philadelphia sailmaker James Forten, who had been active in black
rights causes since the early nineteenth century, believed this kind of
approach was essential to convince white people of the anguish and
pain, the immorality and the outrageousness of slavery. When, led by
Lucretia Mott, women formed their own Female Anti-Slavery Society,
among its founding members were five black women—Forten's wife,
three of his daughters, and a soon-to-be daughter-in-law.[32]

The Pennsylvania Anti-Slavery Society was an offshoot of the American Anti-Slavery Society, established in Philadelphia in 1833. William Lloyd Garrison came to dominate the parent organization in the
early 1840s, and some members of the Philadelphia branch looked to
Garrison and his extremist followers in Boston and New York as role
models. A fanatic, Garrison in time proposed burning the United States
Constitution, calling it a pro-slavery document. Although he and his
followers professed to be pacifists (they believed in nonresistance), they
insisted that every slave had the right to escape and that it was the
duty of moral—Christian, if you will—individuals to help them throw
off bondage. Slaves, they insisted, should rebel, flee, escape to freedom. To Garrison, the very idea of fidelity to the union of American
states was "the latest and most terrible form of idolatry." He told an
audience in New York City in 1854, "If it would be a damning sin for
us to admit another Slave State into the Union, why is not a damning
sin to permit a Slave State to remain in the Union?"[33]

24

Constant agitation, mass meetings, public protests, the publication of inflammatory pamphlets—all were part of the Pennsylvania Anti-Slavery Society's day-to-day operation. Soon Passmore Williamson became involved in its activities as well, and soon, it is apparent, he abandoned the Quaker propensity for anti-violent behavior in favor of the involved, impatient, and aggressive policies of radicals. It would be interesting to know whether Passmore was at all influenced by the words and deeds of an unusual combination of four men, two blacks and two whites, who founded the Radical Political Abolitionist Party. The four militants—James McCune Smith, Frederick Douglass, Gerritt Smith, and John Brown—rationalized violence as a righteous way to sweep away slavery. In a sense they epitomized the integrated approach that the abolitionist movement had stimulated. The new era they were proclaiming would not countenance evil, and slavery was evil and had to be uprooted. Northern newspapers such as the *New York Tribune* and abolitionist-centered publications such as *Frederick Douglass' Paper* and the *National Anti-Slavery Standard* all carried word of this new, militant approach to the question of abolition as well as coverage of the new party's objectives and its inaugural convention in Syracuse, New York, in June 1855. Passmore would certainly have been familiar with all these newspapers.

Passmore's participation in abolitionist affairs prompted him to withdraw from the Society of Friends in 1848, shortly before he married Mercie. Members of the Arch Street Meeting House, where he was a member, tried to persuade him to stay, but at its monthly meeting in January they were informed that "Passmore Williamson entirely declines the attendance of our religious meetings and alleges that he does not recognize any obligation upon him to assemble with us for the purpose of divine worship." A committee was appointed to "treat with him," but it failed to persuade Passmore to adhere to the religion's rules. Members at the March monthly meeting were told that Passmore had even declined to accept notice of disownment when informed of his right of appeal. And the following month, the committee dealing with his case stated that, while he was "no longer" considered a member of the Society of Friends, "Nevertheless we desire that through submission to the humbling and enlightening influence of the Holy Spirit, he may be brought into true christian [sic] fellowship with us." But their hope was dashed, and by the end of May the committee threw up its hands, reporting that "no benefit appears likely to result from further labour."[34]

Passmore liked to say, "They either put me out or I threw them overboard. I don't know which."[35] However, although no longer a practicing Quaker, Passmore was nevertheless infused with the religion's moral posture, with its sense of what was right and what was wrong. Its ethical standards were his guiding principles. By all accounts, he was a serious, sober person. He did not blaspheme, did not cheat, did not lie.

Surprisingly, despite a general prohibition against marrying someone outside the religion (after all, he had been disowned), Passmore and Mercie were wed on August 8, 1848, at the Spruce Street Meeting House, [36] a Hicksite branch that she was then a member of. (She would later join the Green Street Monthly Meeting.) Mercie was twenty-four years old at the time, Passmore two years her senior. She "had accomplished her marriage by Friends' ceremony with a man not in membership," it was noted in the congregation's minutes. The nuptials "had been accomplished as near the order of the society as the circumstances allowed."[37] The couple made their home on Buttonwood Street, between Eighth and Franklin, the latter a street that no longer exists. It was on the edge of the Spring Garden section of the city.[38]

Following passage of the Fugitive Slave Law in 1850, Passmore's name appears increasingly in the minutes of the Abolition Society's meetings. He joins a committee drawing up an appeal to the state legislature, prepares a resolution offering legal aid to defendants in the shooting of a slave owner in what became known as the Christiana Riot, offers a motion to purchase copies of a pamphlet dealing with that riot, acts as secretary pro tem for a meeting of the society, is paid thirteen dollars as compensation for laying out the funeral expenses of "a Manumitted Slave."[39] Even though he was not a lawyer, Passmore became more active in the legal battles dealing with runaways and kidnappings, championing black defendants, appearing at court sessions, writing and offering advice and support. And evidently outraged by the impact of the Fugitive Slave Law's severe provisions, he decided to join the more militant Pennsylvania Anti-Slavery Society.

The burning of Pennsylvania Hall in 1838 and the riots of the early 1840s had led to disarray among abolitionists in Philadelphia. The black community continued as the major conduit for helping escaped slaves, but the role of whites—in particular, the legal and educational supports that they sponsored—fell by the wayside. Even the usually pro-active Vigilance Committee, a pioneer interracial group patterned after a similar committee organized in New York City, floundered; by 1844 it was moribund. The committee might have remained ineffective indefinitely had the Fugitive Slave Law not been enacted. However, its passage in the fall of 1850 immediately resulted in five cases involving allegedly escaped slaves being brought before the district court in Philadelphia. Subsequent cases throughout the North attracted nationwide attention, forcing abolitionists everywhere to take a more vigorous role in opposing it. The law and its immediate consequences brought the Vigilance Committee back to life.

On the evening of December 2, 1852, there was a special meeting of whites and blacks convened at the office of the Pennsylvania Anti-Slavery Society. Passmore Williamson was among those invited. With William Still taking notes as secretary, J. Miller McKim rose to address the gathering. "Friends of the fugitive slave," he said, "had been for some years past, embarrassed, for the want of a properly constructed[,] active, Vigilance Committee." The "old" committee, McKim said, "had become disorganized and scattered." For the past two or three years, he continued, its "duties" had been performed "by individuals on their own responsibility, and sometimes in a very irregular manner." The result was "dissatisfaction and complaint." "It was intended now," he said, "to organize a committee, which should be composed of persons of known responsibility, and who could be relied upon to act systematically and promptly."

Of those attending the meeting, nineteen were elected members of a newly reorganized General Vigilance Committee. Almost half of them were blacks. The nineteen included not only Still, McKim and Passmore, but also wealthy activist Robert Purvis, clothing store proprietor Samuel Nickles, dry goods merchant Charles Wise, shoemaker William H. Riley, plasterer Charles H. Bustill, Rev. Jeremiah Asher of Shiloh Church, coachman Morris Hall, hairdresser Isaiah Wears, oyster seller John D. Oliver and Prof. Charles L. Reason. Reason was a Haitian-born professor of mathematics who had recently been hired to implement a new curriculum for the Institute for Colored Youth, a Quaker school that later transformed into Cheyney University.[40]

From those nineteen an Acting Committee of four members was selected and given "the responsibility of attending to every case that might require their aid, as well as the exclusive authority to raise the funds necessary for their purpose." The four were William Still, who was named chairman, Jacob C. White Sr., Nathaniel W. Depee, and Passmore Williamson. Passmore, who became its secretary, was the only white member of the committee.[41] It is now clear that, in the four years since he became an officer in Abolition Society to now, when he took a pre-eminent post in the Vigilance Committee of the

Anti-Slavery Society, Passmore had abandoned pacifist Quaker principles in order to fight enslavement.

It was undoubtedly Passmore's active commitment to the abolitionist cause that prompted him to change his mind, drop what he was working on, and rush to Bloodgood's Hotel that afternoon in July 1855. He must have hailed a hack and ridden there, because he arrived before Still did even though Still had left the Williamsons' office on Arch Street about three minutes ahead of him.[42] Still was just coming down Walnut Street as Passmore reached the hotel. Together they went up to "a yellow boy"—that is, a light-skinned youngster, evidently the same youth who had brought the note to Still. He was sitting outside the hotel. Passmore asked him whether he had seen any blacks entering the building. The boy suggested he talk to one of the waiters on the second floor. Still, meanwhile, had started to enter the hotel lobby. "Get their description," Passmore called out to him. Still ran into several black employees and began to question them. "She was 'a tall, dark woman, with two little boys,'" he was told. Someone, he wasn't sure who, said the slaves and their master had left the hotel to board the ferry at the wharf. Passmore got the same information from the waiter he accosted. The party they were seeking had just left.

Together, Passmore and Still raced out of the hotel and down to the wharf. Tied up at the dock, the ferryboat *Washington,* a sidewheeler, was making steam, preparatory to leaving. Passengers were striding up its gangway, making their way past stevedores laden with baggage and cargo. Pushing their way up the gangway, the two men entered the main cabin on the first deck. There was no one of the slaves' description seated there. "They are up on the second deck," someone said. Passmore and Still raced up the stairs to the hurricane deck. There, seated in the first row by the pilot house, sitting sideways, was, to Passmore's eyes, "a little old man." Still thought he was "an ill-favored white man" and believed the cane the man had in his hand was a swordcane. Some three or four feet away on the same bench on which the man sat was an "anxious-looking" black woman holding a furled umbrella. Seated close by her on her left were two young colored boys, obviously her children. Passmore and Still approached the woman.[43]

3

The Slave Woman

I pity the slave mother, careworn and weary,
Who sighs as she presses her babe to her breast . . .
O who can imagine her heart's deep emotion,
As she thinks of her children about to be sold.

"O, Pity the Slave Mother," *Anti-Slavery Harp,* 4
(to be sung to the air "Araby's Daughters")

Her name was Jane Johnson, though neither Passmore Williamson nor William Still knew that as they approached her on the ferryboat. The children sitting next to her were her sons Daniel, who was about ten or eleven years old, and Isaiah, about eight or nine.[1] She had a third son, but she had not seen him for nearly two years and "never expected to see him again."[2] It was about that time, New Year's Day of 1854, that Cornelius Crew, a businessman in Richmond, Virginia, had sold her, Daniel, and Isaiah to their current master, who took them to his home in Washington, D.C. Jane's third child had not been sold with them, and Jane had no idea where he was.[3] Jane wasn't even certain of any of the children's ages, nor even of her own or where she had been born. All she was sure of was that her parents were the slaves John and Jane Williams. At one time she would give Washington, D.C., as the birthplace of both herself and her parents; at another time she said she had been born south of the Rappahanock River in Caroline County, Virginia. Similarly, at one time she thought she was about twenty-five years old, at another time believed she was in her early forties.[4] Her current master considered her about thirty-five years old and her children about twelve and seven, respectively. It is likely that Jane had once been married to another slave whose name was Johnson, though she never spoke about him, maybe because their "marriage" was foisted on her by her slave owners, who wanted her to bear children. It is also possible that Johnson was the name of a master who had once owned her, before Crew did. Slaves tended to take on the last name of their owners.

As he approached her, Still noted how "tall and well formed" Jane was. She was of "chestnut color," had a "high and large forehead," was of "genteel manners" and, he added, "seems to possess, naturally, uncommon good sense, though of course she has never been allowed to read."[5] As one white abolitionist who got to know her put it, "She is a remarkably intelligent woman for one wholly without education."[6] Black activist William Cooper Nell described her as being "a woman who can take care of herself."[7] She was, a reporter wrote, "a fine specimen of the best class of Virginia housemaids, with a certain ladylike air, propriety of language, and timidity of manner that prepossesses the audience in her favour." The reporter made a point of saying that she was "very polite in her manners and spoke of 'colored gentlemen,' 'white gentlemen,' and 'colored ladies,' as though ladies and gentlemen had been her associates all her lifetime."[8] Moreover, as it turned out, Jane possessed a strong sense of responsibility.

Jane and her sons had accompanied their master from Washington, arriving aboard a Philadelphia, Wilmington, and Baltimore Railroad train. They had reached the city late that morning, en route to New York City, where they were to board a ship for Central America. Although a major harbor for ocean-going vessels, Philadelphia was not a port of embarkation for ships sailing to Central America. Master and slaves would have to go to New York to catch a ship bound for Nicaragua. Anyway, the master wanted to stop at the home on Fifth Street where his wife's father lived. She had asked him to pick up a trunk of her belongings and bring it with him to Nicaragua.

The trip from Washington to New York was an arduous journey. There was no through train, no one railroad that ran the entire distance, and, anyway, there was no uninterrupted track that spanned the entire route. A passenger had to transfer trains four times, and twice that involved taking a ferry to make the connection between rail lines. The greatest nuisance was the trip between Philadelphia and New York. Traveling northbound, as the slave master was heading with Jane and her two youngsters, required three bothersome transfers: the first, to a ferry to cross the Delaware River to the Camden & Amboy Railroad's depot in Camden; then a transfer from the ferry to the railroad's single-track line to South Amboy, New Jersey; and finally a transfer to yet another ferry. It circled Staten Island, steamed into Upper New York Bay and entered the North River, as the southern end of the Hudson River was called. This second ferry deposited through passengers and their luggage at Pier One in lower Manhattan. The Philadelphia-to-New York leg alone could take anywhere from three and a half to six hours, depending on connections. The entire trip, Washington to New York, took close to eight hours at best, nearly eleven at worst.[9] It was arduous, tiring and, especially with children, prone to making passengers cranky. The master and his slaves had had to wake before dawn to make the trip this day, and it was already mid-afternoon. They would not reach New York until well after nightfall.

Jane was the personal maid of the master's wife, who was currently residing in Nicaragua. For the past nine months, while her mistress was living there, Jane had apparently been placed on the farm of relatives of her owners. Although trained as a house servant and holding, for a slave, the prestigious position of a lady's maid, there is an indication that Jane had been forced to work in the fields and live in a slave hut at the farm. Her experience among the rough field hands and the prospect of living in a foreign country whose language she did not speak had evidently prompted Jane to take her future into her own hands. She had persuaded the master to take her young sons with them. "I didn't want to go without my two children," Jane later explained, "and he consented to take them." Her children were supposed to become the playmates in Nicaragua of her master's young son. What Jane managed to hide from him was that she had prepared a disguise for herself—it was in her trunk—and had every intention to flee with her children once they reached New York.

The stopover at the home of the wife's father had been brief. Jane and the children had a bite to eat there. During the visit, she overheard her master's father-in-law tell him that he "could not have done a worse thing" than to bring slaves into the city. The warning was not baseless. Even before the Fugitive Slave Law had been enacted, free blacks in Philadelphia had shown a propensity to demonstrate if a runaway caught in the city was in danger of being returned to his or her owner. But the master replied that he was certain that "Jane would not leave him."

Brief as the stopover was, by the time they left and made their way to the Walnut Street wharf, the two o'clock ferry across the Delaware

River to Camden had left. So they were forced to wait until the next ferry, scheduled for a five o'clock departure. It could not have pleased the slave master. His father-in-law's remonstrance about bringing slaves into Philadelphia wasn't the first time the slave master had been warned. Friends in Washington had also told him not to do so, and before he left the capital with Jane and her sons, he had warned her not to speak to "colored persons."[10]

With several hours to wait for the next ferry, the master led Jane and her boys into nearby Bloodgood's Hotel, where he decided to dine. The hotel, on the corner of Delaware Avenue and Walnut Street, was built especially to cater to the railroad's passengers. Ticket and freight offices were on the ground floor, while the upper portion of the building was given over to a restaurant and guest rooms.[11] Jane and her sons were left on the second-floor porch or veranda of the hotel, seated on a bench overlooking the street. Her master, Jane noted, seemed particularly concerned about their being in a public place in Philadelphia. If anyone asked, she was to say that she "was a free woman traveling with a minister." The master, she said, "seemed to think I might be led off."

The master sent dinner to them from the dining room, but Jane turned it away. He then came out on the porch to check on them, was satisfied they were sitting where he had left them and returned to his meal. Jane, meanwhile, had already confronted a black waitress who passed by. She told her she was supposed to say that she was free, "but I am not free; but I want to be free," Jane said. She was, she said, a slave woman "traveling with a very curious gentleman, who did not want me to have anything to do or say to colored persons." The waitress expressed her sympathy. "Poor thing, I pity you," the woman said as she walked away. Clearly she did not want to get involved.

His dinner finished, Jane's master left the dining table and walked out onto the hotel's veranda, where he saw someone he knew and joined him. He sat for a while, talking to the friend.[12] Then he decided to make sure that his baggage was being loaded onto the five o'clock ferry, which was now berthed down on the nearby wharf. No sooner had he gone than Jane approached a black waiter who was walking past her. Jane repeated what she had told the waitress. Did she want to go with her master? he asked. "No, I do not," Jane answered. The man told her he would telegraph to New York, where two men would meet her and the children and help them to escape. What the man intended to do, however, was to alert William Still at the office of the Pennsylvania Anti-Slavery Society, anticipating that Still, well known

for his involvement in the Underground Railroad, would alert abolitionists in New York about their coming. The man left her hastily, scrib-
bled a note and handed it to a black boy who was loitering outside the
hotel. He asked the youth to run to the society's office on Fifth Street
as quickly as possible.

It was about 4:45 P.M. when Jane's master returned to shepherd
her and the boys to the ferry. They boarded and climbed the stairway
to the hurricane deck. There, in the open on the top of the vessel, a
welcome breeze could be enjoyed. There were only some women seated
there. The master had Jane and the boys sit down near him in the first
row of benches beside the pilothouse. Other passengers soon appeared,
looking for seats. Suddenly Jane noticed a stranger, "a colored gentleman," beckoning to her. It was William Still, though she had no idea
who he was. Jane nodded her head, but did not move. She was "afraid"
to say or do anything, because her master was seated right beside her.
Then Jane realized that another stranger, a white man this time—it
was Passmore Williamson—was approaching them. "I want to speak to
your servant and tell her of her rights," he said to the "little old man"
whom he took to be her master.[13]

4

The Rescue

Ye spirits of the free,
Can ye forever see
Your brother man
A yoked and scourged slave,
Chains dragging to his grave,
And raise no hand to save?
Say if you can.

"Ye Spirits of the Free," *Anti-Slavery Harp,* 16
(to be sung to the air "My Faith Looks Up to Thee")

The ferry whistle was blowing, signaling late-arriving passengers still on the dock that they had better hurry to board the vessel. Some black porters were struggling up the gangway, trunks hoisted on their backs. Only a few minutes were left before the last bell would ring and the *Washington* would pull away from its moorings. In the last-minute flurry of activity, as the ferryboat made ready to depart, what transpired next happened so quickly that all those present differed in details of what occurred. But they all agreed on the general outline of the event.[1]

"You are the person I am looking for, I presume," said Passmore Williamson, turning from the slave master and directly addressing Jane Johnson.[2] Before she could answer, her master asked what he wanted. "Nothing," said Passmore. His "business," Passmore said, was "entirely with this woman."

"She is my slave," the master said, "and anything you have to say to her you can say to me."

"You may have been his slave," said Passmore, ignoring the master and still speaking directly to Jane, "but you are now free." Her master, he continued, had brought her "here into Pennsylvania, and you are now as free as either of us,—you cannot be compelled to go with him unless you choose." If she wished to be free, he added, "all you have to do is to walk ashore with your children."

"My woman knows her rights," the master declared.

The confrontation had attracted the attention of other passengers, and a crowd formed on the top deck. A few black dockhands and porters no longer burdened with luggage joined the bystanders. Just then, the final warning bell rang out. Passmore warned Jane that if she wanted to be free she would have "to act at once," as the ferryboat was about to leave.

All the while, the slave master was protesting. His slaves, he said, "knew where they were going and with whom."

Passmore told him to hold his tongue. He wanted only Jane to speak. Was she a slave? he asked.

"Yes," she replied.

"Just step on shore and you are free," Passmore said.

Flustered, the slave owner rose from his seat and confronted Passmore. Jane, he declared, "understood all about the laws making her free and her right to leave if she wanted." But, he lied, she did not want to leave. She was "on a visit to New York to see her friends." Then he complained that Jane wished to return to Virginia, that she had "children" in the South "from whom it would be hard to separate her." The master's use of the plural "children" has never been explained; Jane never said that she had more than three children, Daniel, Isaiah, and a third son whom she never expected to see again.

The slave master insisted that Jane did not "want to leave him." Yes, she belonged to him, but, he declared, she was "free." Then, in contradiction to that declaration, he said he was "going to give her her freedom."

All the while the slave master ranted on, Jane kept on saying in a firm, determined voice, "I am not free, but I want my freedom—always wanted to be free! But he holds me." Her entreaties stirred William Still. He had never witnessed "such eagerness as her looks expressed."

The master stooped to embrace Jane, who was still seated. He implored her to say that she wished to remain with him. "Jane, you know you have children and friends at Washington," he said. Watching them, Passmore thought the man "seemed to be prostrated with grief, at the prospect of the separation." But even as the man "clasped her to his bosom," Passmore found Jane "so indifferent as not even to favor him with a reply." Jane, Passmore observed sarcastically, did not even bother to show "any desire to thank him for past favors or protection."[3]

"Come," said Passmore, extending his hand.

Jane took hold of one of her children and started to rise. She wanted, she said again, to be free.

Her master placed his hands on her shoulders to prevent her leaving. But Passmore grabbed the master by the collar and pushed him aside. His display of violence, as mild as it appeared, was an indication of Passmore's mental and emotional transformation from a pacificist Quaker viewpoint to a person who was willing to be physically aggressive.

Jane rose from her seat. Two blacks who had witnessed the exchange of words now took hold of the slave master, one on each side of him. One of them was dockhand John Ballard, the other a hack driver named William Custis, who bore a scar on his neck.[4] Ballard, who was known to his friends as "Rabbit," warned the slave master that if he resisted or drew a weapon, "I will cut your throat from ear to ear."

"Let them alone," said some passenger, a man whom Still took to be a slaveholder. "They are his property." But sympathetic passengers were calling out to Jane, "Go along, go along."

Ballard and Custis let go of the slave master and took Jane's children up in their arms. "Massa, massa," the younger of the two, Isaiah, kept calling out. Frightened and screaming, he and Daniel were carried down the stairs to the main deck, shielded by a cordon of black porters, who cleared the pathway for them as they headed for the gangway.

"The boy cried murder," said Capt. Andrew Heath, who worked for the railroad and saw what was happening. "There were twelve or fifteen negroes forcing the woman and two boys along in a crowd." The boys, Heath said, kicked and tried to get away. "They said they wanted to go to their master."[5]

Robert T. Tumbleston, a traveling salesman from New York who was standing near the prow of the ferryboat, said it looked to him as if "a colored woman and two boys [were] being forced ashore by some colored men." Tumbleston knew both Ballard and Custis. He recognized the latter because of his scar. Passing by him, Custis, who was now holding one of the children by the arm, told Tumbleston that the persons they were escorting were slaves.[6]

As the group came down the gangway and reached the wharf, William Edwards, a messenger boy who carried correspondence to and from the offices of the railroad line, had the same impression as the other eyewitnesses, Heath and Tumbleston. The two boys, he thought, were being "forced away by two colored men," he said. "The boy cried, and was struggling very hard to get away."[7]

William Still had a different impression of the boys' reaction. The youngest boy, Isaiah, who was "too young to know what these things meant," was crying out, "Massa John! Massa John!" But the older boy was taking "the matter more dispassionately, and the mother quite calmly." Jane and the children "were assisted, but not forced to leave." Except for one person calling out—he didn't know who it was—there was no violence or threat that he was aware of. The person who had called out may have been "a colored man," Still thought, for the threat was aimed at the slave master. "Knock him down!" the man, whoever it was, shouted. "Knock him down!"

Like a swarm of bees, the blacks surrounded Jane and her boys and led her away. They turned left at Bloodgood's Hotel and headed down Delaware Avenue. A young black boy had run ahead of them to find a hack. He spotted one, sitting idle on the corner where short, meandering Dock Street crossed into Delaware and Front.[8] The youngster asked its driver, James McIlhone, to wait. Within three minutes, McIlhone saw the crowd coming around the corner, headed toward him. He thought they were "forcing the woman along." The boys had been hoisted up again into the arms of two blacks. They were "crying."

Jane, Isaiah, and Daniel were put in the carriage. William Still, Custis and a third black man got in, as well. Custis told McIlhone that Jane was a sick woman whom they wanted to take home. But McIlhone overheard one of them tell the younger of the two boys that he was "a fool for crying so for 'Massa John.'" "Massa John" would "sell him" if he ever "caught him."

Still told McIlhone to drive to Tenth and Pine streets. They started off, moving slowly, the horse fatigued from a day in the intense heat. As they moved along, the "well-dressed" man that the other black men called "Stille" recounted to Jane the circumstances that had led him and Passmore Williamson to go to the ferryboat. All the way, however, the boys continued to cry. Seated up on the driver's box, McIlhone was aware that the "Negroes were trying to keep them still from hallooing out," but the admonishments went unheeded. "I heard them coaxing them to keep still and not let people hear them going along."

At Tenth and Pine, everyone got out of the carriage. McIlhone saw Custis and the other black man lead the woman and the children down Barley Street, a little byway in the major black section of Philadelphia, which ran from Tenth and Eleventh streets between Lombard and Pine. Jane and her boys would spend a few hours at a friendly "resting-place" until it became dark, when it was safe to move them to Still's own home not far away.

Still did not accompany them. He tipped Custis and the other black man twenty-five cents, then paid the hack driver McIlhone a dollar and a half before walking away in another direction.[9] He felt satisfied that once "the excitement of the moment" had passed, "the mother seemed very cheerful, and rejoiced greatly that herself and boys had been, as she thought, so 'providentially delivered from the house of bondage!' For the first time in her life she could look upon herself and children and feel free!"

Meanwhile, back at the Walnut Street wharf, both Passmore Williamson and the slave master had followed in the wake of the crowd that bore away Jane and her children. Ever since the confrontation on the ferryboat neither man had spoken to the other. Off in the distance on Delaware Avenue, both men saw her and the youngsters entering the carriage. There were two police officers standing nearby. One of them, Thomas Wallace, was wondering what was going on. He had seen what he called "the occurrence on the Avenue" and thought there had been a fight. A woman and two children "were all crying." The slave master approached Wallace and asked him to take note of what was happening and who the persons were who were leading the woman and the boys away. No sooner had he spoken than Passmore intervened. He whispered into Wallace's ear that the persons involved were slaves who were "getting away." Passmore asked the policeman to "protect them." Wallace, however, had no intention of intervening in the matter. The policeman said he would have nothing whatsoever to do with what was going on, no matter whether the request was to protect or to apprehend the slaves.[10]

Passmore then turned to the slave master and introduced himself. He handed him his business card. He said that he would be responsible for any claim that the master might have "for his servants." However, he thought to himself, he "had not designed to do violence to any law but supposed" that he had acted within "the law, and the legal rights" of everyone involved. He was certain that he "had committed no injury whatever" to any right of the slave owner.

The law Passmore referred to was the Liberty Law, which the Pennsylvania legislature had enacted in 1847. The law was meant to strengthen the emancipation act that had taken effect in 1780. While the emancipation act established the gradual emancipation of slaves living within the state's borders, it had exempted domestic slaves who were the servants of congressmen and foreign diplomats, who could "sojourn" in Pennsylvania with their slaves for up to six months; if they remained any longer than that, their slaves were then considered free. The Liberty Law, containing seven provisions, dealt, among other matters, with the kidnapping of free blacks and the capture of fugitive slaves. The law prohibited state courts from taking cognizance of any case involving a fugitive and granted state judges the right "at all times, on application made, to issue the writ of habeas corpus, and to inquire into the causes of legality of the arrest or imprisonment of any human being within this commonwealth." The law also repealed the section of the emancipation act that allowed slave owners to reside with their servants in Pennsylvania for as many as six months. Without exception, the law provided that any slave brought into the state was free as soon as he or she stepped foot inside its borders.[11] It was this provision—a critical point that the federal Fugitive Slave Law of 1850 did nothing to invalidate—that Passmore Williamson had in mind when he told Jane Johnson that she was free.

The slave master was furious. Jane and her boys were his property. They were valuable, worth a great deal of money. He had no intention of letting the matter drop.

Passmore, of course, had no idea who the slave master was. The man had never identified himself. Would Passmore have acted so precipitously to rescue Jane if he had known who her master was? Considering the numerous times he had participated in helping fugitives, the strict moral code he lived by, it is reasonable to conclude that he would not have hesitated, and not regretted for a moment the opportunity, to help free a slave. It is also likely that he would have relished the opportunity to fight openly the battle for slavery's end in the court of public opinion.

One thing is certain. Passmore knew he was taking on the national government. If nothing else, he must have realized that assisting a slave to abandon her master would entangle him with federal authorities. But he had no idea that he was about to be embroiled in a legal and political struggle comparable, metaphorically, to the biblical clash between David and Goliath.

5

The City

Ye Democrats, come to the rescue,
And aid on the liberty cause,
And millions will rise up and bless you,
With heart-cheering songs of applause.

"The Liberty Bell," *Anti-Slavery Harp*, 8
(to be sung to the air "Rosin the Bow")

The rescue had taken great daring. After all, it was not carried out on some dark street at night without witnesses. On the contrary, the spiriting away of Jane Johnson and her youngsters was done in full view of a number of persons, many of whom were white citizens of Philadelphia. Passmore had no way of knowing how they, and/or anyone else aboard the ferryboat, might react. For in a special way, Philadelphia mirrored the nation. It was a divided city, ambivalent about the blacks in its midst, troubled by questions that slavery raised, and particularly hypersensitive when it came to its business interests with the South. Many Philadelphians cared little about the abolitionist cause or about slavery itself except as it affected their lives. Many, in fact, were sympathetic to or condoned the attitude of southerners.

The Philadelphia that Passmore Williamson and William Still lived in was a far cry from the colony that William Penn and his followers set out to establish in the seventeenth century. It was supposed to be free of intolerance. On the contrary, Philadelphia had become by 1855 a city torn between its native born and the newcomers from abroad, between those with money and those without, between whites and blacks.

Underscoring the divisions within the city were the numerous political factions that existed at that time. They represented a nation that had been at odds over many issues in the first half of the nineteenth century—issues as diverse as immigration policy, tariffs, currency and banking reforms, and working-class versus wealthy interests. But now the dominant issue was slavery. There was the Democratic Party, the party in ascendancy, which had won the presidency for Franklin Pierce. It was openly racist and favored southern interests. Then, too, there was the Know-Nothing Party, whose followers within it sometimes called themselves the American Party. The Know-Nothing Party had sprung up in 1850, spurred by the explosion of hatred against immigrants and Catholics, though its followers in Pennsylvania welcomed into its ranks German and Irish Protestants. The Know-Nothing adherents shared with Democrats their pro-slavery stance and an antipathy to abolitionists, who were seen as "disunionists." On the other hand, the once-influential Whig Party had become so divided on the issue of slavery that it had virtually disappeared in the early 1850s, after the party adopted a hands-off policy of not discussing the fractious issue whatsoever.

One of the chief opponents of the ruling Democratic Party was the Free Soil Party, whose members were against the extension of slavery into any new territories. It attracted many adherents of the now-dormant Liberty Party, whose single goal had been the immediate and outright abolition of slavery throughout the nation. There was also a burgeoning group, dissatisfied members of the existing parties, who called themselves Republicans. They represented an olio of factions, a conglomeration appealing not only to frustrated Free Soilers, but also to discontented Know-Nothings and disillusioned Whigs. Although followers of all these groups spoke out against anti-slavery activists, nevertheless abolitionists as well as proponents of both temperance and women's rights were all finding a haven in this new party, too, albeit playing a minority role in its policy making. Republicans at the time fell far short of advocating black equality, and though this new party opposed the expansion of slavery, it would not come out for outright abolition until the Civil War. Passage of the Kansas-Nebraska Act in 1854 had prompted these disparate political elements to coalesce over the slavery issue, because the act not only raised the possibility of opening up a huge area of middle America to slavery, but also kindled the specter of reducing the North to a secondary diminished political force in the nation. If nothing else, anti-slavery-minded Whigs, Know-Nothings and Free Soilers could agree that the enemy was "slave power," which had to be restrained. The party's eventual support of the rights of blacks to freedom and equality was a way to forestall the continued supremacy of the South. As Frederick Douglass put it, the "cry of Free Men was raised, not for the extension of liberty to the black man, but for the protection of the liberty of the white."[1]

From the beginning, Philadelphia had established itself as a major trading center, had jousted, in fact, for years with New York as the nation's most wealthy and enterprising city. Young as America was, the nation as a whole was bursting with energy. The Industrial Revolution—factory goods replacing cottage industries—was in full stride. The smoke fumes that drifted across the landscape came from the coal that fired furnaces, not the wood used for hearths in homes. Factory whistles vied with church bells to announce the hour. Immigration swelled established cities, adding to the babel of languages that was already a feature of the nation. The press for more land, always westward, led to new towns, new states. But with all that—with industrialization, immigration, cultural differences, governments that settlers fashioned—came new problems that even an established city like Philadelphia could not escape.

Although some ninety miles from the mouth of Delaware Bay, the city's deep-water port was an inviting haven for large, ocean-going vessels. Even more so, the city had developed into a hub for inland trade. By 1821, turnpikes north, south, and west connected Philadelphia to New York, Baltimore, and Harrisburg. The highway to Lancaster, completed in 1821 and some seventy miles long, was known alternatively as the Great Conestoga Road or the Philadelphia Wagon Road; it was the most heavily traveled turnpike in the country.[2] Canals came to take over the major task of being the conduit for the transportation of goods—narrow, shallow boats ferrying the coal and iron into the city from upstate Pennsylvania, then returning upstate with manufactured goods made in the city. The first, the Schuylkill Canal, completed in 1825, connected Port Carbon with the city of Reading nearly thirty-six miles away. Then came the railroads. The first line, only twenty miles of track, opened in 1832; within eight years, trains ran north to New York, south to Wilmington and Baltimore.[3] By 1855 there were so many railroads serving Philadelphia, linking it with all points on the compass, that by mid-July the last of the horse-drawn stagecoaches carrying mail to and from Philadelphia and other cities made its final trip.[4] Only New York City could claim a vaster railroad network and a canal, the Erie, that was longer.

Considering all its divisive elements, it was foregone that Philadelphia—a city where the Declaration of Independence had been drawn up and the United States Constitution drafted (the "City of Freedom" was one of its nicknames)—was ambivalent about the presence of blacks in its midst. A few, such as James Forten, had established themselves as what whites considered law-abiding, responsible, middle-class citizens (though Forten and other members of his family were militant abolitionists). But at a time when the city's industrial base was growing rapidly—when its commerce, foundries for the forging of locomotives and shipyards for the building of ocean-going vessels, its leadership in the publishing and medical worlds, made it a bustling metropolis—most blacks, if they were employed at all, held menial jobs, mostly in the construction field as carpenters and plasterers. Others who operated small shops—barbers, dressmakers, and cobblers—catered primarily to fellow blacks.[5]

Employment opportunities as a whole suffered drastically because of the huge influx of immigrants from across the Atlantic fleeing famine and war, in the main Germans at first, then Irish Catholics. The latter in particular were unskilled and competed with blacks for the same jobs. In the decade alone between 1840 and 1850, Philadelphia's population grew rapidly from roughly 258,000 persons to more than 408,000, a gain of almost 60 percent, attributable in large part to the more than 43,000 newcomers who were born in foreign countries. The immigrants vastly outnumbered the free blacks in the city. When the census of 1850 was taken, there were only some 20,000 free blacks who called Philadelphia their home.[6] A study sponsored by the Abolition Society a few years later showed that less than two-thirds of the blacks who had trades actually followed them.[7] William Still's experience in Philadelphia reflected the difficulty that blacks faced when looking for work. At various times, he worked at an odd assortment of low-paying jobs, hauling wood, selling oysters, hawking clothes. He was a waiter at one time, a well-digger at another.[8]

There were other reasons, chiefly economic, that contributed to the attitude of many of Philadelphia's citizens. The city was deeply connected with its neighbors to the south. The city's huge textile mills needed the cotton that plantation owners grew. At the same time, the plantation owners as well as other southern farmers were indebted to the city's banks. In addition, machinery and machined goods made in

Philadelphia found ready markets in the South. Philadelphia's ties to the South grew even more important as New York and Boston became predominant in overseas trade in the second quarter of the nineteenth century, prompting Philadelphia manufacturers, bankers, and merchants to emphasize their business links with the South. And with those ties came a cultural relationship affecting the city's social life and standards that mimicked customs and practices in the South. "Everything Southern was exalted and worshiped," a local journalist at the time remarked.[9]

Moreover, as in other northern states that espoused freedom for blacks, words were one thing, reality another. Blacks suffered discrimination in public schools and on public transportation. They were barred from fraternal organizations, unwelcome at theaters or concert halls, and found they could not rent a room for the night in any of the fashionable hotels that catered to businessmen and visitors.

Blacks reacted by establishing their own fraternal groups. They provided their own entertainments. They formed reform and benevolent associations. They also set up their own schools. By 1841 there were more than fifty incorporated black societies, many of them beneficial organizations founded by groups such as porters and coachmen.[10] Black churches took a critical role in the community, becoming centers of political protest. Two slaves who had purchased their freedom helped to found two of the most noted black churches in Philadelphia, the African Methodist Episcopal Church, known as Mother Bethel, and St. Thomas African Episcopal Church. Together, the two men— Richard Allen and Absalom Jones—organized the Free African Society in 1787, intending at first to assist free but financially struggling blacks. The society's function soon expanded. Its members played a major role in the Underground Railroad, shepherding fugitives to freedom. They also staged protests against slavery. As early as 1817, Mother Bethel sponsored a demonstration against the colonization movement and allied itself with the plight of southern slaves, and Richard Allen joined James Forten in submitting a petition to Congress calling on it to revise the Fugitive Slave Act of 1793. It was at yet a third church, Wesley A.M.E., that blacks convened in October 1850 to protest the passage of the Fugitive Slave Law. They resolved to "resist the law at any cost and at all hazards," and pledged "never to refuse aid and shelter and succor to any brother or sister who escaped from the prison-house of Southern bondage."[11]

Achievements aside, the bigotry all blacks experienced left a bitter taste. Two other slaves who had gained their freedom were especially critical of the city's attitude toward blacks. New York, which also had strong financial ties to the South, already had a reputation as a place where blacks were unwelcome. (In national elections both just before and during the Civil War, Abraham Lincoln would lose that city's vote by a two-to-one margin.) Nevertheless, in speaking of Philadelphia, William Wells Brown declared, "Colorphobia is more rampant here than in the pro-slavery, negro-hating city of New York." Philadelphia, Frederick Douglass said, "has its white schools and its colored schools, its white churches and its colored churches, its white Christianity and its colored Christianity." Even its cultural aspirations, whether concerts or literary institutions, were separate. "The line is everywhere tightly drawn between them," said Douglass. Everything in the city "is mean, contemptible and barbarous."[12] A white English Quaker, who visited Philadelphia about the time that William Still arrived there, said that "there is probably no city in the known world where dislike, amounting to hatred of the coloured population, prevails more than in the city of brotherly love!"[13]

That hatred had been simmering not only in Philadelphia but in Pennsylvania as a whole ever since the Revolutionary War. At first, the state, prodded by the original Abolition Society, was in the vanguard of setting slaves free. The Pennsylvania legislature in 1780 passed the first abolition act in the new nation. It called for the gradual emancipation of slaves. Slaves not registered by a certain date were automatically freed. Those who were registered were freed upon reaching the age of twenty-eight. Those born in slavery were freed upon reaching the age of twenty-six. The only exception to emancipation was domestic servants accompanying congressional delegates and foreign diplomats who were traveling through the state. The act also permitted owners of slaves from out of state to take back runaways who had fled into Pennsylvania.

Attracted in part by the state's liberal stance, so many fugitive slaves had fled into Philadelphia by 1810 that Dr. Benjamin Rush, a member of the Abolition Society, voiced his concern. The society's president, Benjamin Franklin, who owned slaves himself before the American Revolution, had once described most blacks as being "of a plotting disposition, dark, sullen, malicious, revengeful and cruel in the highest degree."[14] His attitude, however, changed after the war, and he was the only founding father to seek a restriction on slavery, satirizing southern justifications of the institution when he was head of the Abolition Society. Franklin aside, the attitude of most whites towards blacks —superior, paternalistic—was a continuing problem. Their prejudice focused not only on free blacks within Philadelphia, but also upon the escaped slaves who made their way to the city. Bias against the run-aways was exacerbated by the fact that most of them were not only illiterate, but also had few skills useful in an urban environment, spoke broken English and had none of the socially acceptable manners that house slaves or black craftsmen had picked up in social interaction with their masters and mistresses. Quakers set aside special sections for blacks to join them in worship, but they did not encourage member-ship in the Society of Friends.

As a result of Pennsylvania's emancipation program, by 1820 there was no longer a single slave in Philadelphia, and the number of blacks had risen from the mere two hundred in 1775 to seven thousand. They were free, of course, and represented about ten percent of Philadel-phia's total population.[15] The total number of blacks continued to grow in the years after 1820; by 1833 there were more than fourteen thou-sand of them in Philadelphia alone and more than twice that number throughout the state.[16] However, although the immigration population had grown even greater, whites feared that the increasing number of blacks would have an impact in local elections. At one point in 1831, an alarm was raised that the legislatures of Virginia and Maryland were going to enact laws to expel the free blacks who lived in those states. The expelled blacks, according to the rumor, would flood ad-joining states like Pennsylvania with "an influx of ignorant, indolent and depraved population" of blacks "fit to be instruments of evil."[17] The reaction to such fears was devastating. The Pennsylvania consti-tution of 1790 had enfranchised "every freeman" who was twenty-one years old and who had resided in the state for two years and had paid a state or county tax. But what did "freeman" mean—a "free man," that is, someone who was not a slave? Some whites argued that the term "freeman" applied only to white men, that no man of color, no matter how "free" or how prosperous, was entitled to vote. This viewpoint was endorsed when, in 1837, a special state convention deliberated the provisions of a new constitution for Pennsylvania.

The principle intention of holding the constitutional convention was to bring Pennsylvania into line with other states that had abol-ished property qualifications for voting. However, the fear that blacks in the future might represent the deciding factor in elections prompted a heated debate. It was a fear that intensified when a legal dispute arose over an election in Bucks County that was decided by a slim mar-gin of votes, which were cast, it was believed, by some thirty or forty black men. During a recess in the convention's deliberations, the state supreme court announced its decision in the Bucks County case, ruling that the 1790 constitution, which was still in effect at that point, excluded anyone of color from voting. Stunned by the turn of events, a number of the city's leading black citizens, including James Forten, drew up a petition, "The Appeal of Forty Thousand," to try to persuade state voters not to deny blacks the right to vote. But an overwhelming majority of white voters subsequently endorsed the new constitution, which took effect in 1838. It limited voting rights to "every white freeman of the age of twenty-one years" or older.[18] At a single, sudden stroke, blacks were completely disenfranchised. It was a stunning blow to the black community. Crepe hung from the doors of a number of the city's most respected black families, in mourning for the loss of liberty.

Perhaps just as destructive were the violent confrontations and race riots that continued to wrack Philadelphia, initiated in large part by newly arrived Irish. The first outbreaks of violence occurred in 1829, others in the 1830s. The fact that the newcomers were white and readily replaced blacks in jobs created a volatile atmosphere, fueling antagonisms. A riot midsummer in 1834 broke out over rides on a carousel on South Street; before it was over the next evening, a black church had been destroyed, another church had been badly damaged, the windows and doors of black homes had been broken, residents had been beaten. In another outburst of violence, triggered by a rally held in Pennsylvania Hall only a day after its opening in 1838, the hall—built by the Pennsylvania Anti-Slavery Society with money from both white and black abolitionists—was burned to the ground after a black man was seen walking arm-in-arm with a white woman. The structure was less than three blocks from the State House, which was now known as the Hall of Independence, or Independence Hall. The angry mob went on to burn a black church south of Independence Hall and a new shelter for black orphans north of the city.

An even worse riot occurred on August 1, 1842, when a group of whites attacked blacks parading in honor of Emancipation Day in the West Indies. The holiday, unlike the Fourth of July, had special meaning for blacks: Great Britain had outlawed slavery in its dominions in 1807 and throughout its empire in 1834. The violence spread between Fifth and Eighth streets in the city's major black neighborhood, an area south and west of Chestnut Street, where Independence Hall was situated. A number of people were killed, others injured, stores pillaged.

The target of one group of rioters was the home of Robert Purvis on Lombard Street. Purvis was a black man who was so light-skinned that a white writer said that it was difficult to forget that he was "not of our own race."[19] But Purvis never denied his black heritage, nor did he make a secret of his abolitionist leanings. He had been a major contributor in 1838 to the writing of "The Appeal of Forty Thousand," the memorial that proved fruitless in preventing Pennsylvania from adopting the new state constitution that disenfranchised black voters. Purvis had been born in Charleston, South Carolina, to a wealthy English cotton merchant and a free-born black woman whose mother was a Moor and whose father was a German Jew. The family moved to Philadelphia in 1819, and Purvis went on to attend Amherst College in Massachusetts. On his return, he married a daughter of James Forten. Purvis helped to form the Vigilance Committee, which met in his home, and he often hid fugitives in a room in the house reached by a trap door. Purvis was credited with helping forty-six slaves achieve freedom.[20] On the first day of the riot, Purvis stationed himself on the steps of his home, armed with weapons, ready to shoot any intruders. Fires at a black church and at a hall in the area distracted hoodlums approaching his house, but they came back the next day. A Catholic priest was able to chide the rioters into moving off, but a local sheriff told Purvis he could not guarantee his safety. Disillusioned and saddened, Purvis abandoned the city, moving to a suburb. The Vigilance Committee was shattered. "I know not where to begin," Purvis declared, "nor where nor how to end, in a detail of the wantonness, brutality and murderous spirit of the actors in the late riots; nor of the apathy and inhumanity of the whole community, in regard to the latter. Press, church, magistrates, clergymen and devils are against us." Purvis said he was "convinced" of the "utter and complete nothingness" in which the public regarded blacks. "I am sick, miserably sick," he added.[21]

Unlike Purvis, most blacks were poor and uneducated. Of nine thousand adult blacks surveyed in the Abolition Society's study in 1853, nearly half of them, more than four thousand, could not read or write.[22] Philadelphia instituted public schools in 1818, but they were only for white children. Not until 1822 could black children attend elementary schools. They were barred from high schools and could not attend professional schools or even sit in on lectures without credit. Underscoring the lack of equal education was the state legislature's decision in 1854 requiring separate schools where there were at least twenty black pupils.[23] Blacks did take it upon themselves to set up their own schools, and by 1854 there were twenty-eight such institutions, including private and charity-sponsored educational groups that catered to blacks, as well as nineteen Sunday schools.[24] However, despite the efforts of blacks to see to their children's education, an estimated two thousand youngsters between the ages of eight and eighteen were not attending school at all.[25]

The Philadelphia that Passmore grew up in and lived in was in sharp contrast to the city that most blacks like William Still inhabited. Notwithstanding its burgeoning population, in many ways Passmore's world was still a small town, where residents in the commercial, publishing, legal, and financial fields knew one another, and those who had not moved to its outlying districts to live resided in the streets in and around the squares near the old State House. It was a close-knit network of the elite. They were members of the same fraternal clubs, attended the same entertainments, saw each other at social functions, did business with one another, intermarried. An observer spoke generously of its citizens' "agreeable and hospitable society, their pleasant evening-parties, their love of literature, their happy blending of the industrial habits of the north with the social usages of the south."[26] Another of Philadelphia's numerous nicknames, "City of Homes," spoke of the genial atmosphere created by the rows of small brick houses that ran along its neat rectangular grid of streets that William Penn had established, stretching from the Delaware to the Schuylkill rivers. Philadelphia was, a local journalist said, "a very well-shaded, peaceful city" reminiscent of "a pleasant English town of earlier times in which a certain picturesque rural beauty still lingered."[27]

That description might hold for what was referred to as the city center, but it was misleading when it came to the rest of the community. As Passmore grew into adulthood, the metropolitan area that was Philadelphia County was changing into a roguish entity of twenty-nine different municipalities, each with its own constables, courts, and set of ordinances. The result was mayhem when it came to law enforcement; thieves, for example, could literally run, or indeed walk, from arrest in one jurisdiction to freedom in another. The county had by then become home to increasing numbers of immigrants—English, Scots, Germans, and Scandinavians, then the Irish. A once-prudish though cosmopolitan county had become a raucous metropolis. In 1849, Passmore Williamson, then only twenty-seven years old, joined seventy-nine other Philadelphians, among them three members of the noted Biddle family, in signing a petition calling for the consolidation of the city.[28] It was ultimately achieved in 1854, all twenty-nine separate communities finally melded into one city.

However, political consolidation did not unify the city's populace. Industry and immigration bred intense conflicts. Brotherly love gave way to hostility between different immigrant groups and between new-comers and old-timers. Mills, foundries, and plants crowded along the river waterfronts. Ramshackle houses infested once serene byways. Except where the wealthy lived, the "City of Homes" was a city of hov-els. And, as for being "The Nation's Birthplace," as of 1850 Indepen-dence Hall housed, on its second floor, the federal district court where southern masters or their agents brought alleged recaptured slaves to establish their ownership. It was understandable why the Fourth of July meant little to blacks.

Philadelphia was a Democratic city, in a Democrat-dominated state, in a nation controlled by a Democratic administration and a Demo-cratic Congress. Tolerant of slavery if not outright pro-slavery. Yet, as a result of the increasing publicity given to the inhumane treatment experienced by slaves in the South, the outrages suffered by free blacks who were kidnapped, the thrilling escapes by and the daring rescues of slaves, a confrontation over the issue seemed inevitable. Slavery tore at the very fabric of the Union. The rescue of Jane Johnson and her children would exemplify the pending conflict between states' rights and federal authority. For Jane's master was no ordinary slave owner.

William Still, who chronicled the stories of escaped slaves passing through Philadelphia, was a key participant in the rescue of Jane Johnson. He was a vital link in the Underground Railroad and continued to champion the rights of blacks after the Civil War. Courtesy of the Photographs and Prints Division, Schomburg Center for Research in Black Culture, the New York Public Library, Astor, Lenox, and Tilden Foundations

Jane Johnson wanted her freedom. She had even contrived a disguise for herself. But after gaining her freedom, she bravely faced her slave master in order to help those who had helped her. Courtesy of The Library Company of Philadelphia

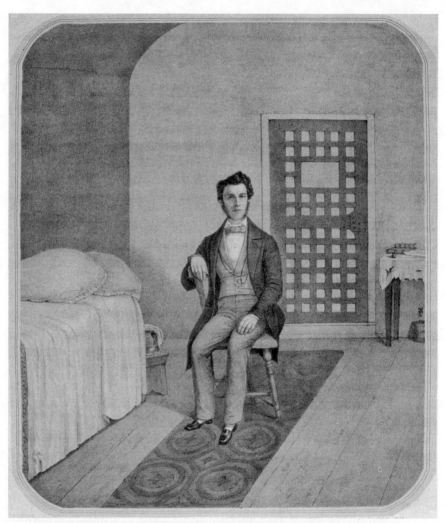

*Passmore Williamson, the Quaker-bred Philadelphian who took responsibility for
Jane Johnson's rescue, posed inside his cell, No. 78, at Moyamensing Prison, on
the sixty-ninth day of his incarceration. This lithograph, based on the original
photograph that Williamson arranged to have taken, was sold as an item of anti-
slavery propaganda for fifty cents a copy, two dollars if framed in gold. His friends
arranged for the decent sitting chair, the rug, and the washstand. They saw to
it that the simple cot that the prison provided for Williamson was comfortably
embellished as well. Courtesy of the Chester County Historical Society, West
Chester, Pa.*

As Jane Johnson looks on, Passmore Williamson fends off her master in an artist's depiction of her rescue aboard the ferryboat Washington. William Still is shown heading down the steps of the vessel's hurricane deck. Courtesy of the Manuscripts, Archives and Rare Books Division, Schomburg Center for Research in Black Culture, New York Public Library, Astor, Lenox, and Tilden Foundations

JOHN H. WHEELER.

Born, Hertford Co., No. Ca. Aug. 2d. 1802.   Died, Washington, D. C. Dec. 7th, 1882.
A. M. Univ. of No. Ca. 1826;   State Treasurer, 1845.   U. S. Envoy to Nicaragua, 1853.
Author Hist. of No. Ca. and of Reminiscences of Eminent North Carolinians.

Slave master John Hill Wheeler was the American minister to Nicaragua with close ties to many federal officials, including President Franklin Pierce. He was continually frustrated in his attempt to regain his "property"—Jane Johnson and her two children. Courtesy of Documenting the American South (http://docsouth.unc.edu), University of North Carolina at Chapel Hill Libraries, North Carolina Collection

Federal judge John Kintzing Kane was a strict constitutionalist—and as stubborn and self-righteous as Passmore Williamson was. He would live to regret his citing of Williamson for contempt. Courtesy of The Library Company of Philadelphia

Formidable-looking Moyamensing Prison, which housed murderers and thieves, became Passmore Williamson's "home" for more than three months. Hundreds of sympathizers flocked to visit him there, including many of the nation's leading black abolitionist leaders. To its right is the incongruous Egyptian archway of the debtors' prison. Courtesy of The Library Company of Philadelphia

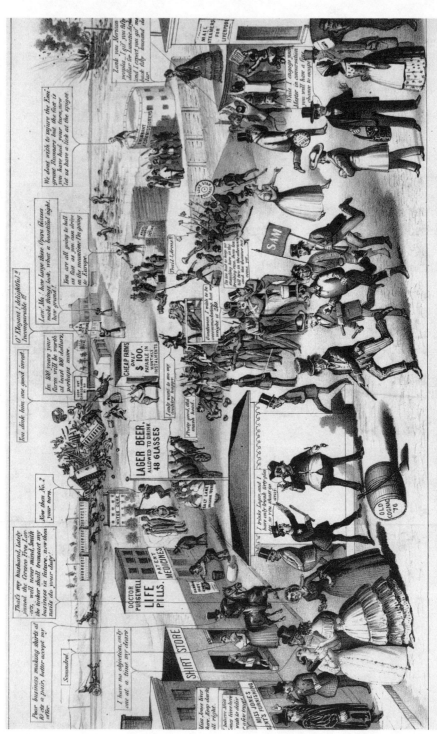

THE FOLLIES OF THE AGE, VIVE LA HUMBUG!!

Overleaf In the lower right-hand corner of this cartoon, which pokes fun at some contemporary antics—"The Follies of the Age, Vive la Humbug!!"— Passmore Williamson tells Jane Johnson, "While I engage your Master in conversation you will have a fine chance to escape." Their inclusion in the cartoon is an example of the widespread notoriety that her rescue received. *Courtesy of The Library Company of Philadelphia*

Above The cruel way blacks were treated was the subject of many cartoons in abolitionist newspapers and publications. In this one, "Effects of the Fugitive-Slave-Law," a posse of armed white men ambushes four blacks in a cornfield. The accompanying text on the left is from Deuteronomy: "Thou shalt not deliver unto the master his servant which has escaped." The text on the right is from the Declaration of Independence: "We hold that all men are created equal." *Courtesy of the Library of Congress*

In a pose similar to the one he took in Moyamensing, Passmore Williamson had this photograph taken within a few years after his release from prison. The portrait became part of the family heirlooms passed on from one generation to the next by his descendants. Courtesy of Shirley Atwood

PASSMORE WILLIAMSON.

This drawing of Passmore Williamson accompanied his obituary in the Philadelphia Public Ledger *of March 1, 1895. He was a few days shy of his seventy-third birthday when he died. His unmarried daughter Mary Elizabeth, who was born when he was in prison, lived with him and was at his bedside when he died. From the authors' collection*

6

The Slave Master

Freely the slave-master goes where he will;
Freemen, stand ready, his wish to fulfil,
Helping the tyrant, or honest or knave,
Thinking not, caring not, for the poor slave.

"Rescue the Slave," *Anti-Slavery Harp,* 28
(to be sung to the air "The Troubadour")

The "little old man" to whom Passmore Williamson had handed his business card was none other than John Hill Wheeler, U.S. resident minister to Nicaragua. Wheeler, a former personal assistant to President Franklin Pierce, had, in fact—on the very day before he traveled to Philadelphia with Jane Johnson and her children—dined with the president, the governor of Virginia, and two federal judges at the White House. Wheeler sat at a place of honor, by Mrs. Pierce's right hand.[1]

The circumstances of his being with such exalted company were not unusual. Wheeler, once a plantation owner in North Carolina who now made his home in Washington, was, like the president, a loyal Jacksonian Democrat. Needless to say, his sympathies were with the South, but he also shared with Pierce an antipathy for political abolitionists and a serious concern that those who fought against slavery were a threat to the Union. The president—a northerner who had made a name for himself as a New Hampshire legislator, then United States representative and senator from that state—pointedly declared in his first inaugural address that both slavery and the Fugitive Slave Law were constitutional. He described abolitionist activities as "fanatical excitement." And his years in the White House, during which anti-slavery forces became increasingly vocal, only served to strengthen his opinion. "Slavery reformers," he would declare in his Fourth Annual Message, "are perfectly aware that the change in the relative condition of white and black races in the slave-holding States which they would promote is beyond their lawful authority . . . that for them and the States of which they are citizens the only path to its accomplishment is through burning cities, and ravaged fields, and slaughtering populations" that would lead "inevitably into mutual devastation and fractricidal [sic] carnage."[2]

Pierce's reaction a year earlier regarding the capture of an escaped Virginia slave was telling. The runaway, Anthony Burns, was seized in Boston by three slave hunters. Two days later, anti-slavery activists tried to storm the courthouse where he was being held. In the melee, a guard was mortally wounded. Federal and state troops were called out to restore order. What happened next demonstrated the intensity of abolitionist sentiment in Boston as well as Pierce's response to the incident. No sooner had a federal commissioner ordered Burns returned to his owner in Virginia than many shopkeepers hung black crepe in their windows. Sensing the possibility of more violence, Attorney General Caleb Cushing urged the president to uphold the law. Pierce ordered two artillery companies, a cavalry detachment and a marine squadron to Boston to see that Burns was returned safely to his slave master. He also had a federal revenue cutter sent to the city to carry Burns back south.[3] On the day Burns was taken to the harbor, surrounded by troops, tens of thousands of protesters turned out to witness the event. It was a troubling indication of northern reaction to slavery and the Fugitive Slave Law. But the president, Wheeler reported, was "delighted with the news from Boston that the slave Burns had been remanded by law to his master." Pierce said that "'the only fear [that abolitionists] had was of lead and steel.'"[4]

The nation was being pulled in one direction by the effects of industrialization in the North and tugged in an opposite direction by the plantation owners, whose fortunes and way of living depended on slavery. Pierce, under the influence of southerners such as his Secretary of War, Jefferson Davis, muddled through. He had already acquiesced to the repeal of the Missouri Compromise, enacted in 1820. It had permitted Missouri to be admitted as a slave state and Maine, formerly part of Massachusetts, as a free state. The compromise had also excluded slavery from lands that were part of the Louisiana Purchase north of latitude 36°30'. However, the law that superseded it, the Kansas-Nebraska Act of 1854, permitted settlers in the territories of Kansas and Nebraska to decide for themselves whether slavery should be permitted when they became states. The act only served to further divide the country. Competing factions, both declaring themselves legitimate state governments, fought for control of the territories. Kansas, especially, became a tortured battleground.

Besides the president, Wheeler had many political contacts with highly placed persons within the government. He had business dealings with or socialized with a number of key administration officers, among them Jefferson Davis, Secretary of State William L. Marcy, Attorney General Caleb Cushing, and Secretary of the Navy James C. Dobbin. His diary is filled with the names of individuals, both civilian and military, with whom he relaxed on outings and at parties, attended the theater or visited on a regular basis. Wheeler was also on familiar terms with many of the leading citizens of Philadelphia. His wife, Ellen, was the daughter of Thomas Sully, the most noted portrait painter in the nation. It was at Sully's home that Wheeler and his slaves had stopped before heading for the ferry at the Walnut Street wharf.

Passmore's description of Wheeler as being "little" was only slightly exaggerated. "He was below the average American, by no means imposing in his presence," wrote a friendly contemporary who wrote a biographical sketch introducing a book Wheeler wrote.[5] As for his being an "old man," Wheeler was a month shy of celebrating his forty-ninth birthday, though when Passmore first saw him he had just recovered from a serious case of cholera. Anyway, Wheeler's furrowed brow, and hair and moustache streaked with gray, made him appear older. A portrait of him shows a grim set to his mouth, but he was actually perceived by those who knew him as friendly, gregarious, a faithful husband, a devoted father, all in all a "quiet, unassuming gentleman."

He was called "Colonel" Wheeler, but there is no record that he engaged in any military activity. It is clear, however, that his family was willing to take up arms to prevent any threat to its property in slaves. A brother had raised a volunteer company in 1831 to take part in suppressing the Nat Turner rebellion across the border in Virginia, fearing, as other slave owners did, that the revolt would spread if it was not put down. However, as far as John Hill Wheeler himself is concerned, there was no obvious reason for the honorific. *Frederick Douglass' Paper* teased that it might have been affixed "merely" to mean "NC.M."—"North Carolina Master" the newspaper apparently meant.

On the other hand, the newspaper said, Wheeler might "have attained his military grade by establishing a line of stages, running a steamboat, or by some other of the thousand and one ways in which that honored title is acquired in our democratic land."[6]

Wheeler traced his family to a Joseph Wheeler, the son of an English admiral who had received a grant of land from the Crown and settled in New Jersey. Despite his English forebears, Joseph's grandson, John, a physician, served in the Revolutionary War, taking part on the American side in campaigns against Quebec and in the South. He was so taken with the genial climate of the South that he decided to settle near Murfreesboro, North Carolina. His wife, incidentally, was the niece of Aaron Ogden, later governor of New Jersey and a United States senator.

His grandson, John Hill Wheeler, was at the peak of a varied and illustrious career and was considered by contemporaries as something of a renaissance man. A confidant of Pierce, he was "a ready, eloquent, and graceful writer," so his contemporary biographer wrote. He was schooled in Greek, Roman, English, and French history. Well-read, he maintained a library that contained more than twelve hundred volumes, and his family customarily read aloud to one another in the evening selections that varied from the Bible to Shakespeare's *Hamlet*.[7] He was himself considered the premier author of North Carolina history, a sobriquet that unfortunately did not survive the test of time. Abolitionists would picture John Hill Wheeler as some sort of devil incarnate, but those who knew him, his contemporary biographer declared, talked of his being "tender and charitable to the afflicted, cheerful and courteous to the prosperous." Friends spoke of his "warm heart, his classic wit, and mirth-creating humor." Anti-slavery advocates and newspapers, however, never recognized any of those attributes. One thing, though, is unquestionable: he sometimes made rash judgments. Certainly, his decision to take Jane Johnson and her children through Philadelphia after repeated warnings from friends was impulsive and ill-advised. Wheeler's tendency to rush to judgment would have serious consequences in his career as a diplomat.

John Hill was born in Hertford County, North Carolina, on August 2, 1806. His father, also named John, was engaged in the mercantile and shipping business and served as postmaster of Murfreesboro.[8] John Hill graduated from Columbian University (now George Washington University), in Washington, before his twentieth birthday in 1826. Two years later he earned a master of arts degree from the University of North Carolina. Next, he studied law under the state's chief justice, and before he was admitted to the bar he was elected in 1827 to the North Carolina legislature.

A follower of President Andrew Jackson, Wheeler four years later ran for Congress but was defeated. As a reward for his support, Jackson appointed him secretary of the Board of Commissioners adjudicating claims of American citizens against France. The claims dated back to 1815, the result of depredations against American commerce during the Napoleonic Wars. In effect, Wheeler supervised the commission's work. In 1836, after that tour of duty was completed, Jackson appointed Wheeler—now thirty years old—superintendent of the branch mint at Charlotte, North Carolina, a position he held for five years. It was during that time that Wheeler married Ellen Oldmixon Sully. She was his second wife. His first, Mary Elizabeth Brown, a minister's daughter whom he wed in 1830, had died in 1836. He and Mary Brown had two sons and a daughter. He and Ellen Sully had two sons.

In 1841, the North Carolina legislature elected Wheeler state treasurer. But once his term ended, Wheeler, still in his thirties, decided to retire to in order to write. His *Historical Sketches of North Carolina*, a collection of local and state history, documents, statistics, and biographical sketches that took him ten years to complete, stimulated others in the state and throughout the South to study their histories. Many years later, after his death, critics would cite the numerous errors Wheeler's work contained, and his partiality to members of his own party would earn it the nickname "the Democratic Stud-Book."[9]

Wheeler did his writing on a plantation on Beattie's Ford in Lincoln County, where he moved in 1842. According to the 1850 census, he owned twenty-five slaves ranging in age from one year old to fifty years old.[10] He was both a supporter of the institution of slavery and a staunch defender of states' rights, regarding "the influence of central power," his contemporary biographer noted, "as dangerous to individual liberty, and constantly tending to imperialism." His belief in states' rights, and his opposition to federal authority in all but national affairs, would prove at considerable odds with his actions as he attempted to recover his slaves.

Wheeler was again elected to the state legislature in 1852, and that same year he labored for fellow North Carolinian James Dobbin in his campaign for the United States senate. Dobbin failed to win the seat, but he was in debt to Wheeler for the work he did, and it is even possible that he also owed a favor to Wheeler for his subsequent appointment to Franklin Pierce's cabinet. For it was likely Wheeler, who, as an assistant secretary to Pierce, brought Dobbin to the attention of the president. Pierce named Dobbin his Secretary of the Navy. Whether it was Wheeler's support in the senate campaign, or Wheeler's recommending Dobbin to Pierce—or both, for that matter—Dobbin rewarded Wheeler's efforts on his behalf by urging his appointment to the critical Nicaragua post.

Wheeler learned of his appointment on his forty-eighth birthday, August 2, 1854. Eight days later he tendered his resignation as a Pierce aide. On August 13, he wrote in his diary that he "had a most instructive interview as regard our relations with Central America."[11] The session must have lasted some time, for there was much to learn. Nicaragua was torn by opposing political factions. William Walker, a soldier of fortune then called a filibusterer, was leading an armed expedition of recruits he had gathered in California with the intent of setting up his own government in Nicaragua. Then there were the British to contend with. They were interested in seeking an interoceanic canal across the isthmus of Central America and had set up a protectorate over the Mosquito Coast territory claimed by Nicaragua. The Clayton-Bulwer Treaty of 1850 between the United States and England was supposed to end encroachments by either nation and provide both nations access to any canal that was built. However, as Wheeler immediately discovered, an English squadron of ships still hovered over the Mosquito Coast.

Wheeler already had strong views that would influence his diplomatic decisions in Central America, in particular a "contempt for the Spaniards and those mongrel races, who occupied with indolence and semi-barbarism one of the finest and most productive regions on the continent." He "knew," his friendly contemporary biographer said, that "it was the destiny of his race to eradicate barbarism, and teach the inhabitants of the wilderness the arts of production, commerce, moral responsibility, social refinement, and intelligent freedom."

Wheeler's journey to Nicaragua began in grand fashion.[12] On October 30, before sailing from Norfolk, Virginia, Wheeler visited the ship-of-the-line *U.S. Pennsylvania*, which greeted him with a thirteen-gun salute. The next day, with Marines drawn up to receive him, he boarded the *U.S. Princeton*. A salute was fired, and at one o'clock the ship was underway, en route to Pensacola, Florida, where Wheeler was to change vessels and board the *Columbia* for the rest of the journey. With him were his wife, Ellen, and their twelve-year-old son, Woodbury. Their other son, Charles Sully, who was about to turn fifteen, was left in school in Washington in the care of a matron.

The voyage was uneventful. Wheeler spent the time studying Spanish and reading a history of Nicaragua. The ship reached San Juan del Norte a week before Christmas, greeted there by "frowning floating batteries of John Bull which view us with distrust," Wheeler wrote in his diary. There, anchored off the coast, were three British Navy vessels —the *Termagant,* a twenty-six gun man-of-war, the *Vesta,* of twenty-one guns, and the *Daring,* of ten guns. They were, he said, "an admirable commentary" on British intentions.

Two days after reaching Nicaragua, Wheeler was involved in talks with the British consul, pressing the American position that the British protectorate "was to have been abandoned long ago—that the result was unavoidable—this country must be under American influence."[13] It took six months of conferences, haggling and compromise, however, to work out an agreement with the British and with the Nicaraguan government then in power, but at last, on June 20, 1855, Wheeler could confide to his diary, "Treaty signed and sealed."[14] The document in hand, three days later, he took leave of his wife and son and headed back to the United States. He was under instructions from his wife to pick up clothing and some other belongings from her father's home in Philadelphia and to bring Jane Johnson back with him.

The voyage home was a nightmare.[15] Wheeler's steamer set out in the morning of June 23, reaching Virgin Bay early that afternoon. But no one went ashore. "Cholera making rapid devastations," he noted in his diary. His subsequent entries took on an ominous tone. "Mosquitoes bad—cholera on the island. . . . At Grenada—War—cholera &c." He had transferred to the *Central America* at Virgin Bay. "Every one seemed happy to be on the Ocean; free from cholera." But at ten that night, Wheeler felt "some pain in the stomach." Two doctors who were passengers stayed by his side all night, "applying blisters and administering in quick succession tonics." The doctors gave him a pill to take every half hour, a concoction that included calomel and opium. A woman in the stateroom next to his died and was thrown overboard. Wheeler was quite certain that his own end had come.

Day after day, though, the epidemic took its toll. "Mr. Russel of Mass. died—thrown overboard—five died today in Steerage. . . two died of cholera—thrown overboard." All during this time Wheeler reported himself as "very feeble" or "still feeble." It was not until the ship reached Cuba that he could say that he was "much better," thanks "to all merciful Providence in whose hands I commit my spirit!"

Wheeler was recovering slowly, but others were not as fortunate. When the ship reached the Florida coast, Wheeler was awakened in the middle of the night by groans from the adjoining stateroom. A young mother with a four-month-old child was dying in great pain. She, too, like the previous tenant of that stateroom, succumbed. The ship's captain asked Wheeler to read the funeral service for her. "Her Body quietly sunk into the ocean!"

Wheeler landed in New York on Sunday, July 8, suffering still from "fatigue" and chills.[16] He continued to complain for several days, at one point so "unwell" from "an attack of Panama Fever" that he stayed in bed the entire day "all company refused." Wheeler's condition—he must have looked haggard after the ordeal—may explain why Passmore Williamson thought of him as a "little old man" when he saw him several days later.

Despite his illness, Wheeler set out for Philadelphia the day after landing in New York. He visited briefly with his father-in-law, Thomas Sully, then set out on the tenth for Washington. By Wednesday, the eleventh, he had delivered the papers he was carrying to Secretary of State William Marcy, who was "pleased with the treaty." He met the president, "who was in excellent health, and happy to see me." He returned to New York for the day on Sunday, the fifteenth, to be with his daughter from his first marriage, returning after tea to Washington to spend the evening with Navy Secretary James Dobbin. The next day, Wheeler conferred with Attorney General Caleb Cushing, who told him he thought that the British had no right to fortify or protect the Mosquito Coast but were justified to have an armed force at San Juan del Norte. The next day, the seventeenth, Wheeler went to the State Department, where he received $242.50 for expenses connected with the drawing up of the treaty. "By invitation," at 4:30 that afternoon Wheeler sat down to dine with the president: "the company," he said, "was select."

The next morning, July 18, Wheeler began the long journey back to Nicaragua, leaving Washington at 6:00 A.M. with Jane Johnson and her two sons. Friends whom he had told that he would be traveling into Pennsylvania with his slaves warned him that it was risky to do so. Hadn't George Washington himself lost two slaves in Philadelphia when the nation's capital was in that city? But Wheeler was certain that "Jane would not leave him."[17] He would have to make a brief detour in the city to stop by the Sully home to pick up his wife's belongings before continuing on to New York. He already had bookings on a steamer bound for Central America.

Sometimes, at the end of a year, Wheeler would include in his diary a rundown of his financial position, listing investments he had made, bonds, debts, and loans, as well as property he owned in Washington—a house on Eleventh Street that he lived in and a lot on the corner of I and Tenth streets. When he sold a farm in Prince Georges County, Maryland, Wheeler noted that he received $485.92 for a slave woman and $360.00 and $400.98, respectively, for two males.[18] But for some reason Wheeler did not make such a reckoning every year, and there is no indication how much he paid for Jane Johnson and her boys when he purchased them from Cornelius Crew of Richmond sometime around New Year's, 1854. A study of the economics of nearby Loudoun County, Virginia, where there was a "growing fondness for 'breeding women,'" stated that a woman with two small children sold for $1,590 in 1858.[19] An earlier general study, one of slave prices in 1850, indicates that Jane would have been worth then about $450 to $500, her son Daniel about $450 and the younger Isaiah $300.[20] No matter what yardstick one chooses, it is clear that the three of them were valuable.

So it is understandable that Wheeler was beside himself as he watched Jane and the children make off in a carriage down Delaware Avenue. The adventures he'd been through in the past year—the success of his diplomacy in Nicaragua, the harrowing voyage home, his recent warm reception by the president—all must have seemed inconsequential at that moment. But he was not a man to be thwarted.

Wheeler immediately sought out the United States Marshal for the Eastern District of Pennsylvania, Francis M. Wynkoop. It was after five o'clock, the Eastern District court was closed, but the marshal was still in his office. Wynkoop, a Pierce appointee who was in his midthirties, was a veteran of the war with Mexico; he had risen from being a lowly private to brigadier general, outranking at the time numerous other officers who would one day in the not-too-distant future lead Union and Confederate forces: Ulysses S. Grant, William T. Sherman, George G. Meade, Joseph Hooker, George B. McClellan, Robert E. Lee, Pierre G. Beauregard, Albert Sidney Johnson, James Longstreet and Braxton Bragg.[21]

Wynkoop had a personal grudge against Passmore Williamson because of an earlier incident involving an escaped slave. He lost no time in sending a deputy marshal named Mulloy to accompany Wheeler to the home of the federal judge for the Eastern District. The judge lived in a section of Philadelphia called Germantown. Wheeler had actually worked closely with the man. Back in the early 1830s, well before he was appointed to the federal bench, the judge had been one of the commissioners on the board dealing with the adjudication of claims against the French, the very same board on which Wheeler had served as secretary. Moreover, it is more than likely that Wheeler and the judge also had met on occasions involving the close-knit Philadelphia social elite, for his father-in-law, Thomas Sully, had painted separate portraits of both the judge and his wife. In addition, the judge, as a member of Philadelphia's Society of Sons of Saint George, had helped underwrite Sully's trip to England in 1838 to paint a portrait of Queen Victoria, and he subsequently represented the painter in a lawsuit related to the portrait and its copies. Undoubtedly Wheeler believed his friend the judge would be sympathetic to his plight.

In fact, Wheeler would find a ready listener in the judge. He would also discover that the judge was worried that Passmore Williamson's actions would prove embarrassing to a Democratic administration in Washington that depended on its close ties with the South. Together slave master and judge would plot—clearly with the administration's approval—how to quash an embarrassing situation that was drawing increasing national attention.

7

The Judge

Are ye deaf to the plaints that each moment arise?
Is it thus ye forget the mild precepts of Penn,—
Unheeding the clamor that "maddens the skies,"
As ye trample the rights of your dark fellow-men?

"Jefferson's Daughter," *Anti-Slavery Harp,* 23

John Kintzing Kane's reputation as a jurist was founded on his decisions in admiralty and patent cases. He had handled slave cases before, but nothing in his career, distinguished as it might have been, could have prepared him for the one that was about to be presented to him. He had no inkling that he was about to be embroiled in a local case with such profound national implications. In ways he could not imagine, it would occupy him for years.

On the surface, as he sat facing John Wheeler in his home in Germantown, the situation seemed simple enough. A federal district court judge, Kane had presided over numerous cases brought by slave owners seeking to recover their property. He considered himself fairminded in such matters. In some cases, he had decided in a slave owner's favor, in others not. This case, however, had a peculiar twist. It was unlike any case that had ever come before him. Wheeler's slaves were not escapees. They had allegedly been kidnapped. Moreover, the supposed culprit, Passmore Williamson, the fellow who had offered Wheeler his business card, was someone whom the judge had encountered several times in fugitive cases before his court. A dedicated advocate of abolition, Williamson had participated in the legal defense of several captured runaways. In Kane's experience, there was something positive to be said about Passmore's "general bearing," but the judge thought one had to make "allowances" about him "for some errors of a too ardent disposition."[1]

Despite Kane's self-professed lack of prejudice, there was an unspoken factor, a subtext, that was wreaking havoc in his family life. At its core was the issue of slavery and the Fugitive Slave Law. Kane's views on the subject were well known. Within months of the act being passed by Congress in the fall of 1850, he made it clear how he felt. The new law must be obeyed, Kane insisted, and penalties for violating it would be enforced without fear, favor, or affection. The Eastern District of Pennsylvania, which he presided over, had suffered "from crimes of excitement, turbulence and force." Abolitionists—he called them "Fanatics of civil discord"—had "convulsed" the nation "in its length and breadth."[2]

Kane himself had to contend with such fanatics within his own family. Two of his sons were abolitionists. One of them had even gone so far as to hide runaways in the family home, under the judge's nose. The other had the gall to appear in court before him to argue in defense of an alleged runaway. Because he was a rigid authoritarian, one can only wonder whether the embarrassing actions of his sons' flouting of federal law had an effect on Kane's decision-making. Is it possible that the events that were about to unfold made Passmore Williamson an unwitting scapegoat for the judge's problems at home?

For Wheeler, the issue was simple. His slaves, his property—Jane Johnson and her two children—had been kidnapped by Williamson and his accomplices. As far as he was concerned, this was a clear violation of the Fugitive Slave Law. But was it?

Wheeler's problem was that "kidnapping" was not, strictly speaking, a violation of that federal law. Jane Johnson had not run away, had not fled from one state into another, was not, in the legal sense of the word, an escapee. Her master had brought her and her boys into Pennsylvania, where they had been abducted. A strict interpreter of federal ordinances, Kane evidently believed that the Fugitive Slave Law could not be invoked in this case. On the other hand, he could make it possible for Wheeler to repossess the slaves if the slaves were brought before him in open court. The solution to Wheeler's problem was simple. It was one that, ironically, abolitionists themselves used to impede implementation of the Fugitive Slave Law by compelling a slave owner to present valid evidence in court that a runaway was his or her property. Kane would order a writ of habeas corpus to be issued, forcing Williamson, their abductor, to produce, in his court, Wheeler's three slaves. At which point, he, Kane, would then order that the slaves be returned to their rightful owner.

Kane was what would now be termed a strict constitutionalist. "The laws of the United States made in pursuance of the Constn. are binding on me, anything in the Constn. or statutes of any State to the contrary, notwithstanding," he wrote in a decision affecting a runaway slave. "My function is not to *criticize* but to *ascertain* what those laws are, I having a [duty] to enforce them."[3]

Others, however, had a less flattering view of the judge. Sidney George Fisher, a friend who often visited in his home, spoke of Kane's being "genial & gracious in his manners, kind & friendly in his relations with others." He had "the accomplishments, feelings and habits of a gentleman." But this same friend "did not approve his course as a judge nor his character in all respects." Kane, Fisher said, "was ambitious and I fear unscrupulous in defending doctrines that tended to gratify his ambition. He wanted high principle." Kane, he added, "was a demagogue even on the bench."[4]

If his portrait is indicative, Kane certainly looked the part of a jurist. He had a high forehead, intense eyes, and a firmness of jaw unspoiled by any facial hair. In all, a handsome individual, though the collar and neck scarf he wears in the portrait make him look stuffy. Perhaps *stuffy* is not the correct word. *Rigid* would be more fitting, or *inflexible,* or even *self-righteous*—adjectives that, ironically, could be applied as well to Passmore Williamson.

Kane came from a family that dated its American connections to 1750, when his grandfather, John O'Kane, a Latin scholar and, so the family believed, a graduate of Trinity College in Dublin, emigrated to New York from Ireland. When the Revolution came, the grandfather raised a company to fight for the colonies, but he was distressed when all connection with the king was to be broken. His own break with the patriot cause was the result of an incident, the details of which are unknown, involving his wife, who was a friend of the wife of the British commander, Lord Howe. O'Kane's allegiance was questioned, and, "disgusted," he refused to take an oath to uphold the new republic.[5] His goods and estates in Dutchess County were confiscated, and he left the country, living in Nova Scotia and then in England during his self-imposed exile. The grandfather returned shortly after the war and before the birth of the judge on May 16, 1795. John was the son of one of grandfather O'Kane's children, named Elisha. Elisha and his second wife settled in New York before moving in 1801 to Philadelphia. John had been given the middle initial E when he was born, apparently he thought, to distinguish him from an older cousin who was also named John, but he later dropped the initial and adopted Kintzing, the maiden name of his stepmother, who raised him, as his middle name.[6]

Kane attended Yale University, graduating in 1814 after attaining the dubious distinction of being what was called the best disclaimer in his class. He said that he made it through those years "without honor after an idle and rebellious career in college."[7] Kane subsequently studied law in Pennsylvania and was admitted to the bar in 1817.

Kane believed he had no prejudices, pointing with pride in his autobiography to the time when, as a young lawyer, he happened to be in court when a judge chose him to defend "certain negro burglars" whose attorneys had gotten into a squabble with both the judge and the jury. One of the accused men had already been convicted. Kane proved that the indictment against all the defendants was in error, the jurors agreed with him without even retiring to deliberate, and the judge even refused to sentence the defendant who had been convicted. Kane felt strongly that it was the "great, primary, controuling [sic] duty of the lawyer, to see to it, that every man has justice administered to him according to the laws of the land." A lawyer has no right, he said, to refuse his services "no matter what the circumstances, *no matter what the circumstances*," he repeated for emphasis. [8]

While in his early twenties in 1819, Kane married Jane Duval Leiper, who many thought to be one of the most beautiful women in Philadelphia. Thomas Sully was so smitten after seeing her at a costume ball in 1824 when the Marquis de Lafayette visited the city—she was dressed as Mary, Queen of Scots—that he asked to paint her portrait. She was the daughter of a Scotsman who had emigrated to the state in 1765 and, after starting out as a tobacconist, came to own lucrative stone quarries in Delaware County. The father, Thomas Leiper, organized the First Troop of Philadelphia City Cavalry and fought at Trenton, Princeton, Brandywine and Germantown during the Revolutionary War. A personal friend of Thomas Jefferson, Leiper served on Philadelphia's Common Council.[9]

The Kanes lived well, residing in the respectable center of the city during the winter and in the fashionable wooded outlying section in the summer. They made their home at first on Walnut Street, then moved about 1827 to Fourth Street. Their residence was also his law office, but in 1840 he separated the two, moving his family to Seventh and Locust streets. Soon after being named a federal judge in 1848, the Kanes purchased a summer place on Green Lane in the north Philadelphia section called Germantown. They called it Rensselaer. In 1852, however, their four-year-old son Willie died suddenly. The trauma of his death was so profound that they could not bring themselves to return to the house, and they sold it.

Kane and his wife were so shattered by Willie's death that it was three years before they were finally able to return to the area. They purchased land next to Rensselaer, and their house, designed by Kane, was built as a memorial to their son. The Kanes called it Fern Rock, after a secluded spot at Rensselaer where Willie liked to play. Kane saw to it that the house was lavishly furnished; the drawing room included pieces that his father had purchased from the first French minister to the United States.[10] Similarly, he oversaw the decoration of the courtroom on the second floor of Independence Hall, where he presided. He took "great pride," a nineteenth-century historian said, "in having everything about him conducted in the most polished style."[11]

By the time he was in his thirties Kane had already been a major actor in Democratic politics. He became prominent in 1828 when he ran, successfully, for the state legislature and was "up to the armpits," as he put it, in the presidential campaign of Andrew Jackson.[12] In addition to calling meetings, collecting contributions and handling correspondence, he was credited with writing a pamphlet endorsing Jackson entitled *A Candid View of the Presidential Election,* which was read throughout the country.[13] He is also credited as the author of statements on national policy made by Jackson when he was president. So it is not surprising that it was Jackson who subsequently appointed Kane to be one of the three commissioners on the board adjudicating claims against the French. Later, in 1838, Kane led state Democrats in the so-called "Buckshot War," a quarrel over a disputed election in Pennsylvania that was so rancorous the militia had to be called out to protect the legislature. Kane gained further notoriety when, as attorney general of the state in the mid-1840s, he prosecuted the men who were arrested during anti-Catholic riots in the Kensington district of Philadelphia.

In 1846 President James Polk nominated Kane to the United States Court for the Eastern District of Pennsylvania. He accepted the appointment, but it was a decision that he came to regret. The appointment, in his eyes, came to mean a life far removed from public and political notice.[14] He soon discovered that his strong partisan views had to be submerged in his role as an impartial member of the judiciary.

Kane believed that as a federal judge he enforced the nation's laws without prejudice and strictly on the merits of each case brought before him, but his rulings in at least one of the critical cases brought before him smack of political partisanship. His behavior in the Passmore Williamson case—his private conferring, for example, with John Hill Wheeler—went well beyond judicial propriety. From the start, both he and his friend, Associate Justice Robert C. Grier of the United States Supreme Court, were concerned that anti-slavery advocates would block enforcement of the Fugitive Slave Law and, quite possibly, instigate violent demonstrations. Grier was a Philadelphian whose circuit covered the Eastern District of Pennsylvania. Like Kane, he was closely connected with the Democratic administration in Washington. Grier, in fact, would later be accused of violating the Supreme Court's confidentiality by alerting the incoming president, James Buchanan, of the court's pending Dred Scott decision in 1857. Worried about the response of abolitionists to the new fugitive law, both judges, Kane and Grier, petitioned Washington for authority to call in federal troops in emergency situations. Millard Fillmore, who was then president, agreed that the law had to be upheld, though he qualified the use of federal troops, saying that they should be summoned "only in the last resort."[15]

Kane's decisions in the first cases he heard regarding the Fugitive Slave Law bore out his attempt to be fair. Soon after its passage, he heard three of the first five cases brought in Philadelphia. The first had purposely been heard by Grier, who wanted to establish the legal protocol for how the cases should be handled. Grier freed the alleged fugitive, a hod carrier named Robert Garnet, because he thought the documents provided by the slave owner, who was from Cecil County, Maryland, failed to prove that Garnet was his slave. The next case that December also involved an alleged runaway from Cecil County, Adam Gibson. It came before one of the commissioners appointed under the new law, Edward D. Ingraham. Ingraham ordered Gibson returned to Maryland, but it later turned out that Gibson had been misidentified and he, too, was eventually set free.

The circumstances surrounding the way Ingraham handled the Gibson case prompted abolitionist lawyers to find a way of avoiding future cases being heard by Ingraham. They felt that Ingraham was pro-southern and, in Gibson's case, had favored the supposed slave owner's petition. When Stephen Bennett, allegedly a fugitive slave from

Baltimore, was seized in January 1851 in Columbia, a small town near the Susquehanna River, the lawyers purposely sought a writ of habeas corpus to remove the case from Ingraham's jurisdiction and bring it before a federal judge. As a result, Kane heard the case. The abolitionists' ploy, however, backfired because Kane decided that Bennett's identity as a runaway was proved. He ordered him returned to his master. Fortunately for Bennett, his neighbors in Columbia raised seven hundred dollars to purchase his freedom.

Similarly, that February, Kane heard another case that had initially come before Ingraham. This one was the result of a writ of habeas corpus that Passmore Williamson and J. Miller McKim sought.[16] It involved Euphemia Williams, a mother of six children, who had been living in Philadelphia for the past twenty-two years. A Maryland man had suddenly appeared in Philadelphia and claimed she was an escaped slave. Finding the evidence porous, Kane dismissed the charge against her. On the other hand, a little over a year later in 1852, Kane ordered a pregnant woman known as Helen or Hannah and her son returned to a Baltimore slave owner, saying she, the boy, and the unborn child were his property.

In all fairness, Kane's early decisions do not appear to demonstrate any bias one way or another, only a rigid application of the law. "Let me say," he wrote, summarizing his view of his role as a jurist, "that considerations like these, however they may affect my feeling as a citizen, or however they might control my action if I were imposing to prescribe the law, can exert but a very limited influence on my judicial administration of the Law, as it stands."[17]

As time went on and more cases came into his court, Kane's biases began to play a larger role in his decisions. A contributing factor may well have been his dismay at the behavior of two of his seven children. He was understandably proud of his eldest, Elisha. Elisha was a physician, naval officer, explorer, and pioneer of the American route to the North Pole. He became a national hero when he led his crew out of the frozen north in an expedition in 1853.

But two of Kane's other sons were a continuing source of personal shame. One, Thomas, studied law with his father and was admitted to the bar in 1846, but he rarely practiced law, working instead at first as Kane's clerk. A committed abolitionist, he defied the very law his father was committed to enforce and used the family home at Fern Rock as a way station for runaway slaves.[18] When Kane discovered what his son was doing, he was furious, so furious that he had his own son imprisoned for contempt of court. However, the Pennsylvania Supreme

Court overruled Kane, saying he had no cause to do so, declared the charge unwarranted, and set Thomas free. Thomas had been named a United States commissioner to enforce the Fugitive Slave Law at the recommendation of his father. But he had quickly resigned the post, saying that its duties conflicted with the dictates of his conscience—and, though he did not say so, also with his activities in defiance of the law. His father, one can imagine, was incensed.

Like Thomas, Kane's third son was also a burden to bear. Robert was a lawyer and abolitionist, too. He had argued before his father in the case of an alleged fugitive, and, as a further embarrassment, had appeared in court before Kane's colleague Grier to challenge the claim of a Baltimore slave master.[19]

In the early 1850s, Kane and Grier were involved in two notorious cases that drew national attention. Both happened to also involve Passmore Williamson. Passmore dubbed one of the cases "the Treason Tizzy." The other, the "Wi[l]kesbarre case," prompted him to take "Notice," as he put it (a roundabout way of saying he was instrumental) in pursuing charges against four federal marshals who had shot an alleged runaway. Passmore's actions did not endear him to Kane, Grier, or the law-enforcement authorities involved.[20]

The first case, known as the Christiana Riot, took place in lower Lancaster County, a gateway for fugitives fleeing north from Maryland across the Susquehanna River, a place that Passmore acknowledged as being "pretty well populated with runaway slaves." There, he said, "fugitive slaves were befriended, harbored, given work, secluded and passed along from one friend's house to another until they reached a place of safety and were free from pursuit."[21] But the area was also a hunting ground for a group of men known as the Gap Gang who tracked down runaways and also kidnapped free blacks. The gang carried away a free black man in September 1850; again in March 1851, in the same area, they tied, gagged, and carried away a second one. Blacks in the Christiana area, whether free or fugitive, were always wary when strangers came into the neighborhood.

Because of the gang's forays, abolitionist sympathizers kept a special eye on Lancaster County. In the fall of 1851, a son of John Kane—which one is unknown—alerted the Pennsylvania Anti-Slavery Society that warrants were being prepared for the arrest of runaways in the area. J. Miller McKim had William Still pass the word immediately along to the fugitives.[22] A day or so later, a slave owner named Edward Gorsuch, who lived near Baltimore, crossed into Pennsylvania and, with the warrants obtained in Philadelphia in hand, set about to seize four of his slaves who had run away. He had learned that they were hiding in Lancaster County. Gorsuch was accompanied by his son Dickinson; a nephew, Joshua Gorsuch; Deputy Marshal Henry H. Kline, and three friends.

Before daybreak on September 11, they reached the home of a fugitive named William Parker and surrounded it. A passing black man happened to see the Gorsuch party and alerted Elijah Lewis, a Quaker abolitionist. Lewis in turn passed along the word to another white man, Castner Hanway. The two men rushed to the Parker house, hoping to prevent violence. Hanway, who was in feeble health, too ill to walk, had to mount a horse to get there. When they reached the site, Kline, the deputy marshal, showed Hanway and Lewis the warrants, ordering them to assist him in making the arrests—which, under the Fugitive Slave Law, they were required to do. The details of what happened next are somewhat fuzzy. A number of blacks, anywhere from twelve to as many as three hundred, accounts say, appeared, armed with guns, corn cutters, staves, clubs, and stones. The blacks rushed the Gorsuch party. Lewis and Hanway were unable to stop them. In the fight that followed, shots were fired. Gorsuch was dead and his son seriously wounded by the time the fighting ended. Parker and a number of other fugitive slaves had fled. Hanway, Lewis, a third white man named Joseph Scarlet, and thirty-six blacks were subsequently arrested. In all, they were indicted on 117 counts of "levying war."[23]

It seemed a foregone conclusion that the defendants would be tried under the Fugitive Slave Law. However, U.S. District Attorney George W. Ashmead believed that the defendants could be charged with treason. Kane concurred, telling a grand jury that on the basis of what he had learned from Deputy Marshal Kline and other witnesses, they could be indicted for treason for, in effect, inciting a rebellion against the federal government. To "successfully" instigate treason, he said, "is to commit it."[24] Hanway was tried first, with Grier presiding.

Although Christiana was in Lancaster County some fifty miles from Philadelphia, the trial took place in the district courtroom in Independence Hall that Kane had had refurbished. Anticipating that there would be evening sessions, the ornate room was now fitted with gas fixtures "of the chastest designs," and ventilators "of the most appropriate patterns" had been placed in the ceiling so that a uniform temperature could be assured. "Nothing was wanting but space," an observer said.[25]

The trial, which began November 24, drew so many spectators that police officers were stationed in the lobbies and on the stairwell to prevent the crowd from rushing up. Passmore and other abolitionists took advantage of the publicity surrounding the trial to raise money for the defense of the accused men and to publish pamphlets in their support. Passmore sponsored a resolution in support of the defendants, who were, he said, moved by "a common sense of humanity and a desire to promote the ends of justice" but too "destitute of the means necessary to secure a proper legal defence" [sic].[26] It is apparent that abolitionists also had a hand in outfitting some of the black defendants in the case who were brought into the courtroom for identification purposes: they all sported around their necks scarves of a patriotic red, white, and blue design.

Defense witnesses questioned the credibility particularly of Deputy Marshal Kline. But it was Justice Grier's charge to the jury that virtually assured the outcome after three weeks of testimony and cross-examination. "Without desiring to invade the prerogatives of the Jury," Grier nevertheless opined that he believed that the charge against Hanway did not rise "to the dignity of treason, or a levying of war" as defined in the United States Constitution.[27] Within ten minutes the jury returned a verdict of not guilty; afterwards all other charges against Hanway were dropped, and he was released. In the following days, treason charges against the other defendants were also dropped, though some of the black men who had been arrested faced state riot charges.

The case served only to exacerbate feelings in the South. Robert J. Brent, the attorney general of Maryland who attended the trial in support of the prosecution, questioned Grier's charge to the jury: "I do not know, and cannot conceive of a more public matter, than the enforcement of an Act of Congress, based on a fundamental article of the Constitution, securing 'the surrender of fugitives from labor,'" he declared. Brent was particularly upset at the jury's swift verdict. "If a portion of the people of Pennsylvania feel themselves insulted and their families outraged by nocturnal arrests, at their houses, of fugitive slaves, they can easily avoid such disagreeable matters by first seeing that they are employing a free colored person and not actually harboring a runaway slave."[28]

The case also must have irked Kane in an unusual, personal way. For one thing, Grier's charge to the jury was an indirect criticism of Kane's ruling to try the case on the ground of treason. Then, too, while the trial was being held, Kane's son Thomas sent six "superior turkeys" and a six-pound cake for a Thanksgiving dinner party provided for the Christiana defendants, both white and black, who were in prison. Hanway, Lewis, and Scarlet had their dinner in the room of one of the jail keepers and were joined by a number of the prison officers. Thomas's largesse prompted the *Pennsylvania Freeman* to comment, "Who will stand best with posterity—the father who prostitutes his powers as a judge to procure the conviction of peaceable citizens as traitors for refusing to aid in the capture of fugitive slaves, or the son who ministered to the wants of those citizens while incarcerated in a loathsome prison?"[29] To add to Kane's further chagrin, his son Robert defended some of the blacks in the state riot trials.

For his part, Grier, despite his ruling on the constitutionality of the indictment, was incensed that abolitionists had, he felt, instigated the Christiana Riot. Grier took particular aim at Lucretia Mott and members of the Female Anti-Slavery Society, who attended portions of the trial, calling them "individuals of perverted intellect." The "guilt" of Gorsuch's "foul murder," he declared, "rests not alone on the deluded individuals who were its immediate perpetrators, but the blood taints with even deeper dye the skirts of those who promulgated doctrines subversive of all morality and all government."[30]

Abolitionists, however, gloried in the outcome of the case. The attention that they had attracted in the nation's press had spurred interest in the anti-slavery cause. Congressman Joshua Giddings of Ohio, an outspoken opponent of slavery, was invited to speak in Philadelphia that December. "The treason trials are making a great deal of talk here now," his hosts wrote him, "and thousands are ready to listen who have long been indifferent."[31] J. Miller McKim told William Lloyd Garrison that the trials "have been a great windfall."[32]

Two years later to the day, the second case involving Passmore Williamson exploded in rioting and gunplay. Again, the details are not clear. A warrant in hand for the arrest of an escaped slave, four deputies seized a light-skinned black waiter named William Thomas at the Phoenix Hotel in Wilkes-Barre, on the north bank of the Susquehanna River in Luzerne County. One of the arresting officers was Deputy Marshal George Wynkoop, the brother of United States Marshal Francis Wynkoop. The deputies sneaked up on Thomas, or "Bill" as he was called, from behind, "knocked him down with a mace" and had partly handcuffed him when Bill broke away and dove into the Susquehanna. As Bill stood in the water, immersed up to his neck, the men ordered him to surrender or they would "blow his brains out." Bill refused. "I will be drowned rather than taken alive," he called back.

The fracas had drawn hundreds of persons to the banks of the river. As they watched, the deputies fired. One bullet hit Bill in the head. He shrieked. While George Wynkoop and the other men huddled to decide what to do next, Bill came out of the water and lay down on the shore, his face all bloodied. Wynkoop and the others thought he was dead. But when a black bystander helped him to his feet, his assailants ran back to Bill, revolvers out. Bill again leaped into the water, prepared, he said later, to "have died contented" if he took "two or three of them down with him." Frustrated and aware that the crowd that had gathered was hostile, Wynkoop and the other deputies decided to retreat. Bill waded up the river and was later found flat on his face in a cornfield. The women who came upon him dressed his wounds and helped him to find shelter. He was never seen again in the town.[33]

That would have been the end of the incident had it not been for William C. Gildersleeve, a local merchant who was an avid abolitionist. Gildersleeve was born in Midway, Liberty County, Georgia. His father, a preacher, was a slave owner. An auction block stood in front of his church, and young Gildersleeve often witnessed men, women, and children being sold. Repelled by what he saw, he finally migrated north, settling first in New Jersey before moving to Wilkes-Barre. His home and store became way stations on the Underground Railroad. In 1837, when he invited an abolitionist lecturer to speak at his house, an angry mob of pro-southern local residents broke into the house and, when unable to silence the speaker, they vandalized the structure. Two years later, when Gildersleeve again invited an abolitionist to speak, this time at a local hotel, a more determined mob forced the speaker to flee and hoisted Gildersleeve onto a tarred fence rail, then poured black dye over his head and hands. Pinned on top of the rail, Gildersleeve was borne on the shoulders of the mob to his home, where they smashed windows and destroyed the furniture. Only the pleas of his daughter and two neighbors who appeared with pistols prevented further violence.[34]

Evidently at the urging of Passmore Williamson, Gildersleeve brought riot charges against George Wynkoop and the three other deputies—James Crosson, John Jenkins, and Isham Keith. Wynkoop, for one, was arrested in Philadelphia. A grand jury in Luzerne County, meanwhile, charged all four deputies with making "a great noise[,] aggravated riot, tumult and disturbance for the space of six hours" as well as creating "both terror and disturbance of the *peaceful* inhabitants" of the town.[35] The federal government reacted by obtaining a writ of habeas corpus, forcing the constable who arrested the men to appear with them before Grier, who was outraged. "I will not have the officers of the United States harassed at every step in the performance of their duties by every petty magistrate who chooses to harass them, or by any unprincipled interloper who chooses to make complaints against them," he declared. He warned Gildersleeve that if he failed to prove the facts set forth in the arrest warrant, he would have Gildersleeve prosecuted for perjury. Furthermore, Grier said, if in retaliation anyone sought any further writ of habeas corpus to bring the deputy marshals before "any tuppenny magistrate," he would see that a federal indictment would be made out "against the person who applies for the writ, or assists in getting it, the lawyer who defends it, and the sheriff who serves the writ." (The judge even told someone he met who knew Gildersleeve that if Gildersleeve was ever brought before him in court, he "would hang him.")[36] Grier promised to see "that my officers are protected." The only thing worthy of blame "in their unsuccessful endeavors to fulfil a most dangerous and disgusting duty" was the officers' "want of sufficient courage and perseverance" in executing the seizure of Bill. Following Grier's admonishment, Kane dismissed the charges against the deputies on the ground that they were only doing their duty.[37]

One can only wonder how long Kane's professed impartiality would hold out. Convinced that a warrant under the Fugitive Slave Law could not be sustained, he evidently told Wheeler that he needed an affidavit from him before he could take action and issue a writ of habeas corpus. And one would have to be drawn up immediately if Wheeler was to have any chance of getting his slaves back. So Wheeler went back into the city to do so and was able to find United States Commissioner Charles F. Heazlitt available. In his affidavit, Wheeler referred to Jane Johnson and her two boys as being "held to labor by the laws of the State of Virginia"—a reference apparently to where he had purchased them. They were being detained by Passmore Williamson, the affidavit read, but not "for any criminal or supposed criminal matter." Wheeler asked that a writ of habeas corpus be directed to compel Williamson to bring his three slaves into district court.[38] Heazlitt witnessed the affidavit, and Wheeler took it back to Kane, who authorized the writ.

The back and forth took time. It was now almost six hours since Jane and her sons had been spirited away from the Walnut Street wharf when Deputy Marshal William H. Miller, accompanied by three men, two of whom were deputies, approached the Williamsons' office on Arch Street to serve the writ. Except for some streetlamps, the area was dark, the city quiet. It was going on eleven o'clock when they rang the front-door bell.

8

Consequences

That flag, my country, I had thought,
From noble sires was given to thee;
By the best blood of patriots bought,
To wave alone above the Free!
Yet now, while to the breeze it waves,
It floats above three millions slaves.

"Freedom's Banner," *Anti-Slavery Harp,* 3

Thomas Williamson was surprised when his son Passmore returned to their Arch Street office within what appeared to him "a very short absence." It did not seem as if even a half hour had elapsed since he left for the Walnut Street wharf.[1] A friend was visiting the father, and Passmore recounted to both men details surrounding "the release of Jane Johnson and her two children from the custody and control of their previous master." The father was supportive. He said he "fully and heartily" approved "every act, matter and thing" Passmore had done.

Once he had apprised the two men of what he called "the circumstances," Passmore returned to his desk and busied himself "uninterruptedly" preparing for his trip to Harrisburg. He took a break to return home to Buttonwood Street for his dinner, then went back to the office and continued to work. About 10:30 that night he left.

Steam locomotives were not permitted to enter the city—the wood and coal burners were considered a major fire hazard—so horses were employed to pull the rail cars across to the west side of the Schuylkill

River, where they were then coupled to a locomotive. Passmore boarded the Pennsylvania Railroad's horse-drawn cars at the line's station at Market and Eleventh streets.[2] Across the Schuylkill, a steam engine that would pull the cars to Harrisburg sat idling. Meanwhile, his father, who had remained with him most of the evening, locked the front door after Passmore left and retired upstairs to his bedroom. He quickly fell asleep.

It was nearly eleven o'clock when Thomas's wife, Deborah, woke him. The door bell had already rung twice. Williamson went to the front window and looked out on the darkened street. In the dim light cast by street lamps he made out what he thought to be "at least" three persons standing on or by his doorstep. He recognized Deputy Marshal William Miller. Williamson asked what they wanted. Miller told him that they wished to see Passmore to serve a writ on him. Thomas informed Miller "distinctly and explicitly" that Passmore did not live on Arch Street; instead, this house was his place of business. Passmore's home was at 32 Buttonwood, but his son, he said, had already left the city on business and was unreachable. Miller expressed disbelief and wanted Thomas to let him and the deputies with him go into the building. Thomas was insulted at the insinuation that Passmore might be hiding in the house. Moreover, was it "necessary for *three* or *more* United States' officers to present themselves at my door, or that of Passmore Williamson, at 11 o'clock at night, for the *only* purpose of serving a writ upon *him*?" Thomas was certain "that it was their intention, under instructions, on gaining admission, to ransack the house from bottom to top with the expectation of finding and taking into custody 'Jane, Daniel and Isaiah.'" Without another word, Thomas returned to his bed. He didn't intend to lose any more sleep on the matter.

No sooner had Thomas lain down in his bed than he heard, far off in the distance in the silence of the night, the parting whistle of a train as it left from the other side of Schuylkill River. He was certain it was the train to Harrisburg that Passmore was on.

Seven hours later, at six in the morning, the door bell suddenly rang again. Already awake, Thomas found Miller on his doorstep once more. The marshal handed Williamson the writ of habeas corpus, then left. The writ required Passmore to appear at ten o'clock that morning, July 19, in Judge John Kane's court. He was to bring with him Wheeler's three slaves. Thomas, of course, realized that there was no way Passmore would be able to make an appearance; his son wasn't due back until very late that night. He took the writ to the Anti-Slavery Society's office nearby and showed it to William Still. "Thee had better attend to it," the father said.[3] Together the two men went to see Edward Hopper. An attorney, Hopper was active in the anti-slavery cause, as might be expected of the son-in-law of the two most noted abolitionists in Philadelphia, James and Lucretia Mott. Thomas asked Hopper to appear in place of Passmore out of *"proper respect to the Court."*

As requested, Hopper showed up in court that morning to explain to Kane the reason for Passmore's absence and to assure him that Passmore was unaware that his presence in court was being sought.[4] However, United States District Attorney James C. Van Dyke did not accept the explanation gracefully. Van Dyke was representing both the federal government and Wheeler, a dual role that would raise an issue of conflict of interest. In the days ahead, his words and actions—his rigidity, lack of any semblance of compassion, and an argumentative attitude bordering on vindictiveness—make one suspect that he harbored personal antipathy against Passmore. It is possible, likely in fact, that the two men had faced off in federal court during a case involving a fugitive slave, though there is no evidence of such a confrontation.

Van Dyke asked that Kane issue another writ, an alias writ of habeas corpus—in effect, a copy of the original writ demanding Passmore's appearance in court, only this time containing the correct address for his residence. Kane agreed. The new writ ordered Passmore to appear at ten o'clock the next morning, Friday, the twentieth. Sometime during the day a deputy marshal delivered the writ to Mercie Williamson at the couple's home on Buttonwood Street.

In the early hours of the next day, sometime between 1:00 and 2:00 A.M., Passmore returned from Harrisburg and received the news from his wife. Immediately after breakfast, he went back to his office on Arch Street. At his father's suggestion, they walked together over to Hopper's office, where Passmore endorsed the writ and wrote a statement couched in the legalese that Hopper dictated: "The within named Jane, Daniel, and Isaiah, or by whatsoever names they may be called, nor either of them, are not now, nor were at the time of issuing the said writ, or the original writ, *or at any other time* [this last phrase was added at the suggestion of Thomas Williamson], in the custody, owner, or possession of, nor confined, nor restrained their liberty by him, the said Passmore Williamson. Therefore he cannot have the bodies of the said Jane, Daniel and Isaiah, or either of them, before your Honor, as by the said writ he is commanded."[5]

Sometime either just before or just after his meeting with Hopper, Passmore saw William Still, his partner in the rescue of Jane Johnson and her children. Their conversation was brief. "Are they safe?" was all Passmore asked. Told they were ("yes" said Still), he smiled.[6]

With his statement in hand, Passmore, accompanied by Hopper, went to Commissioner Charles Heazlitt's office to have the document witnessed. He then appeared before Kane in the district court's second-floor courtroom in Independence Hall. They were to be joined there by another lawyer, Charles Gilpin, a former mayor of Philadelphia, but he was late and missed the opening of the proceedings. Meanwhile, however, word of the impending hearing had spread through abolitionist circles in Philadelphia. As a result, the courtroom was crowded; the atmosphere, said John Hill Wheeler, who of course was there, was of "Great excitement."[7]

A legal battle immediately ensued when Hopper presented Passmore's statement. Van Dyke asked Kane for permission to offer testimony to rebut it. Hopper was surprised. He had not expected that there would be a trial of any sort. Hopper said that if witnesses were to be heard, he needed time to prepare Passmore's defense; there had been "a very meagre [sic] opportunity for consultation" with him, only "a few minutes while the return was being prepared." Van Dyke persisted. Kane remarked that if "the bodies of the three servants were produced in Court," he would consider allowing time for preparation. But, the judge continued, the interference with Wheeler's rights "was a criminal, wanton and cruel outrage." If testimony showed that Passmore had been guilty of contempt in his return to the writ, he, Kane, might "feel it to be his duty to hold the defendant to answer for perjury, without hearing testimony in defence." He said that a prima facie case of perjury could be made out.

The judge's comment stunned abolitionist Mary Grew. Such a "revelation of the feelings of the Judge changed in a moment the whole aspect of the case," she declared. "The Judge had become the prosecutor, and before hearing evidence had allowed his feelings to betray him into a violation of the decency of the Bench, and an outrage upon the personal character of one of the most respectable of our citizens."[8]

It was at this point that Passmore's other counsel, Charles Gilpin, who had finally arrived, rose. Passmore "had complied with the usual form in making a return." He had denied custody of Wheeler's slaves "now or any time." If that was not sufficient, Gilpin said, Passmore would make a more complete response to the writ. Van Dyke could then pursue a civil suit for damages on behalf of Wheeler. Hopper then told Kane that to satisfy the court, Passmore was willing to "amend" his return of the writ in any way compatible with the court as long as it was based upon the fact that he never had possession of the three slaves.

Kane, who had spoken privately with Wheeler two days before, just after the incident aboard the ferryboat, and was well aware of the slave owner's version of the incident, answered that Wheeler's account of the facts was "totally different" from Passmore's. He said that it was the court's "duty to ascertain and satisfy its conscience." If, indeed, Wheeler's story was true, he, Kane, would "bind the defendant over to answer on a charge of perjury."

Over Gilpin's objections, Wheeler was called to the witness stand. What was going on? Gilpin must have wondered. Like Hopper, he was rattled. There were "no direct issues for trial before the Court." There was no jury seated. He would not be able to object to any testimony, or to cross-examine. It was, to say the least, unusual.

Kane not only permitted Wheeler to testify, but allowed several other witnesses to take the stand, as well. Wheeler testified first, recounting in detail the events aboard the ferryboat *Washington*. Passmore, he said, had "pulled" Jane Johnson by the arm. Her boys "said they wanted to go with their master." "Two negroes caught me by the collar," Wheeler continued, "one on each side; one of them said to me, if you draw a weapon or make any resistance, I will cut your throat from ear to ear." Wheeler said he followed the crowd of blacks as they "forced my servants on shore, and hurried them away." He followed after them and saw them "forced" into a hack. Williamson, he said, promised "he would be responsible for any claim that I might have."[9]

The slave master's account was backed up by several eyewitnesses who testified to what had happened on the ferryboat and on the Walnut Street dock. Each of them made it sound as if Jane Johnson and her children had indeed been taken away involuntarily, under protest. Traveling salesman Robert Tumbleston said the "colored woman and two boys" were being "forced ashore." Messenger William Edwards said the two boys were "forced away by two colored men." Capt. Andrew Heath said he saw Passmore "walking along with them." Police officer Thomas Wallace said Passmore was following "the negroes," who "were pushing the woman and boys along." Hack driver James McIlhone said, "The woman and boys were crying."[10]

Neither Hopper or Gilpin was given the opportunity to cross-examine Wheeler or any of the witnesses, and as soon as their testimony was completed, Van Dyke asked that Passmore be cited "for making an insufficient return" and that he "be held" as well "to answer for willful and malicious perjury." Gilpin now asked for time to prepare a defense. Passmore, he said, "could put a different face upon the matter, as to the absconding or escaping of the servants." In support, Hopper rose to say that there might be one witness who could be called to refute the accounts of Wheeler and the witnesses—he was undoubtedly referring to William Still—but the defense needed a delay until the next day to consult among themselves as well as to examine "authorities" for legal precedents.

Kane, however, pointed out that Van Dyke's two motions were still before the court. He had not decided anything as this point, but he was willing to hear Passmore's side if he was prepared to testify under oath. Then he would decide, Kane said, whether to grant the defense a delay. Passmore, Hopper, and Gilpin huddled for a few minutes, then Passmore took the witness stand.

Passmore spoke at length, describing the incident at the Walnut Street wharf from the moment he first learned that "three slaves" wanted "to assert their right to freedom." He traced his movements to the Walnut Street wharf. Then, deliberately pointing to Wheeler, he said, "I saw that man sitting sideways on the bench on the farther side; Jane was sitting next to and three or four feet from him, the two children were sitting close to her." Passmore went on the say how he had approached the slave woman and questioned whether she wanted her freedom. Yes, he had taken hold of her arm and assisted her to rise from her seat when she rose to leave the ferryboat. And he himself, he acknowledged, had at one point taken Wheeler "by the collar and held him to one side." But "colored people who had collected around us" led the woman and her children from the ferryboat, and the last he had seen of them was shortly afterwards, when they entered a carriage at Dock and Front streets. "I saw no more of them," he insisted, "have had no control of them, and do not know where they are. My whole connection with the affair was this."

Although Passmore's own attorneys were not permitted to cross-examine Wheeler or any of the other witnesses, Kane permitted Van Dyke to question Passmore. However, the district attorney failed to shake his testimony. Passmore persisted in his account. He met "the sole person" whom he knew at the wharf just this morning—meaning, of course, William Still, though he did not use his name, simply saying the man worked for the Anti-Slavery Society. "We had some conversation about this case," Passmore said. He was told Jane Johnson and her young sons were safe "and would not return under any circumstances." Passmore then made a point of saying, "I did not enquire where they were, nor did he tell me."

Hopper said the defense declined to make any further argument at this time. But Van Dyke would not let the matter rest. He said that Passmore's testimony was no testimony at all, and he compared him to a pickpocket who steals a purse and hands to a confederate "the plunger" he used to lift the wallet.[11] Van Dyke urged the judge to find Passmore in contempt of court and held to answer a charge of perjury.

Kane hesitated. He wanted "to have time for reflection." The case, the judge said, "was so great, and its consequences might be so very grave" that Passmore "might even pass into the condition of a prisoner." Kane warned that "it would be better" if Passmore produced Jane Johnson and the two children, if it was in his "power" to do so. The judge set a further hearing on Van Dyke's two motions for the following Friday, July 27. In the meantime, considering the gravity of the case, Passmore would have to put up five thousand dollars bail, which he was able to arrange.

As soon as it became clear that it would take time to get back his slaves, Wheeler had put off his return to Nicaragua. It appears certain that he was one of the men who had accompanied Deputy Marshal Miller when Miller, writ in hand, first presented himself at the Williamsons' office at eleven o'clock on July 18. The darkness undoubtedly hid his face. Two hours later—once it was clear the slaves were not going to be immediately surrendered to him—Wheeler himself was aboard a train. So, coincidentally, while Passmore was en route to Harrisburg, Wheeler was on a train bound for New York City. He hoped to retrieve his baggage and his wife's belongings, which had been put aboard the ferryboat *Washington* and trans-shipped to New York.[12] He arrived there at six in the morning of the nineteenth, the same day that the ship he was supposed to sail on with Jane Johnson and her youngsters was scheduled to leave for the Caribbean. He rushed to the dock and was able to have the luggage taken off the ship before it departed. He then met with a friend from Washington named Cottrell, with whom he entrusted the care of his possessions. He asked Cottrell to forward one trunk to Philadelphia, probably with the clothes he would need while he had to be in that city. Wheeler then raced to catch a ferry to take him across to New Jersey, where he could catch the next train to Philadelphia, hopeful apparently that his slaves might in the meantime have been recovered. Four hours after he had reached New York, he was on his way back, arriving in Philadelphia in the early afternoon of July 19. He returned to find that Passmore Williamson was still absent from the city and that there was no word whatsoever about the whereabouts of his slaves.

That same afternoon, Wheeler met with Van Dyke and David Webster, a young state's attorney who was an expert on criminal law, to discuss his case against Passmore Williamson. Afterwards—obviously as a result of their conference—Wheeler swore out complaints against five black porters and dockhands who had participated in helping his slaves to escape: John Ballard, William Custis, James S. Braddock, James Martin, and Isaiah Moore. They were brought before James B. Freeman, alderman for the Sixth Ward, whose functions included legal duties much like those of a justice of the peace. Freeman had the men formally arrested and incarcerated at the Cherry Street police station. The men were left there until the following afternoon. They were denied permission to have visitors and were not given anything to eat until a pitying reporter said, "they begged their keeper, for the love of God, to appease their distressing hunger."[13] Placed in a confined lock-up, the men suffered so from intense heat—the temperature reached ninety-five degrees—that they shed all their clothes.[14]

Even though Freeman was a municipal officer and his court a local jurisdiction, Van Dyke, his federal position notwithstanding, appeared as prosecutor at the proceeding the next day. The five men were not permitted to have legal counsel or to present witnesses on their behalf. Wheeler was on hand again, and his testimony sealed the fate of the five black men. The "whole affair," the slave master testified, "lasted, I suppose, about three minutes." He said that when Ballard threatened him, "I was provoked at the time, but not excited; I was as cool as I am at this moment." Wheeler added, "He took hold of my arm evidently supposing I was about to draw a weapon [but] I had no weapon about me except such as God Almighty gave me—my fists."[15]

When Custis tried to cross-examine Wheeler, Van Dyke chided him for daring to ask any questions. Alderman Freeman then charged each of the men with highway robbery, inciting to riot, and assault and battery. He set their bail at seven thousand dollars each, an impossible figure for the men, all day laborers, to raise. Their trial—and William Still's, too, because he was later charged with the same crimes—was set for August 9. However, because both prosecution and defense attorneys requested more time to prepare their cases, the trial was put off for three weeks until August 29.[16] Still was able to make bail, but the others were imprisoned.

That Friday evening, July 20, Wheeler wrote President Pierce to explain his delay in returning to Central America; then he visited the Sully home. He did not want to unduly disturb his father-in-law's family, so he checked in at the American Hotel, which was popular with merchants and businessmen.[17] It was situated on Chestnut Street, down the street from Independence Hall.

In the days that followed, Wheeler tried to keep busy in Philadelphia, awaiting the outcome of the July 27 hearing involving Passmore and then the trial of the others involved in what he continued to call the "abduction" of his slaves. He again conferred with Van Dyke, though he never confided in his diary what he discussed with him. In the process, however, he struck up a friendly relationship with the district attorney, taking pleasure trips with Van Dyke and his brother, who was a doctor, to Atlantic City and the falls of the Schuylkill. Wheeler also wrote again to the president, called on Marshal Francis Wynkoop to get the latest "testimony" as to "the abduction of my servants," visited with friends at the huge, five-story, three-hundred-room Girard Hotel on Chestnut Street, and went shopping, buying some jewelry for his wife, Ellen, as well as shoes and stationery for himself. On the night before the hearing, on the advice of Van Dyke, he once again visited Judge Kane.[18] What they discussed is not known either. What is clear, though, is that Wheeler, Kane, and Van Dyke were of one mind with regard to the direction the case against Passmore Williamson was taking, and it seemed a foregone conclusion what Kane's decision would be.

As scheduled, the hearing began at 10 o'clock Friday morning, July 27.[19] Passmore had arrived early in order to drop off a document that needed to be certified at the nearby office of the recorder of deeds. Gilpin and Hopper were at his side, but Kane gave them no chance to argue further for the right to examine Wheeler and his witnesses, or even to say another word in Passmore's defense. Instead, he came immediately to the point, reading aloud his decision in the case. He could not, he said, look upon Passmore's return "otherwise than as illusory—in legal phrase, as evasive, if not false."

"[Passmore's response] denies that the prisoners were within his power, custody, or possession *at any time whatever*. Now, the evidence of respectable, uncontradicted witnesses, and the admission of the respondent himself, establish the fact beyond controversy that the prisoners were at one time within his power and control. He was the person by whose counsel the so-called rescue was devised. He gave the directions, and hastened to the pier to stimulate and supervise their execution. He was the spokesman and first actor after arriving there."

Kane then inferentially raised the prejudice regarding black inferiority. "Of all the parties to the act of violence," the judge said of Passmore, "he was the only white man, the only citizen, the only individual having recognized political rights, the only person whose social training could certainly interpret either his own duties or the rights of others under the constitution of the land."

Moreover, Kane brushed aside the argument that state law dictated that any slave brought into Pennsylvania was automatically free. A slave was property, and slave ownership was sacrosanct. "I know of no statute of Pennsylvania," Kane said, "which affects to divest the rights of property of a citizen of North Carolina, acquired and asserted under the laws of that State, because he has found it needful or convenient to pass through the territory of Pennsylvania." Kane was unaware, he said, that "any such statute, if such a one were shown, could be recognized as valid in a court of the United States." Besides which, he added, taking into immediate consideration the rescue of Jane Johnson and her two boys and Passmore Williamson's role in it, "it seems to me altogether unimportant whether they were slaves or not. It would be the mockery of philanthropy to assert that, because men had become free, they might therefore be forcibly abducted."

The judge insisted that his personal feelings had not influenced his decision. He made a point of saying that he had not alluded to "the motives by which the respondent has been governed; I have nothing to do with them; they may give him support and comfort before an infinitely higher tribunal; I do not impugn them here."

Kane's verdict was harsh. He found Williamson in contempt of court and ordered him committed into the custody of Marshal Francis Wynkoop "without bail or mainprize" for refusing to answer to the writ of habeas corpus. Until he did so, he would remain imprisoned. There was no question of putting up bail this time and remaining free. The judge consigned Passmore to the notorious Philadelphia County Prison, familiarly known as Moyamensing. As for the perjury charge, Kane withheld his opinion because Passmore, being now under arrest, might be indicted for that by a grand jury.

Gilpin quickly rose to suggest that Passmore be allowed to amend his return, but Van Dyke interrupted to press for Passmore's being taken immediately to the prison. The judge told Gilpin that if he had any motion to make he should put it in writing. Gilpin argued that Van Dyke's motion for Passmore's commitment was not in writing, but Kane said that he had already granted Van Dyke's motion to remand Passmore to prison, so it wasn't necessary for it to be put in writing. It would be best, the judge added, if Gilpin and Hopper waited until they read his published opinion before offering to the court any motion regarding an amendment of the writ. The opinion had not yet been filed with the clerk of the court and properly recorded, but when it was they would need to study it.

For some reason, Gilpin, who was the senior counsel for Passmore, never followed up on the matter, never filed the motion. Despite the fact that it was the height of the summer and many well-to-do residents had fled the city for the cooler countryside, Kane remained in Philadelphia for weeks. According to Passmore's cousin Edward Williamson, the judge was waiting to receive Gilpin's motion but he had "'heard' nothing but an ominous silence."[20]

Had Gilpin forgotten the judge's recommendation? Had he not paid attention to what Kane had said? Gilpin's failure to read and respond to the judge's published opinion promised to complicate the legal hurdles that lay ahead and raises the question whether his lack of compliance was a purposeful abolitionist maneuver to extend the attention that the case was receiving. Whether intended or not, his dawdling compelled Kane to remain in Philadelphia. How else was the judge to resolve a politically explosive situation if not by freeing Passmore as soon as possible? Kane had accepted that Passmore had told the truth (he would drop the threat of charging him with perjury), but he would not admit that he had made a mistake by citing him for contempt and evidently hoped to settle the question quickly. Why else would he stay stuck in unbearably hot Philadelphia in the middle of summer?

As the audience in the courtroom broke up, Passmore's friends surrounded him. He appeared "perfectly cool and collected," a reporter wrote. On the other side of the room, Wheeler was the center of a circle of sympathizers. The Wheeler party seemed in "high spirits."[21]

Two friends of Passmore, both abolition advocates, accompanied him to the prison. One was Dillwyn Parrish, a druggist by trade who had been president of the Pennsylvania Abolition Society in 1852 and was now its vice president.[22] He was also a member of the Anti-Slavery Society. The other was Charles D. Cleveland, an especially fervent abolitionist proponent who, in a spirited address to the Liberty Party, had lashed out against the South:

> While the slave states are inferior to us in free population, having not even one half of ours; inferior in morals, being the region of bowie knives and duels, of assassinations and lynch law; inferior in mental attainments, having not one-fourth of the number that can read and write; inferior in intelligence, having not one-fifth the number of literary and scientific periodicals; inferior in the products of agriculture and manufactures, of mines, of fisheries,

and of the forest; inferior, in short, in everything that constitutes the wealth, the honor, the dignity, the stability, the happiness, the true greatness of a nation—it is wrong, it is unjust, it is absurd, that they should have an influence in all the departments of government so entirely disproportionate to our own.[23]

The ride to the prison, about a mile and a half away in the southern part of the city, proved awkward. Wynkoop, whose brother had been arrested as a result of Passmore's involvement in the Wilkes-Barre case, escorted Passmore and later claimed that he had offered to make a detour and take him by his home on Buttonwood Street before proceeding to the prison. Wynkoop said he wanted to show Passmore all the courtesy and attention in his power, but Passmore, he said, rejected the offer. [24]

Passmore, however, took issue with virtually all that Wynkoop claimed. The only request he made, Passmore said, was to be taken through the office of the Recorder of Deeds so he could retrieve the document he had left there that morning. "I assured him [it] would not detain us a minute," he said, "but he peremptorily refused to do so, saying he '*had to take me directly down to prison*.'" Passmore acknowledged that before Wynkoop was seated in the carriage, he did offer to extend to him "such courtesies as the duties of his office might permit." But Passmore, demonstrating an obstinacy that would be the hallmark of his imprisonment, said he had no intention of asking for any favors. He told Wynkoop that "I intended to stand on my legal rights, which I presumed would be entirely sufficient."

Not another word was spoken between them as the carriage with Wynkoop, Passmore, Parrish, and Cleveland set off along Library Street, then turned down Fifth Street, heading for Moyamensing.

"My office in the case of Williamson was unpleasant, but not difficult," Kane explained in answer to a letter he received shortly afterwards. There were no hard feelings involved: "My relations with him have always been kindly: he has rendered me personal courtesies; and we have friends in common; he is withal a generous spirited man, and as brave as fanaticism itself.

"But," the judge continued, "on the questions which were, or which might have been in controversy before me, I have never had a doubt. The right of a slaveholding citizen of Virginia or North Carolina, to pass through Pennsylvania, with his slaves, unmolested, has always seemed to me too clear for argument. . . . To limit it by state action would be to regulate commerce between the states. With precisely equal show of right, one state might deny the character of property to intoxicating liquors, another to the products of slave labor, and confiscate the cotton of South Carolina as it comes Northward to the spinning mill, or our Monongahela whiskey as it passes down the Ohio."

Kane added that he had no doubt "as to my power of attaching for a false or evasive return to the Habeas Corpus. It is simply absurd to say, that a formal return is conclusive upon the Court, and leaves the relator to his personal suit. The man may be lynched, the daughter ravished, the slave carried to parts unknown,—and the wrongdoer escape beyond the jurisdiction, or be without a *dock* to respond in damages. The wiseacres have forgotten that the Habeas Corpus is preventive,—or else, they have never known it."[25]

"I have never borne personal ill-will towards that gentleman or any of his kindred," Kane assured another correspondent. "I was grieved when he made it my duty to place him in confinement."[26]

Passmore, on the other hand, had no such amicable feelings about the judge. "I knew he had been nursing his wrath against me ever since the Treason Fizzle, and both he & the mercenary & ruffianly minions under & around him considered they were deeply in my debt for the Notice taken of them in the Wi[l]kesbarre case, and had therefore prepared myself for the worst he could do, and expected that to be done in the most vindictive manner." Passmore said he expected he would be freed on bail. "But I was taken aback when all these matters were so summarily abandoned & I brought to judgment at once upon the pretense of Contempt. He has more courage than I gave him credit for, whether as much discretion remains to be seen. They had evidently taken a survey of matters & come to the conclusion that the only chance they had of punishing me was to adopt the arbitrary and as they no doubt supposed irresponsible course pursued. They are welcome to do their worst. I will never consent or allow the return to be amended or any other concession to be made *until I am convinced I have done wrong*."[27]

9

Pandora's Box

O, kindle not that bigot fire,
'Twill bring disunion, fear and pain;
'Twill rouse at last the souther's ire,
And burst our starry land in twain.

"The Bigot Fire," *Anti-Slavery Harp*, 40

John Kane had no idea that, like Pandora, he had unleashed a series of woes that would plague him personally. Nor, for that matter, did Passmore Williamson realize at first that his stubbornness and self-righteousness would become such a burden to himself, his wife, and his father. But beyond personal considerations, what had started as one woman's escape from slavery quickly became a national cause célèbre that fueled a variety of debates—about states' rights versus the authority of the federal government; about the Fugitive Slave Law; about the application of what was considered the foundation of personal freedom, the writ of habeas corpus; and, ultimately, about how slavery could continue to exist across an invisible border with a population, black and white, that was free. The rescue of Jane Johnson and the subsequent case against Passmore Williamson were turning out to be a blessing for the abolitionist movement.

The problem was that, on the surface, Pennsylvania's Liberty Law seemed to conflict directly with both the United States Constitution and the federal fugitive laws of 1793 and 1850. But Kane's opinion—

that no Pennsylvania law could "divest" a North Carolinian's "property rights"—had never been tested before the United States Supreme Court.

The conflict between a state's rights and those of the federal government had supposedly been resolved in 1842 in what was called the Prigg case. Edward Prigg, acting as the agent of a Maryland resident, had come into Pennsylvania and found and took back a slave woman who had escaped from her owner almost ten years earlier. He had done so without ever obtaining authorization from a state authority permitting him to do so, a procedure that might have enabled the woman to contest her seizure in a state court of law. Prigg was charged with and convicted of kidnapping. Appeals made their way through state courts, landing finally before the United States Supreme Court.[1] It ruled, in an opinion written by Chief Justice Roger B. Taney, that "The right of the master being given by the Constitution of the United States, neither Congress nor a state legislature can by any law or regulation impair it, or restrict it."[2] In other words, Prigg did not need Pennsylvania's permission to secure the escaped slave. Federal authority took precedence. (Taney would underscore the denial of any rights to blacks when, fifteen years later, in his opinion in the Dred Scott case, he denied that any slave or slave descendant could be an American citizen and treated as such in a federal court.)

It was the Supreme Court's decision in the Prigg case that Pennsylvania sought to bypass by enacting in 1847 its personal-liberty law. It prohibited state officials from abetting the capture of fugitive slaves and banned the use of state jails for detaining runaways. More important, in light of the escape of Jane Johnson, the Liberty Law made it clear that a slave owner could not sojourn temporarily or even pass through the state without the slaves automatically becoming free. John Kane, however, dismissed the state law and paid no heed to what abolitionists considered a higher law, God's law. Instead, his words reaffirmed Taney's opinion in the Prigg case and foreshadowed what Taney would say in the Dred Scott decision in 1857, which denied that blacks had any rights whatsoever.

The Supreme Court's decision in the Prigg case did not resolve public controversy over states' rights or discourage abolitionists such as Passmore from invoking the Liberty Law. They interpreted the Pennsylvania statute as a way to legitimatize their actions in assisting runaways or, in the case of Jane Johnson, in helping a slave woman who desired her freedom. Moreover, no matter what Kane asserted, there had never been a constitutional test of the Liberty Law. Kane was overstepping his authority in declaring the state law unconstitutional. Despite what Kane inferred, and southern supporters insisted, Passmore and his abolitionist friends were not breaking the law by helping a slave find freedom. Judicially speaking, Kane was far out of line and, as abolitionists contended, abusing his office. It was more evidence of the domination of "slave power."

The conflict, between state and federal governments, never seemed to go away. Ever since the nation was founded, both northern and southern states had struggled to assert their own authority. At times the assertion of that authority was paradoxical. "In the South," said Carl Schurz, an early supporter of Abraham Lincoln, "it was State-Rights or the supremacy of the Federal power, as the one or the other furthered the interests of slavery; in the North, it was State-Rights or the supremacy of the Federal power, as one or the other furthered the interests of freedom."[3]

John M. Read, a Philadelphia attorney who was the titular chief defense counsel at the Christiana Riot trial, pointed out the irony of the situation with regard to Jane Johnson and her children: here was a case of fugitives being hunted down in a state where, by law, they were automatically free. "The Southern States have always assumed plenary power[;] they have stood for the doctrine of State rights, that what is not given is withheld; that the powers not delegated to the Union are withheld by the State itself, and are by it to be exercised."[4] If that was so, Read asked, what about Pennsylvania's rights?

Abolitionists added to the argument, confused it actually, when they spoke of a "higher law" than the Constitution: God's law. The most radical of them shared the views of William Lloyd Garrison and denounced the Constitution. They believed it condoned states' rights when it came to the issue of involuntary servitude. "Slavery," the American Anti-Slavery Society stated, "obtained sufferance at the adoption of the Constitution through reverence for State Rights."[5]

The controversy—states' rights as against federal authority, the Constitution versus God's law—served only to fuel an already incendiary situation. The riotous Jerry Rescue in Syracuse in the fall of 1851 symbolized the determination of many abolitionists who were willing to engage in violence in the struggle against slavery. Jerry—his real name was William Henry—was a runaway who found refuge in that upstate New York city. He was working in a cooper shop when three deputy marshals and a local police officer seized him. News of his capture spread rapidly throughout the city, church bells ringing the alarm. A convention of the Liberty Party quickly adjourned, and its members and other abolitionist sympathizers crowded into the office of the federal commissioner who would decide Jerry's fate. A number of them surrounded Jerry and rushed him out the door. However, he was recaptured outside and placed in shackles at a police station. That evening an armed crowd besieged the station house and was able to spirit Jerry away. Casualties were, fortunately, light. A marshal wounded one rescuer, then jumped from a window, breaking his arm. Jerry was put aboard a British boat and taken across Lake Erie to Canada. "I have seen that it was necessary to bring the people into direct conflict with the Government," a Unitarian minister from Leicester, Massachusetts, said, "that the Government may be made to understand that it has transcended its limits—and must recede."[6]

In a sense, the South voiced that same argument over the slavery issue when South Carolina declared its secession in 1861. By that time, asserting *their* rights, thirteen northern and midwestern states had enacted laws that either nullified, or rendered impossible to enforce, laws of Congress dealing with slavery. Pennsylvania was one of those states.

Judge Kane's use of the writ of habeas corpus—"you have the body" in Latin—drew widespread condemnation. "The object and intent of the *habeas corpus* are, to restore liberty to such as are held in illegal imprisonment," *The New York Times* declared in an editorial. The judge had "perverted" the writ to accomplish the exact opposite, that is, to "deprive" Passmore Williamson of his freedom. The newspaper said that Kane's action made "every Federal Court a mock auction shop for tricking and swindling, by *construction* of law, citizens of the Free States out of their liberty."[7]

One of most stinging rebukes came from Horace Dresser, a New York City lawyer who was instrumental in the formation of the Broadway Tabernacle Anti-Slavery Society. First of all, wrote Dresser, in a letter to the editor of the *National Era,* the use of the writ of habeas corpus "heretofore has been to *free* men, not to enslave them." Instead, "The great liberator had become the great enslaver." Then, too, Dresser went on, Jane Johnson and her boys "were not *fugitives,*" which would have placed themselves within the provisions of the federal laws. Nor was the writ properly filed, "not so when issued by a Judge out of Court—he has no clerk, seal." A federal circuit court was the proper place in which to seek the writ, not the district court. Kane did not have jurisdiction over the matter, nor any power to cite Passmore Williamson for contempt. Passmore, he said, "should have treated it as an *unlawful writ,* as it was a wicked contrivance of a slaveholder, by perversion, if not perjury, to entrap a poor *woman* and her *children!* What abominations have not been perpetrated in the name of Justice, and by misuse of her most sacred instruments?" Passmore's case "is full of instruction," Dresser added. "It teaches an important lesson upon the question of State Rights; shows how the Federal Judiciary may trespass on the liberties of the citizen, and trample under foot the rights of the person."[8]

The criticisms stimulated by the case became increasingly personal. Both Passmore Williamson and John Kane were targeted, the one by slavery proponents, the other by abolitionist sympathizers. The rebukes often took an ugly turn. Passmore received in the mail a newspaper clipping and a threatening letter from "A Southern man from old Virginia," who wrote that he was "of the same opinion" as the clipping from the *Richmond American* that he enclosed. The newspaper said Wheeler would have been more entitled to its respect "had [he] drawn his pistol and shot Williamson down." If Passmore "were to receive his desserts, he would dangle from a high tree in Independence Square." The man who sent the clipping said, "I am of the same opinion as that paper and if you were to go to the Penitentiary for two or three years perhaps you would learn to keep your nose out of other persons business[.] I would have shot if [I] had been Col. Wheeler."[9]

The decidedly pro-Southern *Daily Pennsylvanian* took the same tack. "We think," it said, "that eight men in every ten would have first shot Williamson dead in his tracks and then the brutal Negro who threatened to cut Mr. Wheeler's throat." "It was an open highway robbery, trampling under foot everything like law and civilization," it stated. "In any foreign country on the globe . . . Mr. Wheeler would have been safe from molestation, together with his servants."[10]

In yet another attack on Passmore, the *Daily Pennsylvanian* brought up a ticklish subject, miscegenation, a topic that was the unspoken reason behind much of the opposition to abolition by many persons in both the North and the South. The newspaper reported on the audience reaction received at a performance of a play entitled *Extremes* at the Walnut Street Theatre. In it, a young white woman falls in love with a black man, who is "so transported" that he cries out, much to the audience's amusement, "Oh, Pathmore—oh Pathmore Williamson!" The laughter lasted a full five minutes, proving, the newspaper said, that in Philadelphia, whether rich, poor, or middle class, all believe that the mixing of races is a subject of "grotesque hilarity."

"Nature," the *Pennsylvanian* said, "has planted a barrier between the Caucasian and the African races more insuperable than the ocean which divides their shores, or the mountains that intervene their homes."[11]

Under the headline "PASSMORE WILLIAMSON, THE NIGGER STEALER," the *New York Evening Mirror,* a Democrat organ, commented, "It has been said, by way of hyperbole, that the meanest of all possible thefts is the stealing of pennies from a dead mother's eyes. But we regard the sneaking Abolitionist, who seduces niggers from their masters, as a more contemptible thief, both in the eyes of God and man, than the robber of corpses or churches." Passmore, the newspaper concluded, should have minded his own business. Slavery "is no evil to the ignorant African subjected to a humane master's care."[12]

Passmore was even chided by the fiery abolitionist Stephen Symonds Foster, who like William Lloyd Garrison, had denounced the Constitution. Slavery in his opinion was "an American and not a Southern institution."[13] Notorious as an outspoken anti-slavery lecturer, Foster condemned Passmore for retaining a lawyer. He should "have trusted to his own tongue before that guilty Court. There is strength in a word fitly spoken. I would give the wealth of a life time [*sic*] for such an opportunity."[14]

For his part, Kane, on a vacation later at Sweet Sulphur Springs, Virginia, was pleased to be approached by other guests, who provided him with ample evidence, he said, "of his just decision from people of the South."[15] But such a response was unusual. Among the correspondence dealing with the imprisonment of Passmore Williamson that Kane donated to the American Philosophical Society—of which he was president at one time—is a letter reflecting ambivalence about his ruling. The writer, from Botetourt County, Virginia, began, "We have examined with pleasure your decision in the Williamson's case, but," it went on, "[I] must say it is generally ridiculed by our Southern judges, for while we claim for our States, 'the rights of States,' we must admit the sovereignty of Pennsylvania." The letter writer said that "so far as it inflicts punishment upon Williamson 'go [for] it,' and although it appears from your local laws he committed no offence, yet he would if he could deprive us of our rightful property, and therefore we say let this punishment be without limitation."[16]

In other correspondence and in newspaper characterizations, Kane was the subject of the most vehement vilifications. One letter writer, a so-called "friend," wrote him, "You have been playing the Devil Since you have been in office. . . . You Son of a bitch."[17]

The judge came under special scrutiny in abolitionist and anti-Democrat northern newspapers. *The New York Times* unfavorably compared Kane with his son, the explorer Elisha Kane: the character of the two "are as opposite as the direction of their looks; while the father turns his gaze constantly to the South, the son turns his to the North, and lays down his noble life in the attempt to benefit his fellow men."[18] His ruling, *Frederick Douglass' Paper* declared, was "as false a piece of sophism as ever disgraced a bench. By it, Pennsylvania, and every other State in the Union, and every rational jurisdiction on the globe, is slave territory! *Slaves are property,* as much so as horses or cattle, sugar or molasses! And no State or nation has the right to say what should be property in another State, nor can it interfere with the owner in carrying his property wherever he pleases!"[19]

Worse still, Kane was likened to Lord Jeffreys, a nefarious seventeenth-century English Lord Chief Justice whose flagrant injustices and brutality were displayed during the "Bloody Azzizes," trials, in which no defense was heard and which resulted in at least 320 executions. The *Hartford Religious Herald* said there was "in this country one who bids fair to rival the infamous English Judge. We refer to Judge Kane."[20] Comparing Kane to Lord Jeffreys, the *National Anti-Slavery Standard* said the judge was "not only a beautiful blockhead, but a first-rate knave." If "any lover of the past" was apprehensive "that the breed of bad judges was running out, we commend to him, for solace or for study, the illustrious Kane, the federal Solon of Philadelphia."[21] The *National Era* said, "The man must be dull who cannot see the daily parallels to the events which preceded the English Revolution of 1689, in . . . the prostitution of the Judiciary . . . accompanied by a degree of insolence which only the progress of civilization prevents from being as ferocious as that of a Jefferies [*sic*]."[22]

In six long editorials, Horace Greeley's influential *New York Daily Tribune* thundered against Kane: "Neither accusations of perjury nor contempt of Court, brought against Abolitionists, can restore the fetters to the limbs of those who have thus been endowed with the supreme right to the control of their own persons and the 'pursuit of happiness' in their own way."[23]

Kane's name lent itself to being spelled "Cain," as in the Biblical sense, which his opponents were quick to seize upon. A satire was published entitled "A Chapter in the Book of Chronicles." It read in part:

"13. And the Lord said, 'The voice of thy brother Passmore crieth unto me from the prison,

"14. And behold thou shall henceforth become a reprobate upon the earth and thy name shall be a reproach unto future generations."[24]

A poem, "A Pas-Kane-ade," related how the Devil gave an "entertainment" one day when a man named Kane showed up:

> "But which of all the Cains?" For Satan's witty[,]
> "Mean you the Judge of Phila. City?"
> "The same, my Lord; I claim my ancestral right
> And entrance seek." Quoth Satan, "I'm in a plight[,]
> Of us, in Pandemonium, there can't be two,
> Therefore, my lieges, my horns and tail unscrew!"[25]

"Cain, CAIN, CAIN," *Frederick Douglass' Paper* cried out, "the voice of thy brother's blood crieth unto thee from the ground. Make ready! The spirit of the avenger is abroad!"[26]

At one point, when Passmore was reported ailing in Moyamensing, the *Free Presbyterian* complained: "Thus the namesake, and the spiritual, if not lineal, descendant of the first murderer plies his work of death. Not by the stroke of the bludgeon, but by the slow tortures of damp dungeons with their foul air."[27]

God's name was invoked by many who rebuked Kane. "A friend to Humanity" wrote him, underscoring his remarks, "God is against you, popular opinion is against you, and even slaveholders themselves are against you."[28] A Quaker woman who identified herself as "a Wife & Mother," said she was "not even" a member of an abolition society and "not a personal friend" of Passmore, but, she wrote the judge: "Sleep has forsaken my eyes, and slumber mine eyelids, as I dwelt on the fearful responsibility resting upon thee, & I have risen from my bed in the silent watches of the night to plead with thee. . . . Let not I beseech thee, the glitter of political aggrandisement [sic]—the promise of Southern friendship, or any fallacious presentation so blind thy eyes & deafen thy ears as that the still small voice in thy inner sanctuary cannot be heard. . . . How knowest thou but the same measure thou metes shall be measured to thee again?"[29]

The Reverend William W. Patton of the Fourth Congregational Church in Hartford, Connecticut, told his parishioners that "every pulpit should have thundered its anathema against judicial tyranny. Every minister of Christ should have been filled with the spirit of Isaiah and Zephaniah to denounce the wrath of God against all who condemn the innocent, until the guilty Judge should have repented in sack-cloth and ashes, or have fled to some heathen city, where no Christian testimony was to be encountered."[30]

One church that did speak out was Philadelphia's Shiloh Presbyterian Church, whose members signed a letter addressed to Passmore Williamson, William Still, and the five other black men who helped in Jane Johnson's rescue. "You are suffering under the shadow of the law, without a shade of justice," the letter read. "Be of good cheer. The God of Justice will defend you."[31]

Newspapers in almost every state commented on the case. Many of those in the North caricatured and vilified Judge Kane and used the imbroglio the case was causing as further reason to condemn slavery, the Fugitive Slave Law, and southern domination of the nation. "Three hundred and forty-seven thousand five hundred and twenty-five Slaveholders in the Republic," the *Evening Journal* of Albany, New York, would note: "The Legislation of the Republic is in the hands of this handfull [*sic*] of Slaveholders. The United States Senate assures it to them. The Executive power of the Government is theirs."[32]

In some states—Ohio, Massachusetts, and Connecticut—other cases involving fugitive slaves were in the local news. But few attained the national notoriety of the Passmore Williamson case. Perhaps because Judge Kane made such a convenient target.

"Why is Williamson in prison?" the *New York Daily Tribune* asked. "What crime has he committed? How long is be to be confined on a charge of contempt?"[33]

10

Moyamensing

What lover of her fame
Feels not his country's shame,
In this dark hour?
Where are the patriots now,
Of honest heart and brow,
Who scorn the neck to bow
To Slavery's power?

"Spirit of Freeman Wake," *Anti-Slavery Harp,* 12
(to be sung to the air "America")

It is safe to say that Passmore Williamson's experience in Moyamensing was unique. Never before in the prison's history, and never again for that matter, was an inmate treated in the manner in which he was. The prison became the scene of some bizarre events.

Moyamensing, a redoubtable crenellated castle, was designed by Thomas Ustick Walter, a prominent Philadelphia architect who would later design the Senate and House wings for the capitol building in Washington as well as its cast-iron dome. The prison and, a few yards away, an incongruous complementary jail built to look like an Egyptian temple, were situated on Passyunk Road, near Tenth Street, just below Federal Street in the southern part of Philadelphia.[1] It was a forbidding neighborhood of ramshackle structures that housed poor blacks and immigrants. A description of the area by a former Philadelphia coroner was so lurid—"Many are found dead in cold and exposed rooms and garrets . . . and others found lying dead in back yards, in alleys, and other exposed situations"—that the Pennsylvania Abolition Society quickly sought to dispel his remarks. "The degradation and wretchedness which mark the infected district in Moyamensing," a pamphlet it published in 1849 read, "are foreign to the real character of our colored population, to whom it would be doing a gross injustice, not to point out clearly the broad line of separation." Blacks in the city, the society felt necessary to emphasize, were "to a considerable degree, sober, industrious, and independent."[2]

The county prison was constructed in the 1830s to replace out-moded jails on Walnut and Arch streets in the city proper. The castle was a massive square building of Quincy granite that was meant to capture, according to the description in a contemporary guidebook, the "Tudor style of English Gothic" architecture. The entranceway in its center rose three stories and was topped by a tower. Wings on either side were two stories high and were flanked by formidable octagonal towers. The prison cells were in two extensive halls, with three tiers of cells on each side. Convicted felons were in the wing to the right, those awaiting trial in the wing to the left. There were separate sections for black, white, and women prisoners. Cells in the two upper tiers were reached by corridors extending the entire length of the halls, which were lighted from apertures in the roof and in the outside walls of the cells themselves. In all, the prison held a little of over four hundred cells, each of which could be shared by two prisoners. A novelist who once visited Moyamensing thought the structure "not severely prison-like," but he saw it on a snowy night when "the few lamps that were used in it glowing feebly in the dark, presented an eery [sic], fantastic, almost supernatural appearance."[3]

In startling contrast was the county prison's odd-looking mate, which was originally built to house debtors and later turned into a separate prison for women. The color of the temple, the guidebook said, was "very peculiar," though it did not explain what it meant by that remark. Its portal consisted of two huge red sandstone columns supporting a pediment "of like dimensions." The edifice was a reminder of the "vivid description of the architectural beauties of ancient Egypt, in the times of the Pharaohs."[4]

Interested sightseers could take a tour of the county prison for twenty-five cents. A fifteen-member board of inspectors managed the prison with some success, if the contemporary guidebook is to be believed. "The health of the Prison is good," it said. "Great care is taken to furnish wholesome food, and to have it properly cooked; every prisoner is allowed as much as he wants, this being found more economical than the mode of individual rations."[5] Reality was something else again. Passmore Williamson found it necessary to arrange to have his meals delivered to his cell from home.

Moyamensing was the name of the section of Philadelphia in which the prison stood, a name derived from an Indian word for "unclean place" or "place of pigeon droppings."[6] The prison had a terrible reputation. Seven months before Passmore entered Moyamensing, coal-gas escaped from a defective heating apparatus into many of the cells. Guards found thirty prisoners unconscious; they were able resuscitate all but one of them.[7] Moreover, the prison and its adjoining debtors' prison were unusually insecure. Escapes were commonplace; at least one a month occurred. The iron bars in the cell windows had been cemented into the mortar in such a way that a prisoner reputedly needed only a knife to dig them out. During the Christiana Riot trial in 1851, two prosecution witnesses who were being detained in the debtors' section escaped using blankets to wiggle down to the ground below from their cells.[8] Perhaps it was to discourage such escapes that a gibbet fashioned out of bars of iron in 1781 to display the body of a convicted pirate was afterwards hung for a time in Moyamensing.[9]

Passmore was placed in Cell No. 71, a white-washed, stone room on the second tier of the building's right wing, the one reserved for criminals. It had previously been occupied by a man held on conspiracy charges.[10] The Philadelphia correspondent of the *National Anti-Slavery Standard,* who visited him in the days following his incarceration, described the cell as "an apartment" of "I should say—10 feet by 15, and the furniture consists of a rickety Windsor chair, a small pine table, and a cot bedstead—all of the commonest kind and second-hand—and two yards and a half of threadbare ingrain carpet. They were hired for Mr. W.'s use by one of his friends." The cot, the reporter said, "reminded me of the answer to the old conundrum, 'When is a bedstead not a bedstead?' Answer—'When it is a little buggy.'"[11]

It soon became obvious that the prison officialdom harbored friendly feelings towards Passmore. On August 6, eleven days after he arrived in Moyamensing, the door to Passmore's cell was unlocked to allow him to roam the corridor during the day if he wished.[12] No other prisoner was granted that freedom. It was a special privilege but it could not, however, have been a relaxing diversion. According to the *National Anti-Slavery Standard* reporter, "the associations are not very pleasant in the large hall. Oaths and rude treatment of rude men to ruder women are not very pleasing to a refined mind."[13]

Passmore had to be back in the cell at 6:00 P.M., when the inside door was locked and he was left, as he put it, "to my own reflections until about the same hour in the morning. I could have a light in my cell if desired, but I have declined it on account of the insects which would be attracted by it, preferring to court 'Nature's sweet restorer' at an early hour by walking my floor. The exercise & monotony, aided by a clear conscience and a sense of my unusual Security soon prepare me for a sound nap." Passmore evidently suffered from allergies during summer months. But, he wrote to assure his uncle, William Williamson of West Chester, Pennsylvania, who had been speaker of the state senate in 1848, "So far I have enjoyed as good health as usual & by observing those precautions always necessary for me at this Season I feel no apprehension on that account."[14]

The freedom to roam the corridor was but one of a number of privileges permitted Passmore. His having meals sent in to him from outside was highly unusual. Then, too, a friendly night watchman unlocked his cell door to allow his wife Mercie, entering her ninth month of pregnancy, to pay him visits. He was disappointed when he did not see her one night but, he explained to her in a letter, the turnkey was away. Mercie came by frequently, sometimes staying the entire day,[15] though it must have been a difficult for her. Buttonwood Street was more than two miles away, and although omnibuses ran down to the county prison, the ride would have been jolting to someone in her condition. Perhaps she took a carriage, for come she did. One visitor recalled finding her in the cell seated on Passmore's cot. His four-year-old son Tom came one day and "enjoyed himself here so well that he wanted to stay" the night.[16]

He was "perfectly contented," Passmore assured cousin George Pyle. His only worry was about his family. His twenty-two-month-old daughter Sarah, cousin Edward Williamson had reported to him, was coughing "terribly at night, and, altogether, poor Mercie has a weary time of it."[17] A reporter picked up the story: the child's illness as well as "her other trials, is having a very bad effect upon Mrs. Williamson. Her physician is very solicitous about her."[18] Passmore said the "only cause of anxiety that I have at any time felt has been on Mercie's account. She is with me to day and appears quite reconciled & happy."[19]

An even more amazing relaxation of prison rules occurred when Mercie finally gave birth at their home on Buttonwood Street to the couple's third child. A prison officer escorted Passmore to his home so he could visit mother and child.[20]

The response to Passmore's imprisonment was swift and over-whelming from the very first days that he arrived at Moyamensing. It was abundantly clear to him, his father, and his supporters that the interest he was attracting would provide a windfall for the abolitionist cause. Indeed, the fact that a respectable white citizen could be incarcerated without the opportunity to vindicate himself was, among other things, proof positive of the influence and power of southern interests. It was a point that other anti-slavery advocates had recognized: riots and protests against abolitionists had an opposite effect, turning many people into sympathizers, as James Thome discovered. After Thome, an Ohio anti-slavery lecturer, was attacked by an egg-throwing mob in Boston, he was pleased to remark, "Egged the first night. Hatched abolitionists fast."[21] So it would be a boon for the cause if Passmore stayed a while in prison, drawing attention in both the press and in the country's pulpits. In fact, Lucretia Mott wrote some friends that Passmore's father Thomas "says he is only afraid Passmore will come out of Prison too soon."[22] On the day she wrote, August 7, her husband James went to see Passmore,[23] perhaps to make that point as well himself. A letter of encouragement along the same line came from Senator Charles Sumner of Massachusetts, an ardent advocate of abolition whose outspoken antagonism to slavery would provoke a South Carolina congressman to attack him on the Senate floor in 1856. Sumner wrote Passmore, calling his imprisonment an "outrage [that] is rendered more outrageous by the way in which it was done." Sumner congratulated Passmore for his responsibility and dignity. "It is privilege to suffer for truth," he added.[24]

Like Sumner's letter, the mail Passmore received was, almost without exception, supportive, whether from family, friends, or complete strangers. His plight inspired a sympathizer from Maple Grove, Pennsylvania, who was evidently a woman, to pen a poem in his honor that read, in part:

> The axe, the cord, the stake, perform their task
> At once, and in their very sharpness prove
> Yes! there are many kinds of martyrdom—
> Most merciful. But who shall say that he
> Who, lingering, drags the weary hours along
> Within a felon's prison—shut from all
> The kindly intercourse of social life
> While waiting for his country's tardy justice,
> To break his bonds, and give him back to freedom—

Is not as much a martyr as the man
Whom tyranny condemns at once to death?

Women of Pennsylvania! behold the man,
The champion of your sex, who dared to brave
The frowns of those high in official station,
That stoop to Slavery's o'ertopping baseness,
And in this prosperous State, which we call free,
Would the woman-catcher in his work,
Set on the bloodhounds, and secure the prey![25]

So what was happening to Passmore seems carefully orchestrated, an abolitionist ploy to make the most of his predicament and to show how southerners and southern sympathizers both abused and misconstrued the Constitution as a way of oppressing northerners. It soon became clear that Passmore's stubborn refusal to give in to Democratic authorities was part of a strategy to play his imprisonment for the publicity it was worth. Northern newspapers sympathetic to the abolitionist cause followed his incarceration on almost a daily basis, spreading the word of Passmore's resolute adherence to his moral principles. The newspapers would report on every legal twist and turn in his case, pounce on every rumor, revel in the attention that he was attracting nationwide. Passmore had become a martyr to the cause. One thing is certain: Passmore needed no prodding to play out his role. Several days after James Mott's visit, it was reported that, during a visit to the prison, Thomas Williamson had been reading to his son articles in the *New York Tribune,* one of which opined that Passmore "will neither break nor bend." "That's true," the elder Williamson confirmed. "He will neither break nor bend."[26]

Day after day, Passmore's cell was flooded with friends and sympathizers who came from virtually every state in the North. They even included a few persons from the South. Visitors were asked to sign a ledger, but it is certain that not all took the trouble to do so. Mercie, for one, never signed it, nor did Passmore's father, Thomas, or any of the lawyers who conferred with him. Not all the pages of the ledger still exist, and those that survive cover less than half of the time that Passmore spent in prison. Yet they alone bear the names of 489 individuals, including many of the leading black abolitionists of the day—Frederick Douglass, Harriet Tubman, Charles Lenox Remond, Mary Ann Shadd Cary, and William Cooper Nell, among them. The last, Nell, who is considered the nation's first black historian, brought Passmore a copy of his book *The Colored Patriots of the American Revolution*, which Nell inscribed "in token of admiration for his willingness to be a Martyr in Moyamensing Prison for the Cause of Liberty."[27] Incredibly, Nell, however, forgot to tell Passmore that Jane Johnson and her two boys were living in Boston. He had personally escorted them from the rail depot in Boston upon their arrival there in his capacity as a member of that city's Vigilance Committee. Or perhaps Nell purposely did not inform Passmore of Jane's situation because Passmore's knowing it might have complicated his insistence that he knew nothing of her whereabouts. Passmore did not like to lie. It was not until a month and a half after his visit that Nell finally wrote Passmore to inform him of Jane's circumstances, telling him that he had been able to secure a home and a job for her. He said she was grateful to Passmore and his friends for rescuing her.[28]

At times, so many visitors crowded into Passmore's cell that it was difficult to elbow one's way in. He must have yearned for some breathing space himself, because when Edward Williamson and his sister Clara visited him one day they found him in the room of the warden, Charles Hortz.[29] The opposition *Philadelphia Times* quoted some Philadelphians as claiming that Passmore's "apartment is luxuriously furnished" and he holds daily "Levees of friends" in it.[30]

Another letter that Passmore wrote, this one to cousin George Pyle, indicates his state of mind and his firmness in seeing justice done. He had no intention of saying he had custody of Jane Johnson and her boys. That would be a lie. He was now a member of the "Can't get away club," he said. He was enraged at the "Damnedest set of rascals that ever managed to keep off the gallows! Without the courage to make them respectable Ruffi[a]ns the[y] have undertaken to use, what they certainly have mistaken, their irrespo[n]sible arbitrary power to punish me for sundry little annoyances I have heretofore subjected them to." Passmore said that a North Carolina lawyer who had served with John Hill Wheeler in the state legislature told him that he didn't agree with what Passmore had done, but "*Cain* [the judge, that is] had committed the greatest outrage ever committed in this country by a Judicial office[r]." The lawyer thought that "there was but one plea by which he could defend himself and that was ignorance."[31] Passmore told his uncle William Williamson: "I have always regarded the desire for the approbation of the just and good as an honorable and laudable ambition, and have now felt its attainment to be second only, as a sustaining influence, to the conviction of being right. Both I have experienced since my imprisonment, the former to an extent far beyond any expectation, & the latter without a moment's interruption."[32]

A contretemps that developed demonstrates Passmore's stubbornness. After eight days in prison, he wrote Pyle, "I am perfectly contented, have enjoyed good health, plenty of company and altogether am as happy as any individual in My favored condition ought to be."[33] However, a reporter visiting him about a week later wrote that although Passmore was still as "undaunted as ever . . . [of] Simple, stern, unbending integrity of motive and action," he was "considerably wasted, from confinement and disease."[34] Within a few days of his confinement, Passmore had had to send for medicine when he came down with a case of diarrhea,[35] then he subsequently caught cold, suffered from an inflamed tooth and complained of a headache "& general soreness & debility."[36] He was next reported to be suffering from rheumatism, produced by the dampness of his cell, which was on the north side of the second tier and did not get much sunlight.[37]

Sometime in the latter part of August, Dillwyn Parrish, who had accompanied Passmore to Moyamensing, and Dr. Elwood Wilson, the Williamsons' family physician, appealed to Judge John Kane to change Passmore's cell. They purposely did not tell Passmore they were going to make the request, believing that he would refuse any appeal to Kane for special treatment. They did not even tell Passmore's father what they were doing. Parrish and Wilson were particularly concerned that a Democratic newspaper might find out about their request and make it seem as if Passmore was putting himself in the position of pleading for help. As it was, Kane "jumped" at the opportunity to do something for Passmore.[38] There was even a rumor at one point that the judge had gone down to the prison to see him, but this was doubted by an observer friendly to Passmore. "The Judge," he said, "has made mistakes enough in this case, and he had better not make the matter worse by another blunder."[39]

Kane did ask Parrish and Wilson to submit their request in writing, and when that was done, he acceded to their appeal. However, he left it up to Marshal Wynkoop, in whose custody he had placed Passmore, to determine whether the change of cells was really called for. Putting it up to Wynkoop to decide was, in the opinion of the *National Anti-Slavery Standard*, a slap at Passmore. Wynkoop was "Mr. Williamson's personal enemy," it said. Kane's action was "as much as to say, Mr. Williamson is suffering no needless hardships which are not of his [own] imposition. If he has not heretofore had the benefit of all proper courtesies, he has to thank his own obstinacy for it; and as it is, any time he chooses to make application himself to the Marshal, all that he needs shall be promptly forthcoming."[40]

Passmore was terribly upset when he learned of what had transpired. As the newspaper's correspondent pointed out, "It looked, at first blush, like an acknowledgment on the part of Mr. Williamson of what he had before strenuously denied—Judge Kane's jurisdiction; and it also bore the appearance of an appeal to the Judge for mercy."

Maybe Wynkoop was worried that Passmore's illness would worsen and his failing condition become fodder for the abolitionist press, because, despite Passmore's objections, he had him moved across the hall to Cell No. 78, on the south side of the tier, which was sunnier during the day and less damp. Visitors continued to crowd his cell, and its neighboring environment was still repugnant. Together with a "lady friend," the reporter for the *National Anti-Slavery Standard* visited him on Saturday, August 25. It was the twenty-ninth day of Passmore's imprisonment:

A number of persons had gone before us, and, when we entered, his cell was full as it could *comfortably* hold. Soon others presented themselves for admission, and we left to make room for them. So you see that, hard as is Mr. Williamson's lot, *solitariness* is not one of his trials.

Before leaving the building, my friend and myself took a walk along the corridor, she to look at the construction of the edifice, and I to examine the inscriptions upon the slates hanging at the door of each cell, indicating the crime of the inmate.

Mr. Williamson's cell is No. 78. On the slate at his door is inscribed his name and his *crime*—"CONTEMPT"! No. 79, on his left, has two occupants; one for False Pretense and the other for Larceny. No. 80 has also two, one for Larceny and the other for *Murder*. No. 81 has but one—he, too, for *Murder*. I went no further in that direction. Coming back, I found No. 77, on the other side of Mr. Williamson, occupied by two persons, one for False Pretense and the other for Robbing the United States Mail. In No. 76 was a man for Assault and Battery on the High Seas; and in No. 75 was one known to you and of your own profession (poor fellow!)—for Forgery. These are Mr. Williamson's neighbours [*sic*]; murderers, thieves and robbers.

My friend had undertaken to go the rounds of the corridor, but her heart failed her and she came back. She could not longer endure, she said, the looks of the unhappy creatures, who peered at her through the doors of their cells, as she passed. "If this," said she, "is what is meant by the 'privilege of the corridor,' it is one which I should not want more than once to avail myself of. If I were Passmore Williamson, I would rather stay in my cell, if it were twice as close, than walk where I had to meet such dismal sights."[41]

11

Votes For and Against

I'll be free! I'll be free! And none shall confine
With fetters and chains this free spirit of mine:
From my youth have I vowed in my God to rely,
And despite the oppressor, gain Freedom or die.

"I'll Be Free, I'll Be Free!" *Anti-Slavery Harp*, 19
(to be sung to the air "Sweet Afton")

Well aware of the role he was playing as a martyr for the abolitionist cause, Passmore realized that his self-sacrifice would lose its effectiveness if it ended too quickly. One can only speculate whether he also had in mind that martyrdom, an obsessive—some would say masochistic—sacrifice for one's beliefs had been a staple of Quaker history from its origins in England. George Fox, the most important figure in the founding and spread of the religion in the seventeenth century, was imprisoned eight times. By 1689, when the Act of Toleration was finally passed, an estimated total of 15,000 Quakers had been jailed, about 450 of whom died in prison.[1]

Even though Passmore no longer attended services, he clearly was embedded with Quaker ethics and rigidity. The tenacity of such indoctrination was demonstrated that September when Republicans held their first state convention in Pittsburg (as the name of the city was then spelled). Passmore was not immune to seeking public office. He reminded cousin George Pyle in 1848 that he had run for office in the past and was considering being "a candidate for a share of the loaves & fishes again this fall" and wanted to be "careful to say nothin[g] which might interfere with my availability." It is not known what office he had sought in the past or wanted then to seek. But Passmore claimed to be a supporter of the Liberty Party, whose sole raison d'être was the abolition of slavery. He intended, he said, to stick by the party until he could find "a more ardent, efficient and consistant [sic] opponent of the peculiar institution."[2]

That opportunity came on September 5, 1855, the forty-first day of his imprisonment, when the newly formed Republican Party met in Pittsburg. Passmore's imprisonment symbolized the threat of the loss of political freedom throughout the North, so it is no surprise that he was the party's very first nominee, supported unanimously to run for the Canal Commission, an important and critically influential state agency that regulated not only canals but also railroads in Pennsylvania. When a delegate wondered how it would be possible for Passmore to serve on the commission if he was in Moyamensing, another delegate vigorously called out, "We will take him out!"[3] But Passmore's father advised him against his accepting the nomination. Cousin Edward Williamson said that "Uncle Thomas" thought it would be best to *avoid the possibility* of any suspicion of desiring to make capital out of his peculiar circumstances, or to use them as a stepping stone to political preferment." Thomas thought Passmore should "respond as soon as he is officially informed of the nomination, declining it absolutely, but with a proper appreciation of it as an evidence of the people's approval of his conduct." Thomas asked that his brother William, a prominent lawyer and Edward's father, prepare a draft of what would be Passmore's rejection.[4] Passmore's name was withdrawn, but he still received more than 7,000 votes that fall. That was nowhere near the two leading candidates, who received more than 150,000 votes each,[5] but it was an indication of the fact that his name and his cause were linked and well known.

During his first month in prison, Passmore tried to get the Pennsylvania Supreme Court to issue a writ of habeas corpus that would compel Wynkoop to bring him into a state court where he could plead his case. Five days after he first entered Moyamensing, Passmore petitioned Chief Justice Ellis Lewis, asking him to personally intervene and issue such a writ. His petition claimed that Judge Kane had no jurisdiction in the Jane Johnson case inasmuch as she had been "voluntarily carried" into Pennsylvania and was "not a fugitive from labor or service within the true intent and meaning of the Constitution."

Therefore, the petition read, Kane could not issue a writ of habeas corpus. Passmore asked that Lewis issue such a writ, so that he could appear before the state supreme court and vindicate his rights.

Lewis responded quickly. The very next morning, he turned Passmore down, saying in a brief opinion that no court had any jurisdiction in contempt cases that were pending before another court.[6] Once Kane had cited him for contempt, the state court could not interfere, he wrote.

Lewis's rejection was so abrupt that Passmore never forgot it. Two years later he filed suit against him for refusing to grant the writ, but nothing evidently ever came of it.[7] The justice's denial, however, was applauded by the *Washington Union,* a Democratic organ. "If, yielding to the clamor of abolition maniacs," Lewis "had undertaken to release Williamson," Wynkoop would, of course, have disobeyed the order. The newspaper went on:

> In that case, the Chief Justice, having entered upon the career
> of error, would have been constrained to persevere in it, and to
> order the commitment of the Marshal by a State Sheriff. There-
> upon, the Marshal would have himself have applied for a writ
> of *habeas corpus* to the United States Court; and if the Sheriff
> refused to obey this writ and release the Marshal, then the
> Sheriff would be committed by the United States Judge; and
> so on, *ad infinitum,* until the Sheriff and all his deputies, and
> the Marshal and all his deputies, were held in confinement
> one by the other, and all law and all justice utterly prostrated in
> Pennsylvania, in order to enable Passmore Williamson to commit
> robbery and perjury with impunity.[8]

Following Lewis's turndown of Passmore's appeal, his lawyers, Charles Gilpin and Edward Hopper, enlisted the services of William M. Meredith, a former United States district attorney for the Eastern District of Pennsylvania. Meredith had been a precocious youngster, graduating from the University of Pennsylvania at the age of thirteen. The three counsel—"lawyers of learning, high reputation, and social position,"[9] according to a biographer of the legal world—petitioned the entire five-member state supreme court, asking to be heard. Evidently the notoriety the case was receiving caused the court to grant their request.

Ordinarily, the state supreme court was in recess during the month of August, but its members agreed to listen to what Gilpin and Hopper had to say, setting a hearing for Monday, August 13. The meeting was to take place in the courthouse in Bedford, a sleepy town in the Alleghenies, near the resort area of Bedford Springs, where the court planned to hold a general term session away from the stifling heat of a city. Passmore's attorneys presented a written argument for the writ and were told to return on Thursday to present oral arguments. Meredith came for the hearing that day, together with Passmore's father and a bevy of reporters representing Philadelphia and New York newspapers.[10] Both Gilpin and Meredith spoke for an hour, citing authorities, pointing up the fact that a writ of habeas corpus was a matter of personal liberty not related to the loss of property. Kane had been in the wrong, but the state justices could rectify that error, they said.

The justices, however, decided to put off a decision until Thursday, October 4, when they were scheduled to hold a session in Sunbury, on the Susquehanna River in the middle of the state. Ordinarily they met in Sunbury only in the month of July.[11] The postponement of their decision was a devastating blow. After a summer recess, the court regularly met in Pittsburg in September, just a few weeks off. That session usually lasted eight weeks. Why such a delay? Why Sunbury at that time of year? Why not Pittsburg, which was more convenient? There was no hope now that Passmore would have the chance to be free before October, a good six weeks away.

Again, the attention the case continued to attract throughout the state and the nation may have spurred the justices to work quickly on their opinions. They had apparently decided in advance to write them and forward their remarks to Justice Jeremiah S. Black, who wrote the majority opinion.[12] As a result, the court was able to advance the date for handing down its decision. On Saturday, September 8, twenty-three days after hearing the arguments of Gilpin and Meredith, the justices came together in an unusually scheduled session in the district court courtroom in Independence Hall in Philadelphia. It was crowded with spectators. Four of the five justices—all of them, incidentally, Democrats elected the previous year—concurred in denying Passmore's plea for a writ of habeas corpus. Their rationale was that they had no right to interfere with a federal court. Justice Black, an outspoken critic of abolitionists, declared: "The writ of which the petitioner is convicted of disobeying, was legal on its face. It enjoined upon him a simple duty, which he ought to have understood and performed without hesitation." Black said, "I say the writ was legal, because of the act of Congress gives to all Courts of the United States the power 'to issue writs of *habeas corpus,* when necessary for the exercise of their jurisdiction.'" He said that Passmore "carries the key of his prison in his own pocket. He can come out when he will, by making terms with the Court that sent him there. But if he choose to struggle for a triumph, if nothing will content him but a clean victory or a clean defeat, he cannot expect us to aid him."[13]

Associate Justice John C. Knox rendered the only dissenting opinion. He agreed with Passmore's counsel that the federal district court did not have jurisdiction in the case. "The right of a master to reclaim" a slave brought into a free state "is not a question arising under the Constitution," Knox wrote.[14] But his opinion did nothing to change Passmore's circumstances.

A rumor later circulated, based on an article in the *Cincinnati Gazette,* that Knox and two other justices—Walter H. Lowrie and George W. Woodward—were actually in favor of granting the writ. However, when the court assembled in Philadelphia, John Kane and some of his friends told them that if the writ was granted, President Pierce planned to order Passmore's removal from Moyamensing to a navy ship, in a repeat of how Anthony Burns had been treated in Boston. Passmore was to be guarded by Marines and army troops against any force the state might send to free him. As a result, so the rumor went, Lowrie and Woodward changed their opinions, and the writ was not granted. Newspapers such as the *Provincial Freeman* and the *Lancaster Independent Whig* repeated the story, but it has never been confirmed by any reliable source.[15]

After nearly six weeks in prison, there was no sign of relief in sight. In fact, a month earlier, on August 8, two days after Lewis denied his petition, Passmore was indicted by a grand jury. So now he not only faced charges of contempt but more serious charges of riot, assault and battery, as well. The grand jury also indicted on the same charges William Still and the five black men who had helped in the rescue of Jane Johnson.

Still was able to post a bond, with J. Miller McKim acting as his guarantor, and, undaunted, he continued to aid runaway slaves who came to his attention, recording at one point in August the "sundry arrivals" whom he assisted—five women and nine men, most of whom were in their twenties. One of them, "a young mulatto woman" who was considered a "fancy article" and had been sold four times, escaped by being secreted by a black deckhand aboard a steamer from Richmond. Four of the men, including two brothers, "selected" an oyster boat from their master and sailed it north of Baltimore, where they landed and then proceeded on foot across the Pennsylvania border. The brothers eventually reached Hamilton, Canada, where, one of them wrote, they came upon "a gret meny" acquaintances from Virginia and asked Still to inform their wives of their whereabouts and tell them "we live in the hopes of meting them once more this side of the grave, tel them if we never more see them, we hope to meet them in the kingdom of heaven in pece."[16]

Still's unabated assistance to runaway slaves aside, everyday operations at the Anti-Slavery Society office were otherwise suffering. McKim was beginning to complain that he had become "so engrossed" with the case "and the varied duties growing out of it, that I am obliged to neglect a good deal of the ordinary routine business of the Anti-Slavery Office." Of particular concern was fund-raising. Donors were giving money to Passmore's defense. Edward Williamson reported that two individuals had offered Passmore one thousand dollars each, and two others pledged five hundred dollars each "to defray the expenses" of his suits. "Others have stated their intention to contribute when needed, to the extent of their ability," he said.[17] McKim was annoyed. He usually spent the summer months raising funds, collecting subscriptions for the society's newspaper and catching up on finances in general, "but this year," he said, "I have hardly made a call or raised a dollar, except what has been necessary for some specific purpose connected with Passmore Williamson's case."[18]

In early September, just a few days after the decision of the state supreme court turning down his request for a writ of habeas corpus, a reporter for the *New York Tribune* and a friend of his visited Passmore. They found him reading, "his silver-haired father" at his side. The reporter said that "notwithstanding his delicate constitution," Passmore's "countenance give assurance that he is possessed of all that fortitude which his trying situation demands. His body is confined within the walls of his narrow cell, the companion of criminals, but his soul is free thank God; over that no tyrant judge has power!" The reporter thought it "incredible" that "under such circumstances a man can keep his temper. I found myself ever and anon carried away with indignation, and my friend was obliged to gently check me lest it should disturb his father."[19]

Passmore wrote in answer to a letter inquiring whether there was truth to the report that there would be new legal efforts to obtain his freedom:

> I may say that I contemplate no further legal proceedings with
> reference to my liberation from this jail, in which I am now
> confined. I have now been kept here for more than two months,

and I can see no prospect of liberation. I am a native, and have always been a citizen of Pennsylvania, and believing myself atrociously wronged, I applied to the highest tribunal known to our laws, but relief has been withheld. I can expect none from the authority that placed me here, without dishonorable submission. Having been guilty neither of falsehood, dissimulation, nor contumacy, I am sure that it is no case for a degrading capitulation. Such a course would bring with it a diminution of self-respect more oppressive than the power now seeking to crush out the highest attribute of State sovereignty by immuring me within these walls.[20]

12

Stranded

With luxury and wealth surrounded,
The Southern masters proudly dare . . .
To mete and vend God's light and air;
Like beasts of burden, slaves are loaded,
Till life's poor toilsome day is o'er;
While they in vain for right implore.

"Ye Sons of Freemen," *Anti-Slavery Harp,* 6
(to be sung to the air "Marseilles Hymn")

John Hill Wheeler found himself forced to remain in, or close to, Philadelphia. He was hoping for some break in the case of Passmore Williamson and the others who had taken part in the rescue of Jane Johnson and her sons. As far as he knew, his slaves were still in hiding in Philadelphia. He still expected to get them back.

On Saturday, July 28, the day after Judge John Kane committed Passmore to Moyamensing, Wheeler attended the Court of Common Pleas as a witness. The occasion was a hearing on a writ of habeas corpus that defense attorney William S. Peirce, who appeared frequently in fugitive-slave cases, had been able to obtain. It directed that the five blacks who had helped to rescue Jane Johnson and her sons—John Ballard, James P. Braddock, William Custis, James Martin, and Isaiah Moore—be brought before a court to determine the reasons for their being arrested.[1] The presiding judge was William D. Kelley, a former deputy prosecuting attorney for the city and the county. It soon became evident, that, unlike Alderman James Freeman, who had earlier set the rescuers' bail at seven thousand dollars each, Kelley was no friend of the South. He had testified as a defense witness at the Christiana Riot trial of Caster Hanway in 1851, impugning the reputation of the federal government's chief witness, Deputy Marshal Henry H. Kline, whose testimony, he said, was untrustworthy. William Still later commented that neither Kelley nor the state prosecutor at the hearing for the black men, William B. Mann, "sympathized in the least with Wheeler or Slavery."[2]

Wheeler's testimony was essentially a repetition of what he had said at the initial hearing for Passmore before Kane on July 20. Ballard had "caught him by the arms rudely" and "said that if I resisted they would cut my throat from ear to ear." Under cross-examination by Peirce, Wheeler explained that Jane Johnson and her boys had never actually been with him in North Carolina. He had only referred to their being slaves "under the law of North Carolina, because I am a citizen of that State." He had purchased them in Virginia. He said that, following custom, he "presumed she would be known as Jane Wheeler." Wheeler said he had done "all I could to prevent" his slaves from "being taken away" from him. He had lost them and some of his other property with them—"an umbrella and other articles." Yes, Jane had told Passmore Williamson that "she wanted to be free but that she knew where she was going." Wheeler said he thought she did not go "voluntarily." He denied that he had promised to set her free.

At this point in the hearing, Mann said he thought the charge of highway robbery against Ballard was "simply absurd" and it was dropped. He also recommended that the charge of inciting to riot be merged with that of riot. Peirce requested that the bail set for all the men be reduced because it was "exorbitant and oppressive," which Kelley agreed with. The judge, in fact, took Alderman Freeman to task for setting it so high. "The defendants," he said, "were evidently poor men and it was not probable that they were very enlightened or deeply skilled in international law, and as to the rights and privileges of Ambassadors above men." Kelley reduced Ballard's bail to one thousand dollars.

Wheeler next testified against Custis, whom he said was one of the men who had restrained him. Kelley reduced his bail to one thousand dollars, too. Some of the eyewitnesses to the rescue then testified to the actions of Braddock, Martin, and Moore. Both Capt. Andrew Heath and police officer Thomas Wallace agreed that, while the slave children kicked and cried "murder," there was otherwise very little excitement on the dock. Heath said "the thing was done quietly and quickly." On the basis of their testimony, Mann said he could not see how the charge of riot could be sustained against the three men, but he did not recommend that it be dropped. Their bail was also reduced to one thousand dollars. The case against all five of them, as well as against William Still and Passmore Williamson, would now be in the hands of a grand jury.

The Philadelphia correspondent of the *National Anti-Slavery Standard* had a conversation with four of the five black rescuers who had worked on the dock the day of Jane Johnson's rescue. He did not say which of the four defendants he had talked with. "They are very respectable looking persons, and instead of being sorry for what they did, would like nothing better than to have a chance to repeat their offence," he wrote. "A handsome purse for their benefit, and to pay all legal expenses incurred, or to be incurred in their behalf, has been raised by merchants in Market street and others, and I had the pleasure of handing to each an instal[l]ment to meet immediate necessities. It was a pleasant duty, and they were grateful and worthy recipients. The only drawback on their pleasure, they said, was the thought that Mr. Williamson was still in prison."[3]

Meanwhile, stuck in Philadelphia, Wheeler tried to make the most of his forced stay while awaiting the trial, which in the days ahead was postponed until the latter part of August to give both sides, prosecution and defense, time to prepare their cases. Wheeler was still suffering from the ordeal he had gone through on the cholera-ridden voyage from Nicaragua.[4] He was "quite unwell at night" that Saturday of the hearing, but the next day he was able to attend Christ Church in the morning, and in the evening he joined some friends and his niece Esther for dinner at the La Pierre House on Broad Street, near the Academy of Music. On Monday, July 30, he had a "long consultation" with Judge Kane. As usual, he made no comment in his diary as to what they discussed other than they had conferred. Wheeler also met with Van Dyke, who advised him to go to Washington "forthwith" and consult with the president. The federal district attorney persisted when he and Wheeler met again the next day, Van Dyke urging Wheeler to write up a statement of the case to present to Franklin Pierce. Wheeler finally heeded the advice. He reached Washington in the early evening and went directly to see the president. They had "a long conversation." Pierce asked Wheeler to return the next day to the presidential mansion.

On the next day, Wednesday, August 1, Wheeler returned to the White House. With the president were Attorney General Caleb Cushing and Justice Roger B. Taney of the United States Supreme Court. The men talked at length about the case, though Wheeler did not confide in his diary as to what was said. However, the State Department that day issued instructions to him to stay in the country until August 20.

The following day, August 2, was Wheeler's forty-ninth birthday, but he did not record in his diary that there was any celebration. His only comment was plaintive: "May God give me grace to grow wiser in truth as I age, until I am fitted to depart in peace." He conferred during the day with Attorney General Cushing before leaving Washington in the afternoon. He reached Philadelphia at midnight.

On a Sunday sometime about then, if the *New York Tribune* is to be believed, Wheeler walked into a drugstore in Philadelphia to have a glass of soda. Standing by was a group of young men, one of whom, "J.G.T.," was reading aloud from a local newspaper an article entitled "Wheeler Slave Case." Wheeler identified himself and said he was "the man whose slaves were stolen." J.G.T. voiced his sympathy with Passmore Williamson, who "did no more than his duty in taking the people." Wheeler responded, complaining that he "wa'n't disturbing anybody . . . simply passing through on my mission." He insisted that the "Constitution of the United States recognizes" his right to the slaves. J.G.T. said he would not obey a law remanding a slave to his owner. "Then you are a traitor, sir, a G__d d____d traitor," Wheeler declared, "and you ought to be taken out of here and hung upon the first lamp-post." When J.G.T. said that "it would be the proudest period" of his life if he were in Passmore's place in prison, Wheeler rejoined: "Well, you'll be there one day. You Abolitionists have got to be put down. If I had had a revolver Passmore Williamson would not be where he is now; I would have put a bullet through his head. Unless Philadelphia acquits herself, Southerners will not come here, and Southern trade is worth a million dollars a year." "I hope we hold our principles higher than dollars and cents," J.G.T. replied. Wheeler declared that if a man came to him in his official capacity as a minister and said "he came from the Free States," he, Wheeler, would tell him "to go to h__l!" The *Tribune* concluded that after Wheeler "left abruptly," the bystanders to the exchange in the drugstore agreed "in pronouncing Mr. Wheeler to be, personally a black-guard."[5]

The days wore on. Wheeler's entries in his diary become repetitive and monotonous as he waited out the time until the trial. He talks about the case with Van Dyke, twice goes to the theater with him, attends church, visits the United States Mint with niece Esther, suffers an upset stomach "from eating bad watermelon at dinner," gets a haircut, buys a pipe, purchases shoes. On the eight of August, Wheeler learns that a grand jury has indicted William Still, Passmore Williamson "and his coloured associates for riot and assault." He goes again to New York City, where he is introduced to Democratic boss Fernando Wood. (Wood, who was New York's mayor on the cusp of the Civil War, would urge that the city secede from the Union.) Then Wheeler receives what to him must have been startling and disturbing news. Jane Johnson has reached New York, also. More specifically, she had been across the East River in Brooklyn, where she made out an affidavit before a local judge, swearing that she had never been in Passmore's custody. Illiterate, she signed the document with an X. The affidavit was sent to Judge Kane as a proof of Passmore's declaration that he never had her or her children in his custody.

It is now painfully clear to Wheeler that he has no chance of recovering his slaves. While in New York himself on August 16, he goes to the Protestant Servants Association, whose offices were in the Bible House on the corner of Bowery and Eighth. There he hires two servants—Margaret Benin and Margaret Wood—with the intention of taking them to Nicaragua to wait on his wife. [6] Both Margarets are white.

In his diary, Wheeler calls Jane's affidavit "all stuff!" but he otherwise keeps to himself his reaction to this new development and does not comment on it in his diary. However, as soon as he returns to Philadelphia he meets with Van Dyke once again, apparently to discuss what if any are the legal ramifications of her statement. His only recourse seems to be to force Passmore to make restitution for the loss of his property. However, the original contempt case against Passmore is still in the court's jurisdiction, and no matter what the outcome is, he must totally abandon the idea of ever seeing Jane and her children again.

At about the same time, Wheeler hears from Washington that the president now wants him to remain until the riot case is heard on August 27. With yet even more time on his hands, Wheeler visits West Point, where a stepbrother, Junius Brutus Wheeler, a twenty-five-year-old veteran of the Mexican War, is a cadet. On his way back through New York City, he writes his wife Ellen that the steamer *Northern Light* sailed that day from the city for Central America "full of passengers— How I wished to be in her." Instead, he goes with friends to the Rockaways on Long Island, "took a bath in the sea," but is "very Lonely—

thinking of Home and my family." Returning to New York City, he takes in a performance of *Henry IV,* then revisits West Point.

The only excitement Wheeler experienced during those weeks was when he learned that William Still, in the company of J. Miller McKim, had gone to the office of a Philadelphia alderman and made out a complaint against him. The complaint said that Wheeler "attempted to carry away said Jane in a violent, tumultuous and unreasonable manner, contrary to the act of Assembly of March 3, 1847." The act, the Liberty Law, forbade the transport of slaves through the state. A warrant for his arrest was issued on August 11, but a constable reportedly was unwilling to serve it on Wheeler, and the matter fizzled out.

It rained very hard on the day before the trial, Sunday, August 26. Despite the inclement weather, Wheeler met yet again with Van Dyke, who advised him "to keep very quiet, and not to allow persons to know that I am in Phila. so that we can su[r]prise them into a trial tommorrow [*sic*]."

It is not clear what the federal district attorney hoped to accomplish. It is odd that Van Dyke even suggested keeping Wheeler's presence in the city a secret. Wheeler had made no attempt to seclude himself the past week or so. Someone might have recognized him at the hotel where he was staying, when he was walking along the street, at the theater he attended, or certainly when he went to Christ Church for Sunday services. The church was situated at the corner of Fifth and Arch streets, only two blocks from the Williamsons' office and near the headquarters of the Anti-Slavery Society. Wheeler never did explain the reason for the subterfuge. Perhaps he and Van Dyke hoped that defense witnesses would not bother to show up to testify if Wheeler did not appear and they had no need to deny his accusations. Or perhaps it was it an attempt to try to limit the number of spectators attracted to the trial, whose presence might influence the jury.

The next day, Van Dyke attempted another maneuver, asking that the trial be postponed for twenty-four hours because of the absence of witnesses. Another rumor, meanwhile, circulated around the hallways off the courtroom in Independence Hall that Wheeler had left Philadelphia for New York City a week earlier, that his name was on the passenger list of a steamer bound for Central America.[7] He was not expected to testify.

It is possible that Van Dyke and Wheeler started the rumor when they learned about the surprise witness that the defense planned to call at the trial. Did they believe that the witness would feel safer if Wheeler was not in the courtroom? What was the prosecution up to?

13

Two Surprise Witnesses

Our grateful hearts with joy o'erflow,
Hurra, Hurra, Hurra,
We hail the Despot's overthrow,
Hurra, Hurra, Hurra,
No more he'll raise the gory lash,
And sink it deep in human flesh,
Hurra, Hurra, Hurra, Hurra,
Hurra, Hurra, Hurra.

"Jubilee Song," *Anti-Slavery Harp,* 10
(to be sung to the air "Away the Bowl")

The first thing in the morning of Wednesday, August 29, John Wheeler went to a gunshop called the Pistol Gallery. He had his revolver examined, fired and reloaded.[1] Wheeler was experienced in the use of firearms. While in Nicaragua the past December he had gone on a "most charming" river excursion, shooting alligators and iguanas, and had in fact killed an iguana "as we passed along."[2] Perhaps the slave master had his revolver checked in anticipation of his return there. Or perhaps he was concerned about possible violence in the courtroom.

The trial of William Still and the other blacks who had participated in the rescue of Jane Johnson hadn't yet started. It was scheduled to begin at 10:00 A.M. in the Pennsylvania Court of Quarter Session on Courthouse Row by Independence Hall. But at the last minute. U.S. District Attorney James Van Dyke asked for a delay until 11:30 because an important witness from New York was expected. The important witness was, of course, Wheeler, who, of course, was not in New York. But he was late, perhaps because of his stop at the gunshop. When he did finally appear in the courtroom, his presence, surprising as it may have seemed, apparently did not cause a stir in the audience, nor did it have any special impact. By this time, the stories about Jane Johnson's rescue—Wheeler's version and Passmore Williamson's—were common knowledge throughout Philadelphia.

If their maneuver was intended to diminish public interest in the case, it failed. The courtroom was crowded with spectators as well as reporters from a number of Philadelphia, New York, and Washington newspapers.

A jury of twelve men was quickly sworn and seated.[3] Then, when Wheeler was called to the stand, the ruse that Van Dyke and he had in mind, of springing him as a witness at the last minute, had, an observer said, only a "partial effect on popular interest in the case."[4] Edward Williamson, who was in the audience, had immediately suspected that the important witness was Wheeler, who "was announced to have sailed 9 days since."

A reporter for the *National Era* thought Wheeler's testimony was "positive as to the forcible abduction of the woman."[5] Wheeler was in tears as he once again recounted the incident aboard the ferryboat *Washington,* prompting a reporter for the *Philadelphia Evening Post* to believe that the emotion displayed by "the weeping minister, the great bereft," was intended "partly for theatrical effect."[6] Edward Williamson thought the slave master's testimony offered no new information about the incident. His statement, Edward said, was very well put together though "a little 'highfalutin'" and contradictory at times. Edward offered no examples for his remark other than to say that the slave master managed to get through "a searching and long cross-examination pretty well, though some of his answers conflicted a little."[7]

Eyewitnesses who were there on the day in July when Jane Johnson was rescued at the Walnut Street wharf testified next, among them Joseph Mirkle and Samuel Smith, neither of whom had appeared at any earlier court hearing. The latter was a merchant from New York City who subsequently ran into Wheeler on one of his trips to West Point and volunteered to go to Philadelphia to testify on his behalf. Smith, however, agreed under cross-examination that Jane had said she wanted to be free. Edward Williamson reported that almost all the witnesses concurred on that point and upon hearing the threat "by one of the negroes to cut Col. Wheeler's throat if he showed any weapons."[8]

After they testified, the prosecution rested. Judge Kelley recessed the court until the next day, when the defense would present its case.

There was talk that day that the defense lawyers—Charles Gibbons, who was representing William Still, and William Peirce, who was appearing for the five other black defendants—had petitioned Judge William Kelley for a writ of habeas corpus *ad testificandum*. They wanted to bring Passmore into court to testify as a witness for the defendants. But Kelley pointed out that Passmore was a co-defendant and could not be a witness.[9]

That night, Wheeler joined a theater party that included Thomas Sully and his daughter Blanche. They attended a well-known Philadelphia entertainment attraction, a troupe of "Negro Melodists" known as the Sanford Minstrels, who performed in a theater on Eleventh Street off Chestnut.[10]

That night also, Mercie Williamson went into labor. She gave birth to Mary Elizabeth, Passmore's and her third child. Edward Williamson reported "all doing well," and that Thomas Williamson went down to tell his son Passmore the next morning.[11]

While the elder Williamson was visiting Moyamensing the morning of August 30, the defense opened its case. The courtroom was again packed. Only two witnesses were scheduled to be heard. The first was a plumber named George M. Sandgram, who worked along the wharves dotting the Delaware River. He had witnessed the events on the Walnut Street dock and contradicted a number of statements made by Wheeler as to Jane Johnson's willingness to be led off the ferryboat.

As Sandgram finished his testimony and stepped down from the witness stand, the court officer called out in a shrill voice the name of the next witness. There was "a breathless silence," then "a buzz of incredulity" as the name echoed through the courtroom: "Jane Johnson."[12] Everyone realized that for Jane to appear in court in Philadelphia put her in immediate danger of being seized as an escaped slave and returned to her master, Wheeler. Jane was risking her freedom to help the very persons who had helped her to gain it.

It was, the Female Anti-Slavery Society reported, "a trying hour for the heroic woman who had dared so much, and was willing to dare still more, for the assertion of her own freedom, and for the sake of her deliverers." Despite the risk she was facing, she seemed calm and firm "in that hour of jeopardy to her newly-found freedom."[13] She had "willingly returned to Philadelphia," the society insisted, "at some peril to her liberty."[14]

The fact that Jane would jeopardize her freedom was as astonishing to all those present in the courtroom as it was remarkable. Her appearance was bound to be a publicity coup. Her abolitionist friends had assumed that her arrival in Philadelphia would be a well-kept secret, but somehow word of her presence had leaked out. A reporter for the *Philadelphia Evening Post* later learned that the previous day and again that morning, "the Courtroom was infested by the ill-favoured slave-hounds kept about the U.S. Marshal's office for dirty business."[15] Somehow Jane's enemies had discovered that she was back in the city and were on her trail. Wheeler and Van Dyke certainly knew.

Purposely veiled to keep from being recognized, Jane had been sitting outside the courtroom in company with Lucretia Mott and several other members of the Female Anti-Slavery Society—Rebecca Plumly; J. Miller McKim's wife, Sarah; and Sarah Pugh, the president of the organization. Jane entered the courtroom and, "in a lady-like manner," answered to her name.[16] William Still, who was seated with the other defendants at the defense table, was undoubtedly aware that she had returned to the city and planned to testify, but he was nevertheless astounded at the effect Jane's appearance made. "Never before had such a scene been witnessed in Philadelphia," he said. "It was indescribable."[17] "Thrilling" was the way the correspondent for the *New York Tribune* put it.[18] The *Evening Post's* reporter said Jane "ascended the witness box amidst the deepest sensation of an immense audience. Some minutes elapsed before order and silence were sufficiently restored to proceed."[19]

As Jane took the stand, U.S. District Attorney James Van Dyke appeared in the courtroom, followed by several deputy marshals. One of them was Francis Wynkoop's brother George, who had been involved in the shooting of William Thomas in Wilkes-Barre two years earlier. The marshals intended to seize Jane as soon as she finished. But District Attorney Robert Mann, sensing that Jane was in danger, anticipated what Van Dyke planned. He quickly summoned a squad of city police officers. Some entered the courtroom, others lined the hallway as well as the corridor of a rear exit.

So, as Jane stepped to the witness box and began her testimony, there, taking their stand against the wall of the courtroom by its entranceway, were a number of federal marshals ready to seize her—a "ruffian force," the Female Anti-Slavery Society reported, which was "employed to kidnap her." And not far away, positioned by the other walls, were several uniformed policemen, ready to protect her.[20]

Jane was sworn in and, fearlessly, did not hesitate to tell her side of the story. Her testimony, an observer said, "was simply and naturally delivered."[21] She proceeded without hesitation to refute Wheeler's account. She had planned to run away with her children when they reached New York City, and had even made a dress to disguise herself. It was in her trunk, which her former master now possessed. No one had forced her to leave her slave master. After her rescue, she had been spirited away to New York and then on to Massachusetts, all of her own free will. "She spoke what was evidently the truth," the reporter for the *Philadelphia Evening Post* reported, "tearing to tatters all the ingeniously devised lies of the prosecution as to her 'forcible abduction.' Poor Wheeler! For the first time I pitied that unfortunate man."[22] Jane's testimony was "a crusher," said Edward Williamson, who sat in the spectators section.[23]

Some members of the audience in the courtroom thought Wheeler had been surprised by Jane's appearance, but they misread his reaction. One of those who was mistaken was the correspondent of the *National Anti-Slavery Standard.* He reported that the slave master was sitting "inside the clerk's desk, where every eye could read his shame." When Jane stepped up, "he laughed immoderately and nervously, then became deadly pale, and as the testimony went on, red and pale by turns. At last, he could bear it no longer but picked up his hat and disappeared."[24] Another reporter said Wheeler's surprise "was so great that he turned pale, and then, 'like a boiled lobster, turned from white to red.'"[25]

The truth was that Wheeler was fuming. Jane had quietly but firmly made false his testimony about her rescue and mocked his version of their relationship. And despite what observers thought, Wheeler was actually not surprised by Jane's appearance in the courtroom. He had, in fact, earlier sworn out two warrants for her arrest in the presence of Supreme Court Associate Justice Robert Grier. One warrant was for her arrest as a fugitive slave, the second for larceny for stealing the apparel that she was wearing at the time of her rescue. The federal marshals were in the courtroom to carry out the warrants.

As Jane finished her testimony and was about to step down from the witness stand, Judge Kelley called a recess, saying he would charge the jury the next day. Van Dyke approached Mann, prepared for a confrontation. He told him that he had the United States army at his command and that he intended to arrest Jane. Mann responded that Van Dyke had better not touch her. He quickly had the police officers surround Jane. "The most intense suspense pervaded the court-room," a

New York Tribune reporter said, "and for a while it seemed that nothing could avert a bloody scene."[26] The *Evening Post's* reporter experienced "strong apprehensions" that the federal marshals would attack the officers summoned by Mann.[27] As the policemen began to lead Jane from the courtroom through the crowd of spectators, Lucretia Mott and her companions, anxious but determined, joined the procession.

The federal marshals expected Jane to leave through the same door by which she had entered the courtroom. They had gathered there to intercept her. But the police officers, Jane, and her companions suddenly reversed direction and rushed out through a rear door, on the opposite side of the crowded room, catching the marshals completely off-guard. J. Miller McKim and police officer George Corson joined the procession. With Jane in the middle, McKim, Corson, the other police officers, and the women with Lucretia Mott at their head escorted her out into the street.

Van Dyke's "courage," said the *Evening Post's* reporter, had "paled before the stern determination of District Attorney Mann and Judge Kelley to vindicate the dignity of the Courts of Pennsylvania." If an attack had been made by the federal marshals, the reporter added, "it would have been received by one hundred as true hearts and many breasts as exist in the old Keystone State. But the Marshal and his men who thought it great sport to shoot at William Thomas in the waters of the Susquehanna, went quietly back to their dens when they found themselves face to face with the freemen of Pennsylvania."[28]

Edward Williamson had witnessed the confrontation between Van Dyke and Mann, but as the courtroom cleared, much to his "chagrin," he had no idea what happened next. He heard from others that "when they left the court room, they passed out to the carriage door between files of Police officers, without molestation, got into the carriage and drove off."[29] As security, a second carriage with police officers followed the one in which Jane sat, in case the federal marshals tried to intervene.[30]

"We didn't drive slow comg. home," Lucretia Mott wrote in her abbreviated style several days later to her sister Martha Wright. "Miller, an officer—Jane & self—another carriage followg. With 4 officers for protection and all with the knowledge of the states attorney—Miller & the slave passed quickly thro' our house, up Cuthbert St. to the same carriage—wh. Drove around to elude pursuit—I ran to the storeroom & fillg. my arms with crackers & peaches, ran after them & had only time to throw them into the carriage."[31]

That night, Jane Johnson had dinner at the Mott home on Arch Street. "Brief shelter and help in eluding pursuit, being furnished her," the Female Anti-Slavery Society reported, "she was rapidly borne on her way to a place of greater security; and other homes, on whose thresholds the footsteps of the fugitive slave are ever welcome, received her."[32]

The next day, McKim introduced Jane at a meeting of "friends of freedom called to take into consideration the present aspects of the question of slavery." It was held in Norristown, on the Schuylkill River some ten miles from Philadelphia. Her appearance, according to the *Provincial Freeman,* "produced a great sensation. The audience demanded her appearance upon the platform." Jane rose to "tremendous applause, and took her place quite overcome by the warmth of her reception." McKim said her appearance was proof that Passmore Williamson never had custody of her.[33]

That same day, Saturday, September 1, Judge Kelley, in his charge to the jury, totally disregarded any constitutional provision or federal jurisdiction in the matter. They didn't apply to a nonfugitive case such as this. Kelley said that Jane was free the moment Wheeler crossed the Pennsylvania state line with her. The jury's verdict, announced the following Monday, acquitted Still and all the other defendants on the charge of riot. And, in effect, the verdict also served to drop the same charge against Passmore Williamson. Ballard and Custis, however, were convicted of assault and battery. In sentencing them, Kelley said he was taking into account the "outrageous holding to bail in an enormous sum" that Alderman Freeman had imposed on them as well as "the sufferings they had been subjected to" in the Cherry Street police station. He sentenced both men to one week's imprisonment in Moyamensing and ordered them to pay a fine of ten dollars each. They had already served five weeks in prison.

Completely frustrated, Wheeler, meanwhile, had left Philadelphia for Washington late Friday night after Jane's testimony and subsequent getaway. There was nothing left that he could do to change things. It was about time for him to resume his duties as America's envoy to Nicaragua. So he called on Secretary of War Jefferson Davis the next day, Saturday, then went to see his friend, Secretary of the Navy James Dobbin. He had a "long and interesting conference" with Secretary of State William Marcy, called on Attorney General Caleb Cushing, and in the evening visited with the president.[34] As usual, he confided nothing to his diary about any of the details of those meetings, nor what he thought of Jane's escape from the federal marshals.

On the afternoon of Sunday, September 2, Wheeler left Washington for New York City. He had already arranged to return to Nicaragua aboard a vessel that was scheduled to sail soon. He reached the city at six in the morning, Monday, "very tired," but nevertheless he went down to the waterfront to board the *Star of the West,* evidently to check on his sailing accommodations and those of his traveling companions, James Van Dyke's brother and sister-in-law, Dr. and Mrs. John Van Dyke. Wheeler had his luggage put on board the ship the next day.[35] The *Star of the West* was not scheduled to sail until Wednesday, September 5, so on both Monday and Tuesday nights Wheeler attended the theater, seeing a performance of a play by the French playwright Pierre Corneille one night, the comic opera "The Daughter of the Regiment" by Donizetti the next.

The *Star of the West* set sail at 3:30 Wednesday afternoon. "Enjoyed a quiet night of rest in State Room A," the weary Wheeler noted in his diary.[36]

As for the trial and Jane Johnson's testimony, the entire proceeding, he said, amounted to the "most barefaced perjury committed by her and her black confederates."[37] What Wheeler failed to say, however, was that he was far from finished with the case. Undeterred by the outcome of the trial, he felt robbed and intended to do all he could to get restitution.

14

Legalistics

The finger of slander may now at you point,
That finger will soon lose the strength of its joint;
And those who now plead for the rights of the slave,
Will soon be acknowledged the good and the brave.

"Ye Heralds of Freedom," *Anti-Slavery Harp,* 28

Days turned into weeks, and the weeks became a month, and then one month began to slip into two months. Visitors continued to flock to Moyamensing to pay their respects to Passmore Williamson: William Still, who had gone to Canada after his acquittal to check on the plight of runaway slaves who had fled there; a delegation from the House of Correction in Boston led by its master chaplain, the Reverend I. T. Burride; Mary Grew, who would write the narrative of his case that the Pennsylvania Anti-Slavery Society subsequently published; a five-member committee from the National Convention of Colored Americans, which was being held in Philadelphia.

There seemed to be no end in sight for Passmore's confinement in the prison. At the time Jane Johnson attended the abolitionist conference in Norristown on September 1, Williamson had been in jail thirty-seven days. The Republican state convention nominated him for the Canal Commission on September 5, his forty-first day in prison. When the Pennsylvania Supreme Court rejected his application for a writ of habeas corpus on September 8, Passmore had been in prison forty-four days.

"Where this is to end, I shall not attempt to decide," Passmore's cousin Edward Williamson wrote his father, "but I fear that we have not seen the worst of it yet. If there is no relief in Court or Legislature, it seems to me that there is nothing left . . . but 'opposing force to force'; if a resort to this last appeal *must* come, to preserve our State Sovreignty [sic] and independence (which may God in his mercy prevent) I am ready for it and will strive to do my duty, and may He, as He will, defend the right."[1] That was tough talk from a man raised as a Quaker.

The *Daily Pennsylvanian*, never one to hide its hostility to abolitionism, gloated that Passmore's confinement "is perpetual at the pleasure of the prisoner," for "the wrong doer [sic] continues from hour to hour repeating the wrong which the law is endeavoring to redress. To let him loose would be to give him the victory,—it would be in one case to allow him to commit murder under the forms of law; in the other to barter away the life-long liberty of a citizen against the temporary imprisonment of his kidnapper."[2]

Edward Williamson believed that the question of Passmore's incarceration would "ultimately" rest with the United States Supreme Court. For now, however, "nothing definite has been talked of, and there is nothing in contemplation, unless it be an appeal to the Legislature." Edward said, "I saw Passmore this morning and *he* has no idea of getting out, *over Kane's head,* until the Legislature shall meet." Edward wondered whether the legislature had the power to annul the state supreme court's decision. He said that some persons had proposed to sue the four judges who concurred in rejecting Passmore's request for a writ of habeas corpus.

In the meantime, Edward reported, he heard that "a voluntary testimonial to character" was being drawn up by persons who were not abolitionists or friends of the Williamson family.[3] The testimonial, signed by "several of the most prominent merchants" in the city, "many of whom do not sympathize at all with Mr. Williamson on the slavery question," read: "We, the undersigned, who know Passmore Williamson well, desire to testify to his entire truthfulness, and to his upright character, and to express our firm belief that he is entirely incapable of evasion or equivocation, under any circumstances. . . . It will clearly appear to every unprejudiced mind, that his return was 'the truth, the whole truth, and nothing but the truth,' and entirely correct in all particulars, without evasion or omission."[4]

The testimonial may have been reassuring to the Williamson family, but a lawsuit that was filed on behalf of John Hill Wheeler after he

had left the country proved a momentary concern. However, the paperwork of the lawsuit, which was for an unspecified amount of damages,
contained a number of errors in it, and no attorney's name was attached to it. Its technical faults were never corrected in any subsequent
paperwork, so nothing came of the matter.[5] The *National Anti-Slavery
Standard* reasoned that the suit had been filed only for appearance's
sake, to keep alive the slave master's claim for restitution: "If Wheeler
had quietly yielded the position that Jane Johnson and her children
were free, by refraining from prosecuting for damages," the newspaper
reasoned, "it would have withdrawn every shadow of a plea for holding Passmore Williamson in prison."[6]

As time passed, the criticism of Judge John Kane seemed to grow
in direct relation to the number of days Passmore served. Moreover,
Passmore's confinement was proving to be an embarrassment to the
Democratic administration in Washington. Meetings were being held
"all around our country" and "nearly every day," the *National Anti-
Slavery Standard* reported. "Abstract principles are not readily grasped
by the great mass of men; but when they see them incarnated in the
person of Passmore Williamson, and that incarnation lying in a loathsome dungeon, the quick instincts of the heart outrun the cool deduc-
tions of reason, and every one [*sic*] not smothered in cotton responds
to the voiceless appeal which he makes."[7]

Delegates to a meeting that fall of the Free Will Baptist Anti-
Slavery Society held in Dover, New Hampshire, adopted a resolution
calling on "brethren throughout the denomination" to unite in peti-
tioning Congress for the impeachment and removal of Kane from the
federal judiciary. The resolution said that the society regarded the
imprisonment of Passmore "as an illegal stretch of authority, and as
indicative of servility to the Slave Power, which has impeached the
ability and stained the dignity of the Judicial bench."[8] In the months
that followed, petition after petition was filed with the House of Representatives from towns and counties in Illinois, Indiana, Massachusetts, Michigan, and Ohio, all "praying for the impeachment" of Kane.[9]
Passmore himself drafted a petition—a portion of a working copy with
his corrections still exists. In it, Passmore charges the judge with causing "a general and settled mistrust of his official integrity" and also
accuses him of being guilty of "divers misdemeanors in office, by igno-
rantly or corruptly assuming power and jurisdiction of cases not delegated to him, nor authorized by the Constitution or laws of the United
States, but which jurisdiction was, and of right ought to be exclusively
in the legal tribunals of this State."[10] However, there is no record that

Passmore ever sent a corrected version of what he wrote to the House of Representatives. Perhaps, he was merely drawing up a sample petition as a model for others to copy.

Kane was not only vilified in the press, but also was reportedly ostracized by his neighbors. Edward Williamson said he had been told that someone who lived near Kane in Germantown witnessed the judge being snubbed by many of his friends on train rides to and from his home and the district court courtroom. The judge "goes up and down *alone*" with the exception of two personal friends. "None in the cars speaks to him, goes near or recognizes his presence." Edward said, "If it [the snubbing] is entirely matter-of-fact I can hardly think of anything more painful to a sensitive mind, than to find men shrinking from one as from contamination, and more galling, still to find that it has made one an *object of pity* to kind hearted friends."[11]

The "someone" Edward alluded to was undoubtedly George Sidney Fisher, a lawyer who not only knew Kane but also had been a visitor to his home. Fisher, who kept an extensive diary, was convinced that Kane was "in error." He felt that the judge's decision to imprison Passmore for contempt was "contrary to law, oppressive & the result of a desire on the part of the Judge to please the South & thus open the way to preferment." Fisher believed that "a respectable man has been imprisoned because he is an abolitionist, on the pretext that he was guilty of contempt of court." Fisher, who reviewed Harriet Beecher Stowe's *Uncle Tom's Cabin*—an influential and phenomenal bestseller when it was published in book form in 1852—wrote, "The truth & importance of the doctrine I advanced in my review of *Uncle Tom,* that slavery was domestic relation & that a slave is not property, is made manifest."[12]

It is not known for certain whether Fisher ever openly expressed his opinion to Kane, but they did discuss the case, and, in fact, Kane attempted to use Fisher as a conduit to Passmore. Kane evidently knew that Fisher and Passmore had friends in common. One morning in the second week of September, Fisher and the judge ran into each other on a North Pennsylvania Railroad train as they were going from their homes in Germantown to downtown Philadelphia. "He spoke to me without reserve and very fully about Williamson's case," Fisher recorded in his diary. "He says he is willing to discharge him as he asks for it, declares he meant no disrespect to the Court, and submits to answer all legal questions."[13] Kane authorized Fisher to pass on what he had said to Passmore's friends, obviously in the hope of trying to break the impasse.

Fisher passed on the message to a friend named William Wister, who, he knew, would in turn tell J. Miller McKim at the Anti-Slavery Society's office. The next day, McKim called on Fisher. Was it true, he asked, that Kane had spelled out "the terms on which Williamson could be discharged?" Fisher assured him that it was, indeed, true.

That evening, on the way back to Germantown, Fisher again ran into Kane on the train. He told him of McKim's visit and that he had relayed the judge's message to McKim. Kane said that Fisher had correctly "stated the whole & no more, that he meant to convey to me." Upon reaching his home, Fisher "thought of the matter" and decided on his own to draw up "such a petition as I thought Williamson ought to sign & which would meet Judge Kane's views." He then took advantage of obtaining a lift in the carriage of a neighbor who was headed into town to see McKim. He read to him the petition he had drawn up. McKim approved it and said he would pass it along to Passmore.

Two days later, McKim reported back that Passmore had refused to sign the petition, "giving reasons satisfactory McKim said to him, & said he would be happy to see me in his *cell* and explain them to me." Fisher did not bother to ask McKim what the reasons were, nor does he record in his diary that he visited Passmore to find out. He thought Passmore was wrong in declining to sign the petition. "He makes the mistake," Fisher said, "of thinking Judge Kane should concede to him[,] & his position now, after Judge Kane's offer, is one of contumacious resistance to law."[14]

Edward Williamson thought he knew the reason why the judge's offer was rejected. "Passmore, I am certain," he said, "will not amend his return until, at least, the Judge shall indicate in what particular points it was disrespectful or untrue."[15] Despite Kane's conciliatory gesture, an uncompromising Passmore wanted full vindication of his role in Jane Johnson's rescue.

Fisher learned that Passmore had rejected the petition on Monday, September 17, the fifty-third day of his incarceration. "Passmore's counsel seems to be somewhat adrift as to what is best to be done," Edward Williamson reported to his father five days later. Passmore and his lawyers planned to meet at the prison that morning, but, Edward said, "The decision of the Supreme Court appears to have Shut all available passages from the prison."[16]

Passmore remained adamant. He had not disregarded the judge in any way, he had not told a lie, he had not ever had custody of Jane Johnson. He had no intention of surrendering to the judge. Indeed, well aware of what he was doing, he planned to take advantage of his incarceration to further publicize his case. Sometime in late September or the first days of October, when two of the Williamsons' children were ill and Mercie was obviously too busy tending to them, Passmore took the occasion of a visit by young Charles Downing to make a request. Downing was an office boy who worked for him and his father. He ordinarily brought Passmore his food in prison. Passmore asked Downing that on his next visit, he also bring his best suit of clothes to Moyamensing. The boy was told to ask his stepmother to pick up the garments from his home. The weather had turned cold very suddenly,[17] necessitating warmer apparel, but Passmore wanted the suit for an entirely different reason. He also asked Downing to arrange to bring a photographer to prison. He had an idea about another way to broadcast his martyrdom.

On Wednesday, October 3, on the sixty-ninth day of Passmore's imprisonment, Thomas Curtis took Passmore's photograph as Passmore sat—suit, vest, shirt, and cravat—posed in a chair in his cell. Curtis sold copies of the photograph at his Philadelphia bookstore. The cost was fifty cents a copy, two dollars if a gold frame came with it.[18] A lithograph of the photograph was also available. The setting—a cell door behind him, the cot, the washstand, the threadbare rug—was a visual reminder of the ordeal Passmore was enduring. It was effective propaganda.

Meanwhile, Jane Johnson, who had returned to Boston, again tried to help Passmore. On the same day that Passmore's photograph was taken, two attorneys representing her—John Read, of the Christiana Riot defense team, and Joseph B. Townsend, a young real-estate specialist—presented a petition addressed to Judge Kane at the federal district court. The petition was an affidavit that Jane made out in Boston on September 26 before a United States commissioner for the District of Massachusetts. She again signed with an "X" mark. In the affidavit, Jane once more swore that she had wanted to be free, that she had "voluntarily and most willingly left the boat, aided in the departure by several colored persons, who took her children, with her consent, and led or carried them off the boat." Passmore, the petition read, "did not accompany the colored persons who assisted your petitioner to get away, but remained some distance behind, and your petitioner has never seen him since she left the steamboat." She was never "in any way or manner whatever, in the custody, power, possession or control of Mr. Williamson, nor has she received from him any directions or instructions, directly or indirectly, whither she should go."[19]

Although Passmore's own attorneys were at a loss as to what to do next, Jane's counsel were able to obtain a hearing before Kane. At their request, the judge set the sixth of October to hear their arguments why he should accept the affidavit.[20]

It seemed simple enough on the surface. If Jane's petition and her statements were accepted, all the proceedings against Passmore under the writ of habeas corpus would necessarily cease. That was the gist of her lawyers' argument when they appeared before Kane on the sixth, a Saturday—the seventy-second day of Passmore's imprisonment. Townsend made a point of not challenging Kane's decision citing Passmore for contempt. He made it clear that he agreed that the decision at the time was correct because of the evidence then before the judge— namely, Wheeler's testimony and the eyewitness accounts.

"I do not in any way represent Mr. Williamson," Townsend declared, "nor has [sic] he, his friends or his counsel been consulted in regard to the present application." What he was asking, Townsend said, was that "the party most interested" be allowed "to declare her knowledge of the subject matter, to disclaim and repudiate" Wheeler's story. Townsend then went on to cite a number of precedents in English law related to the case. Using precedents from English law was not unusual. Both American and English law share a common-law tradition, and it was routine for American lawyers to cite cases in the substantial record of judicial rulings and decisions in English law. The precedents, Townsend said, "show that it is the rights and liberties of Jane Johnson and her children that this Court is charged with protecting in this proceeding, and not the rights of Mr. Wheeler. If he has suffered injury, the law is open to him to redress, but not in this form." Townsend added that "the sole question" was whether there was "any detention or restraint of this woman against her will."

Read, who followed him, argued that the petition be heard. He said that it was "a general principle that the writ of habeas corpus must always be *issued by or on behalf of the party whose liberty is restrained.*" But Jane, he said, "never consented to the issuing of the writ," which, Read was quick to point out, was one of common law, as established in England, and "not specially restrained by any statute." As for Pennsylvania's right to declare slaves free once they were on its soil, Read said that southern states "have always assumed plenary power; they have stood for the doctrine of State rights, that what is not given is withheld; that the powers not delegated to the Union are withheld by the State itself, and are by it to be exercised." In effect, Read was arguing that there was a double standard that permitted southern states to employ the doctrine of states' rights to defend slavery while at the same time they ignored a northern state's right to outlaw the institution because it didn't suit them.

Kane said he would take the matter under consideration, but his mind was already made up. He had intimated as much when Jane's petition was first offered three days earlier. At the time, he expressed "a doubt of the petitioner's having such *status* as would entitle her to be heard," and he specifically directed her counsel "to address their remarks to that point" when they came before him to argue for admission of her petition.[21]

The judge could be as stubborn and unbending as Passmore was. In all fairness, however, Kane did not treat the issue lightly. His ruling, issued on October 12, was a lengthy, reasoned argument that ran to nineteen pages when published.[22] In it, Kane first dealt in detail with the history of the case against Passmore Williamson, then he covered every point raised by the defense counsel. The writ of habeas corpus, dating back even before the Magna Carta to Roman law, was issued, he noted, "whenever a citizen was denied the exercise of his personal liberty, or was deprived of his rightful control over any members of his household, his wife, his child, his ward, or his servant." The writ, he said, "left no discretion with the party to whom it was addressed." As a judge, Kane said, he himself had granted the writ "at the instance of a negro, who had been arrested as a fugitive from labor," and "from that day to this, often as it has been invoked and awarded in similar cases that have been before me, my authority to award it has never been questioned." The Constitution, its history, congressional policy— all, he said, "meant to require of the Courts of the United States, that they should dispense the privileges of the writ of habeas corpus to all parties lawfully asserting them, as other Courts of similar functions and dignity have immemorially dispensed them as the common law."

As for Pennsylvania's Liberty Law, Kane repeated that he knew of no state statute "which affects to divest the rights of property of a citizen of North Carolina, acquired and asserted under the laws of that State, because he has found it needful or convenient to pass through the territory of Pennsylvania; and I am not aware that any such statute, if such a one were shown, could be recognized as valid in a Court of the United States." And, then, in a bit of convoluted reasoning, Kane insisted that the Pennsylvania law freeing slaves upon their reaching the state "did not affect to vary or rescind the rights of slave owners *passing through* our territory. It applied to persons *resident* and persons *sojourning* . . . [over whom] the State had lawful dominion: but it left the right of transit for property and persons, over which it had no jurisdiction, just as it was before." (Here Kane's distinction between "sojourning" and in "transit" suggests both a legal and a logical ambivalence: he seemed to be acknowledging Pennsylvania's right to determine for itself the matter of "sojourning" but not of the state's authority with regard to a slave owner in transit.)

When the American Constitution was drafted in 1787, Kane continued, "slaves were recognized as property, throughout the United States," and "as late as the year 1830, they were found in every State of the original thirteen." He questioned whether "a State may single out this one sort of property from among all the rest, and deny to it the right of passing over its soil—passing with its owner, parcel of his travelling equipment, as much as the horse he rides on, his great coat, or his carpet bag."

Kane indicated that he was not unaware of local feeling and attitudes about slavery:

> We revolt in Pennsylvania, and honestly no doubt, at this association of men with things as the subjects of property . . . [but] we distinguish against the negro much as our forefathers did; and not perhaps, with quite as much reason. They denied him civil rights as a slave; we exclude him from political rights, though a freeman. Yet no stranger may complain of this. Our constitutions and statutes are for ourselves, not for others. They reflect our sympathies, and define our rights. But as to all the rest of the world; those portions especially, towards whom we are bound by the "supreme law" of the federal constitution; they are independent of our legislation, however wise or virtuous it may be; for they were not represented in our conventions and assemblies, and we do not permit them to legislate for us.

If slavery is "unjust and oppressive," Kane added, "the sin is on the makers of laws which tolerate slavery: to visit it on those who have honestly acquired, and lawfully hold property under the guarantee and protection of the laws, is the worst of all oppression, and the rankest injustice towards our fellow men." The judge said that Passmore's "duty then, as now, was and is to bring in the bodies; or, if they had passed beyond his control, to declare under oath or affirmation, so far as he knew, what had become of them: And from this duty, or from the constraint that seeks to enforce it, there can be no escape."

Kane said that because Jane Johnson was not actually named in either Wheeler's petition for a writ of habeas corpus nor in the writ itself that was served on Passmore, she "is a stranger to any proceeding that is or has been before me." (The judge was stretching a point here. Wheeler's affidavit refers to a "Jane," though not to "Jane Johnson" as such.)[23] Kane said, "Our records cannot be opened to every stranger who volunteers to us a suggestion, as to what may have been our errors, and how we may repair them." In conclusion, Kane said, "She asks no judicial action for herself, and . . . Mr. Williamson has not sanctioned her application. She has therefore no status whatever in this Court."

George Sidney Fisher read Kane's "long opinion" in an afternoon newspaper. It affirmed "the extreme *new* Southern doctrines on slavery, that the laws abolishing it in the North are unconstitutional etc." Fisher thought the opinion "badly written & argued."[24]

The rejection of Jane's statement could only mean that Passmore's incarceration would continue indefinitely. His only recourse seemed to be to give in to the judge and lie about his having custody of Jane and her children. But before the full impact of its meaning penetrated, an unexpected turn of events occurred.

In court as an observer as Kane delivered his decision was John Cadwalader, who had been elected to Congress the previous year. Cadwalader had been vice provost of the Law Academy of Philadelphia for twenty years and was known for his thorough preparation and wide knowledge of law in general. He rose from the spectators' section of the court and asked Judge Kane if he could speak as *amicus curiae*— a friend of the court. There was a point that had been publicly misrepresented, "an incident of the original proceeding," he said.

Cadwalader had been present in July when Kane committed Passmore to Moyamensing on the charge of contempt. He recalled that one of Passmore's attorneys, Charles Gilpin, had asked the court for permission to amend Passmore's return but had been refused. However, Cadwalader said, Kane had subsequently told Gilpin to put his motion to amend in writing—which the judge in recounting now the details of the case had forgotten about. "But," Cadwalader continued, "no motion to amend was then or afterwards made, although the Court paused to give an opportunity for making it, and invited the counsel then or afterwards, to make any motion which their client might be advised to make."

Kane agreed with Cadwalader. That was his recollection, too. He made the offer but never received any motion and never expressed "any purpose to overrule such a motion, if one should be presented."

Cadwalader said he was "induced" to point out the lapse in Kane's account "by the best feeling towards a worthy but mistaken man." And he hoped his remarks, which he made to correct also a false impression in newspaper reports of the case, "might lead to the adoption of such a course as would end" in Passmore's liberation.[25] This last comment was something of a surprise. Cadwalader was a Democrat, a principal speaker, in fact, at party rallies. Perhaps he wanted to help bring an end to what had become an embarrassment to both Kane and the Democrats.

The door was finally open to resolving the impasse between the judge and the prisoner. But it would take more than two weeks of legal semantics and arguments before a resolution could be affected. Kane, unbending as ever, was especially persnickety. Maybe it was a matter of ego, of who was right and who was wrong, of who knew the law better, or who was going to be the winner and who the loser. Or maybe it was a question of how it would look in the eyes of the judge's colleagues in the legal community if he gave in. For the next week was taken up with insistent haggling over details. And all the while, Passmore sat in Cell No. 78, as unyielding as Kane, as unwilling to give in. They were like two mountains that could not be moved.

The judge refused at first to accept an affidavit made by Passmore, because his counsel did not follow proper procedure in presenting it. They should have first filed a petition asking permission to present the affidavit. That was Wednesday, October 17—the eighty-third day of Passmore's confinement. On Monday, October 22—for Passmore, his eighty-eighth day in prison—his lawyers presented a petition in support of the affidavit. What the petition said is unknown, because it never became part of the court record. Kane insisted that the petition was merely a kind of remonstrance against Passmore's imprisonment and not a purgation of the charge of contempt. He said Passmore first had to apply for leave to purge himself before he could be reinstated with the court and have some rights. The judge, however, did agree to hear arguments on Passmore's desire to relieve himself from contempt. He set October 26 for the hearing.

J. Miller McKim was furious. "Did you ever know Such a Scoundrel?" he told Edward Williamson. "He said the other day that he must appear by petition and now when he does so, refuses to hear it." Edward thought that "the matter will be presented in another form, but what, I don't know."[26]

The arguments began on the Friday, the twenty-sixth, continued on the Saturday, the twenty-seventh, then were recessed to continue on Monday, the twenty-eighth.[27] Passmore was represented by the three attorneys who had initially appeared in court for him—Edward Hopper, William Meredith, and Charles Gilpin. They wanted to offer, over United States District Attorney James Van Dyke's objection, the petition from Passmore, but Kane persisted that Passmore had to purge himself first. The back-and-forth between Meredith and Van Dyke got particularly testy, with Meredith asking that the judge prohibit Van Dyke from appearing as a federal officer inasmuch as he was representing Wheeler. "I do not appear as such," Van Dyke claimed, insisting that he was simply representing the United States in the matter. To which Meredith remarked, "Then I decline taking any notice of the District Attorney, as I consider that he has nothing to do with the matter at all." Not to be outsnubbed, Van Dyke responded, "The gentleman may consider me as acting in any position he pleases; it makes no difference, one way or the other."

The two men continued to quarrel over Van Dyke's role, until, finally, Kane rejected Meredith's request, saying that Van Dyke could remain. Once that was settled, however, the argument about the Passmore's petition resumed. It seemed to go on for hours.

Kane again refused "to hear a paper which does not propose to be offered to purge from the contempt." Meredith persisted. There was no rule about not being able to present a petition. He said he could "find nothing in the books which I am aware of" dealing with a case similar to Passmore's, who "is simply in custody for omitting to do something which he was directed to do."

Gilpin finally intervened, offering to present the petition, saying he understood that the judge was objecting to the form in which the petition was made but not its contents. He was disappointed when he learned that the court ruled it could only be approached by a direct application for purgation. On and on the argument went.

A layman now reading the official, verbatim transcript of the hearing cannot help but nod off. The arguments are circuitous and repetitive. It's as though Passmore's lawyers were not listening to the judge, and the judge was not listening to the lawyers. Finally, however, after much haggling between the adversaries, Kane agreed to accept the petition, but only to peruse it and decide if it was admissible to be put in the record. Whether he would agree that it represented a purgation of contempt was another matter. He said he would look at the document and get back to Passmore's counsel the next morning at ten. Van Dyke now objected to the judge's even looking at the petition, and so the argument began once again. Kane decided to let the matter rest until the following day, October 27, the ninety-third day of Passmore's confinement.

In the interim, Kane read Passmore's petition and was not pleased. It did not contain a purgation of his contempt or, as the judge put it when court reconvened on the twenty-seventh, "the expression of any wish, on his part, to make such purgation." But he was still willing to hear Passmore's counsel on the matter. Meredith, however, came up with a new argument. He said he had studied an English authority and determined that the court was required to make interrogatories in a case such as Passmore's. If it fails to do so within four days, the contempt is "actually purged, *ipso facto.*" He cited case after case to make his point, reading court records of testimony and rulings, almost all of them of English origin. Passmore, he said, "has never refused to answer any thing [*sic*]."

Meredith's argument over the question of interrogatories only led to the judge and Meredith disputing the cited cases, quibbling, as lawyers will, over definitions, semantics and relevance. Kane reiterated that if Passmore declared "his willingness to make a full return," he would put forth interrogatories. That none had been asked before, the judge explained, was because "there could be none filed addressed to a party who is at the time in contempt."

Meredith now tried to apologize for his colleague Gilpin's failure months earlier to file the proper amending motion. Meredith described the dereliction as a "very unfortunate" misunderstanding on Gilpin's part, hoping apparently to appeal to Kane's better nature and forgive Passmore. But the judge was adamant about the legal procedure involved and getting testy himself about the continued wrangling. He was willing to proceed with interrogatories as soon as Passmore indicated "that he is prepared to answer when called upon," and, he added sarcastically, he was surprised that Passmore's attorneys, despite "repeated intimations that have fallen from the bench," had not pursued such a course.

Van Dyke finally interrupted to say that it was "too late for the defendant, so long as he thus remains in contempt, to ask this Court or any other Court in contempt of which he remains, to do anything [until] that contempt is purged and that he is reinstated as he was in the Court immediately." That prompted Meredith to question again Van Dyke's presence: who was he representing, Wheeler or the federal government? Meredith asked Kane to decide, once and for all, whether Passmore could purge his contempt if he answered interrogatories. The judge decided to put off any ruling until Monday, October 29—the ninety-fifth day that Passmore spent in Moyamensing.

The answer again was "No." The judge that Monday decided against accepting Passmore's petition. It would not be filed or put on record. Passmore was still in contempt. There was no indication in writing that "he thereby pray that he may be admitted to make such purgation." As a result, Kane declared, "Passmore Williamson hath not, at this time, a standing in this Court." However, the judge threw out another sop to Passmore's lawyers. If he "desire to purge himself of the contempt" and "is willing to make true answers to such interrogatories as may be addressed to him," then he could be brought "before the Court, if in session, or if the Court be not in session, then before the Judge at his chambers."

Kane's remarks were taken as a hint that he was willing to compromise if Passmore did, too. "This is a small hole for Kane to crawl out of," *Frederick Douglass' Paper* remarked, "but then he is a very small man."[28] Passmore's father evidently felt that the time had come to end the matter. He asked Edward Williamson to bring U.S. Commissioner Charles Heazlitt to Moyamensing. Thomas wanted Heazlitt to notarize a petition that Passmore was going to make, the nature of which, Edward said, "I am ignorant." "Uncle T. has said nothing about it to me," he wrote his father, "and I don't want to ask any questions."[29]

On Friday, November 2, Hopper, Meredith, and Gilpin presented a petition from Passmore indicating that "he desires to purge himself of the contempt because of which he is now attached, and to that end is willing to make true answers to such interrogatories as may be addressed to him by the Court." There was a discussion as to why the word "legally" was omitted in the phrase "of which he is now attached" —an omission that surely was Passmore's way of showing that he was unlawfully imprisoned. However, without demanding the insertion of the word, Kane agreed to have Passmore called into court the next day, Saturday, November 3.

Finally, seventeen days after the courtroom disputes began, Passmore stood before Judge Kane in the second-floor courtroom in Independence Hall. As a marshal escorted him into the district court, a reporter thought he looked "exceedingly well, and but little paler and thinner than in July." Passmore "appeared perfectly cool and collected throughout the proceedings this morning and evinced no emotion whatever."[30]

It was Van Dyke, in his role as United States district attorney, who posed the interrogatories: did Passmore at any time seek to obey the mandate of the writ of habeas corpus and bring before the court the slaves therein mentioned? If yes, Passmore was to state fully what he did to do so.

Passmore did not answer at first. He and his three attorneys withdrew outside the courtroom for a brief period. On their return, Gilpin read a reply. Van Dyke objected to it as being evasive. Only a yes or no was required. Kane intervened. It seemed to him that what Gilpin replied was "a distinct negative," but an expanded answer was proper. Passmore and the attorneys conferred again. The answer was amended to read:

> I did not seek to obey the writ by producing the persons therein mentioned before the Court, because I had not, at the time of the service of the writ, the power over, the custody or control of them, and therefore it was impossible for me to do so. . . . The parties not being in my possession or control, it was impossible for me to obey the writ by producing them. Since the service of the writ I have not had the custody, possession or power over them; nor have I known where they were, except from common rumor or the newspaper reports in regard to their public appearance in the city or elsewhere.

Van Dyke again said he thought the response was evasive. He and Gilpin now argued about whether rephrasing the question was called for. The judge suggested how the answer could be fashioned—"I did not so seek, *because,* &c." But that suggestion led to a dispute over the definition of the word "seek." Kane finally said he thought the "difficulty" could be overcome by amending Passmore's answer once more: "I did not seek to obey the writ by producing the persons in the writ mentioned before this Court. I did not so seek, because I verily believed that it was entirely impossible for me to produce the said persons agreeably to the command of the Court."

Van Dyke said he had another question. He wanted to ask Passmore whether he had "made any mental reservation" in his answer. But Kane, without waiting for Passmore's counsel to raise an objection, immediately overruled Van Dyke. Van Dyke then offered another question dealing with the extent of the financial "injury" done to Wheeler. But Kane overruled that, too. He rebuked Van Dyke, reminding him that he was no longer representing Wheeler. The only inquiry that was proper was "an inquiry as to what injury had been done the process of the Court."

Having said that, Kane accepted Passmore's statement as he, as judge, had suggested that it be amended. "The contempt," he declared, "is now regarded as purged and the party is released from custody. He is now reinstated to the position he occupied before the contempt was committed. Mr. Williamson is now before me on the return of the writ."

Van Dyke, however, would not let the matter drop. He said that he was switching hats and representing Wheeler. Taking a paper from his pocket, he read a statement explaining the slave master's intent to seek damages in a United States circuit court because he had been unable to obtain "a more ample remedy" in district court. In the document, Wheeler stated that he was withdrawing his complaint from the current proceedings. In effect, the slave owner had abandoned his request for a writ of habeas corpus against Passmore. He would not pursue that matter further. Instead, he would rely on the circuit court for a remedy for his loss.

Once Van Dyke was finished, Meredith asked simply, "Is Mr. Williamson discharged?"

"He is," said Kane. "I understand from the remarks of the District Attorney that a *nolle prosequi* has been entered in the case, in this Court."

Passmore was finally a free man. He had been in prison for one hundred days. He was immediately surrounded by friends and supporters, congratulating him and rejoicing. The months of imprisonment, the needless legal wrangling, the battle of principles and the stalemate caused by two stubborn egos—all eventually were reduced in the end to what appeared to be a simple legal technicality, rather than a profound issue of the law. The case was a victory for the abolitionist cause, and, as *The New York Times* pointed out in summing up the meaning of Passmore's martyrdom, it was one more critical reminder of just how capricious the courts could be when they were motivated by a political agenda:

> In all cases similar to the Williamson case those decisions, until
> set aside, will be regarded as precedents, and wherever they are
> so regarded the Northern man will be completely divested of his

privileges, and exposed naked and defenceless to the envenomed shafts of power and oppression. There Magna Charta [sic] and the Bill of Rights—there Federal and State Constitutions—there Anglo-Saxon and American liberty, will be alike trampled in the dust. . . .

But what chance have Americans of getting rid of those precedents, as long as the Federal Judges are appointed by the government, and the Government is the tool of the slave-owner? Before those arbitrary and unconstitutional decisions can be expunged from our law-books, the Federal government must be made independent of the Slave Power, or the Federal Judiciary made independent of the American Government. Either of these reforms would enable the Northern citizens to sweep away those odious precedents; but without effecting one of them they need not hope to do so.[31]

15

Revenge

I am an Abolitionist!
Oppression's deadly foe;
In God's great strength will I resist,
And lay the monster low.

"I Am an Abolitionist," *Anti-Slavery Harp,* 7
(to be sung to the air "Auld Lang Syne")

On Monday, November 5, 1855, just two days after he regained his freedom, Passmore Williamson decided to seize the opportunity to prolong public attention to his case. He also wanted, it is clear, to get back at Judge John Kintzing Kane. Passmore issued a complaint against the judge, seeking damages for his imprisonment. A warrant was issued requiring Kane to appear in thirty days before a court in Delaware County, across the Schuylkill River from Philadelphia.[1]

Passmore was clearly physically depleted by his ordeal in Moyamensing, apparently angry over the separation from his family at a time when his wife needed his support, irked as well as by the sums of money he had had to spend to gain his freedom. On the other hand, he must have been fully aware that abolitionists were always keen to make the most of an incident that would suggest to the public the costs of the persecution of slaves and the prosecution of anti-slavery activists.

According to the *Chester Republican,* the warrant against Kane was followed by a declaration, filed on behalf of Passmore by attorney

Joseph J. Lewis, claiming damages against the judge of fifty thousand dollars for having unlawfully imprisoned him.[2] It was reported that Passmore's incarceration had cost his father, Thomas, alone four thousand dollars by mid-October,[3] and that was before the dragged-out final hearings in Kane's court attended by three attorneys representing Passmore. The sum did not include moneys Passmore himself had spent on attorney fees. Despite the nature of his case, his lawyers did not serve pro bono; they charged legal fees.

Evidently, Passmore's suit was filed in Delaware County because Kane was visiting there. The judge was the administrator of the estate of a relative of his wife's, Samuel Leiper, and guardian of Leiper's children. A deputy sheriff arrested Kane while he was sitting at breakfast in the family home.

The *Daily Pennsylvanian* was convinced that abolitionists had maintained a surveillance of Kane's movements, because his visits to Delaware County were not frequent, and how else would the sheriff have known that Kane was in the county? The newspaper believed that the reason for arresting him there, rather than in Philadelphia, was because there was "a fair chance" that an abolition-friendly judge would preside over the case, "selecting the Court" that "would best suit his purpose." "This is not a matter between Passmore Williamson and Judge Kane," the *Daily Pennsylvanian* declared. "It is a contest between the Constitution and the designs of a band of wretched fanatics. . . . The rabies of the Abolitionist must be either killed or cured. There is no intermediate mode of treatment."[4]

The embarrassment of the arrest, temporary though it was, then the lawsuit itself and the ensuing legal battle—all must have been a constant source of aggravation for the judge. The litigation continued for more than two years, costing him considerable time and expense. An attempt in the state legislature to have the lawsuit shifted to Philadelphia County ran into a snag when state senator Charles R. Buckalew, an influential Democrat, opposed it, effectively squelching the effort. Even though Kane himself was a Democrat, Buckalew said the bill for a change of venue had been introduced against the advice of a large number of Democratic lawmakers, who felt it was inappropriate to interfere with a legal process.[5]

Buckalew was commenting on a "petition or memorial" that Passmore Williamson had presented to the state legislature, arguing against a change of venue in his case against John Kane. On January 24, 1856, John Hancock, a Democratic member of the Pennsylvania house, had introduced a bill to change the venue to Philadelphia County. It was referred to the Committee on the Judiciary System. (Coincidentally, on that date, both the Pennsylvania house and the senate passed a resolution giving "thanks to Dr. [Elisha] Kane, his officers and crew, for the successful result of the recent expedition to the Polar regions.")[6]

Passmore had traveled to Harrisburg to attend a hearing on the bill before the House Judiciary Committee. Unforgiving of Kane's judicial rulings in his case, he wrote cousin George Pyle, "I think he has run to the end of his rope. He will begin to find that he is not much different from other men. His Judg[e]ship will not save him from having to answer the exegency [sic] of the writ from Del. C. just like a *common man*. Poor fellow, I pitty [sic] him for[,] from his peculiar character of mind & the Servile Circle by which he has associated[,] he has learned to feel the Superiority of his position both social & official to such an extent as to make it very mortifying to be drag[g]ed down to the level of one who has never been an Honorable."[7]

When his initial lawsuit against the judge was quashed for a technical reason because it contained a clerical error, Passmore wrote Pyle that "although it was not deemed a matter of any importance it was deemed best, if possible, to avoid every thing [sic] which might be made the matter of exception." Without hesitation, Passmore had a second suit filed. "This will delay the case one term," he wrote, "but will deprive the Supreme Court of one handle by which to lift him out of the Scrape if it should ever be brought before them."[8]

Passmore's suit charged, in the awkward legal phrasing, hyperbole, and repetitious jargon that were customary at the time, that Kane

> did beat[,] ill treat and imprison him[,] the said Passmore Williamson . . . without reasonable cause for a long time[,] to wit for the space of three months did keep and detain and other wrongs to the said Passmore Williamson . . . caused him to be seized and arrested and also then and there forcibly and violently coerced and compelled the said Passmore Williamson to go in and along divers public streets in the City of Philadelphia . . . to a certain public prison called Moyamensing . . . and caused him to be kept and detained in prison there without any reasonable or probable cause whatever for a long space of time[,] to wit for the space of three months . . . [where he was kept] maliciously[,] wickedly[,] oppressively[,] wantonly under pretence of judicial authority . . . by means whereof he[,] the said Passmore Williamson[,] was then and there exposed to public ignominy[,] scandal and disgrace . . . and was also thereby then and there

greatly injured and prejudiced in his health and was then
and there also thereby obliged and compelled to lay and expend
another large sum of money[,] to wit the sum of two hundred
dollars for his board and maintenance in the said prison house
. . . and also thereby obliged to lay out and expend another large
sum of money[,] to wit the sum of two thousand dollars in
endeavouring to procure and obtain his discharge. [9]

As a result, the suit read, Passmore was prevented from "pursuing his usual business and occupation and obtaining and acquiring the great gains and profits of said business and occupation, and whereby also his said business was greatly deranged[,] disordered[,] damaged and prejudiced."

The sequence of the legal motions that followed in the Court of Common Pleas in Media, Pennsylvania, seems to a lay reader to be tedious, the procedures time-consuming, the briefs that were filed repetitive and extraordinarily lengthy. A Summons in Trespass (an unlawful act in unlawful manner injuring another's person or property) was issued December 18, 1855. Passmore entered a Rule (an order made by a court) upon Kane to plead in thirty days on February 27, 1856.

Kane filed responding pleas on the twenty-fifth of the following month. A replication (reply by the plaintiff, Passmore) was filed on April 18, 1856. Passmore's attorney asked for a court order on July 3 of that year in order to take the depositions of witnesses who were residing in Washington. (Who he had in mind was not recorded.) Kane filed demurrers (exceptions to the point of law alleged) and rejoinders (a second pleading to the plaintiff's replication) on August 16, and Passmore responded to those defense maneuvers on August 19.

On August 20, 1856, it was agreed that the validity of the suit would be put on the trial list for the November term notwithstanding a pending decision to another demurrer that Kane had filed. The case was argued on December 17. On May 25, 1857, the court ordered that all special pleas be stricken together with all subsequent pleadings, and following that, on June 6, Kane entered a plea of "not guilty."

All these legal maneuvers by lawyers for both the judge and Passmore involved costly written documents. A so-called Paper Book—an argument for the defense replete with a history of the case and citation after citation—ran forty-eight pages. A Demurrer Book traced Passmore's charge, Kane's response, Passmore's answer to the response and a subsequent answer by Kane to Passmore's response.[10]

The lawsuit wasn't Kane's only problem. There were the accumulating petitions to Congress for his impeachment—which, eventually, were pigeonholed in the Democrat-dominated House Judiciary Committee. To add to the judge's public humiliation, a supplement covering the entire proceedings in the contempt-of-court case against Passmore was added in 1856 to the American edition of a book compiled by Lord Chief Justice John Lord Campbell of England. The book was entitled *Atrocious Judges: Lives of Judges Infamous as Tools of Tyrants and Instruments of Oppression.*[11] The supplement compared Kane to the most venal judges in English history.

Above all was the anguish Kane suffered on losing his son Elisha, the much-heralded explorer. Elisha succumbed shortly after his thirty-seventh birthday in the winter of 1857. He died in Havana, where he had gone, seeking a warmer climate, to alleviate his deteriorating state of health. His body was brought back to the United States and lay in state in New Orleans, Louisville, Columbus, and Baltimore. From Baltimore, an honor guard of troops escorted his casket to Philadelphia, where he lay in state in Independence Hall, a rare honor. Pallbearers included Associate Justice Robert Grier of the United States Supreme Court and Pennsylvania's chief justice, Ellis Lewis.

John Kane was beset in his last years by the frustration of trying to obtain recompense for the financial expenses of the lawsuit brought by Passmore. Two days before Elisha died, Kane wrote Grier that Secretary of Interior Robert McClelland had "intimated" to him that a certificate from Grier as to the propriety of the legal fees he had incurred would be "desirable" if he was going to be repaid. Kane pointed out that he had had to fight two suits. A first one was defeated because of a printing error in the brief submitted by Passmore's attorney, but a second, corrected one was then filed. He said that he had required the assistance of six "professional gentlemen." "It seems to me just," Kane went on, "that each of the three first referred to, should receive a fee of $250, and that the three last should receive a fee of $500 each; making an aggregate of $2,250. Besides this, I have paid for their expenses on sundry visits to the Court, where the causes were pending, $200;—and for printing pleadings, paper books, and briefs of arguments, $94.25. The amount of my claim must therefore be $2,544.25."[12]

Grier endorsed Kane's claim the same day, and Kane sent it off to McClelland on February 16. "I think the charges reasonable and proper," the judge wrote. The sum represented "the amount of charges incurred by me in the defence of two suits, brought against me in one of the local Courts of Pennsylvania for acts done by me as a Judicial Officer under the laws of the U.S."[13]

When he didn't hear from McClelland for five months, Kane wrote him again in June 1857 to remind him of his claim. By then, James Buchanan had been inaugurated as president, succeeding Franklin Pierce, and McClelland was no longer secretary of the interior. "You were good enough then," Kane wrote, referring to his February correspondence with McClelland, "to express your approving judgment of the claim and of the adequacy of Judge Grier's certificate as the voucher of it, and to add a promise that I should be advised of the President's action upon & in the course of the week." Kane noted that after placing the documents in McClelland's hands, "a family calamity" —news of Elisha's death—forced him to leave Washington. "I thereupon addressed a personal note to you, apologising [sic] for my sudden departure and praying you to expedite the settlement."

When, again, he received no word for months, Kane wondered whether McClelland's response might have reached Philadelphia but been mislaid. He had to go to Washington on other business, so he took the opportunity to renew his claim. However, he was "mortified to learn that none of the papers relating to it remain among the files, though other letters from me, of the same date, but upon other subjects, are there." Kane asked that McClelland inform the new administration of "what disposition was made of it,—and in what quarter I may hope to find my letter and the voucher that was appended to it,— as well as the evidence of the Department[']s action upon them."[14]

McClelland wrote back immediately. As far as he knew, Kane's claim was submitted to Franklin Pierce, "who, so far as I have any knowledge, did not return it. As it is not to be found among the files there, it must either have been retained by him, or perhaps referred to the Attorney General."[15]

That July, Kane repeated his claim, writing directly to President Buchanan, a fellow Pennsylvanian whom he knew. He noted that Passmore's second suit was "still pending after full and repeated arguments on sundry motions and demurrers." He said the judge handling the suit had "for now nearly a year held it under advisement. Indeed I have begun to doubt whether between his proclaimed political opinions on one side and his responsibility to professional opinion on the other, he has not resolved to let the cause die in his portfolio." In the meantime, he added, "the Defendant in these suits, your humble servant, has been Subjected to considerable expenses by reason of them, and is honorably indebted." Kane related in detail the history behind the submission of his claim. However, he noted that a clerk of the executive department had intimated to him that the administration had adopted a rule that would exclude his claim altogether. He asked Buchanan to look through the papers he was enclosing—copies of those that he had previously sent McClelland—"and to advise me as a friend what I ought to do, or whether I ought to do anything. I feel some delicacy in making the request; but I hope you will at least excuse it, seeing that I am without recourse save to God and your Grace."[16]

Evidently Buchanan referred Kane's appeal to the acting secretary of the interior, Moses Kelly, because Kelly reported to the president in late August 1857 that neither his department nor the executive department "had any official knowledge of these suits." Nor was Kelly aware of any case where compensation had been made "to Counsel employed by any Judicial Officer of the United States, in the defense of suits instituted on account of acts done in the discharge of the duties of his office, unless previous authority had been given."[17]

Sometime in the intervening months between August and November, the original papers that Kane had left in Washington were found. In another letter to Buchanan, Kane said he was told "that the claim they developed was not without the sanction of precedent, and that a favourable opinion of its merits had been expressed by" Attorney General Jeremiah S. Black (who, when a Pennsylvania state supreme court justice, it will be remembered, wrote the opinion rejecting Passmore's appeal for a writ of habeas corpus). Kane pointed out that Buchanan had promised at an interview during the summer to get back to Kane with a decision after the next meeting of his cabinet. But, Kane wrote on November 13, 1857, he still he had not heard what the decision was.[18]

A day later, Secretary of Interior Jacob Thompson officially notified Kane. The decision had been made nearly three months earlier, but no one had informed him. Kane's son Thomas, now a colonel in the army, was present as Thompson wrote a brief note to the judge. The president, acting upon the report of Moses Kelly, had, on the previous August 25, rejected his claim. "Judge Kane being a Judicial and not a Ministerial officer of the U.S., I do not possess the power, under the 11th Section of the Act of August 31st, 1852, to allow the payment of his claim."[19]

A little more than three months after John Kintzing Kane learned that he had been turned down in his appeal for compensation, he contracted typhoid pneumonia and died at his home in Germantown. His death on February 21, 1858, put an end to the lawsuit that Passmore

Williamson had brought against him. It was officially terminated in mid-April of 1858 upon the formal notification to the court of Kane's death.[20]

It is interesting to speculate how Kane would have felt about the subsequent careers of his abolitionist sons, Robert and Thomas. Ironically, Robert for a time during the Civil War replaced James Van Dyke as United States District Attorney for the Eastern District of Pennsylvania. At the same time, he also served with the Philadelphia City Cavalry. Thomas, a career army officer, had befriended Brigham Young in the 1850s and played a leading role in an amicable settlement of the government's dispute with the Mormons in Utah. Thomas founded the town of Kane in northwestern Pennsylvania, and there, at the outset of the Civil War, he organized the 13th Pennsylvania Reserves, better known as the Bucktails Brigade.

Thomas's career in the army was notable. Leading a regiment known as the Kane Rifles, he was wounded at the Battle of Dranesville, and subsequently, while rushing with his regiment to the aid of another regiment that had been ambushed, he was wounded again and this time taken prisoner. After a prisoner exchange, he returned to his regiment with the rank of brigadier general and took part in the Chancellorsville Campaign in the spring of 1863. At the time of the Battle of Gettysburg that July, Thomas, who had contracted pneumonia, was on sick leave. Despite his illness, he was entrusted with carrying a message to General George Meade, warning him that the Confederates were in possession of a critical Union cipher. He delivered the message after great difficulty, at one point disguising himself as a civilian to avoid capture by Jeb Stuart's rebel cavalry. Thomas resumed command of his unit on the second day of fighting at Gettysburg, but he was too weak to sit on his horse. He was afterward cited for gallantry and brevetted a major general but had to resign for reasons of health.

John Kintzing Kane was sixty-two years old at the time of his death. Passmore Williamson would probably have enjoyed learning of the judge's financial travails and frustrations, but there is no evidence that he knew anything of Kane's failure to be reimbursed for the complaint suit. Passmore, however, would have certainly learned of Kane's death from local newspapers if not from friends in Philadelphia. But if he commented on the judge's demise, his remarks were not recorded. However, J. Miller McKim did have something to say, writing a friend that the news of the judge's death would be a blessing for runaway slaves: "Judge Kane died last night! The fugitive will feel more secure in his hiding place."[21] A friend of Passmore, Benjamin Harris Brewster, believed that "remorse" over Kane's action in Passmore's case was "the cause of his death."[22] George Sidney Fisher had dined with Kane two weeks earlier, but Fisher was not invited to his interment, probably because the family knew all too well his opinion of the judge. "I regret the loss of Kane," he wrote in his diary. "I did not approve his course as a judge nor his character in all respects." He and Kane had had their differences, Fisher continued, "but this never interrupted our friendly intercourse." He thought Kane "had ability, acuteness, some learning, plausibility, but he was without moral principle." It was "easy to see," Fisher added, "that he wanted truth & sincerity."[23]

16

Aftermath

The fearful storm—it threatens lowering
Which God in mercy long delays;
Slaves yet, may see their masters cowering,
While whole plantations smoke and blaze! . . .
Have pity on the slave;
Take courage from God's word;
Pray on, pray on, all hearts resolved—
These captives shall be free.

"Ye Sons of Freeman," *Anti-Slavery Harp*, 6
(to be sung to the air "Marseilles Hymn")

Jane Johnson, the focus of such a critical chapter in the abolitionist cause and so much public notoriety and private turmoil, spent the rest of her life living peacefully and quietly in Boston, helping other escaped slaves when she could.

Jane continued to reside in the same black community on Boston's Beacon Hill that she first reached in the summer of 1855. She did move, in all about a dozen times, but always within that same neighborhood, an area on the north slope of Beacon Hill populated by active, influential blacks. At one point, she lived next door to Lewis Hayden, an escaped slave who led the Boston Vigilance Society; he and his wife Harriet housed hundreds of runaway slaves.[1] One of Jane's closest friends was William Cooper Nell, who had met her at the Boston rail depot when she first arrived in Boston in late July 1855. The Vigilance Society underwrote Jane's board when she first reached the city and also doled out expense money for shoes, furniture, and other items. One of her benefactors was Robert Wallcut, a white member of the society, who published the abolitionist newspaper *The Liberator.*

Jane married twice. The first time was to Lawrence Woodfork or Woodford, a thirty-nine-year-old laborer who sometimes worked as a cook. Woodfork had been born in Essex County, Virginia. The couple was wed on August 13, 1856. It was the second marriage for both of them. Oddly, Jane's age then is listed on the marriage register as twenty-five. She and Woodfork are known to have taken into their home escaped slaves on two occasions, once on Christmas Day, 1857, and again in April, 1859. Woodfork died in December 1861. Two and a half years later, on July 20, 1864, Jane married William Harris, a thirty-seven-year-old mariner who was originally from Allegany County, Maryland. The couple was wed in Boston by a bishop of the African Methodist Episcopal Church. It was Harris's second marriage, and, for some inexplicable reason, according to the marriage register, it was recorded again as her second marriage. Jane's age then was given as twenty-six. The marriage did not last long. Jane was widowed again a year later.[2] There is no explanation for the difference recorded between her age at the time of her marriages and the age that was later recorded at the time of her death.

Once she settled in Boston, Jane learned to read and write, possibly because, besides the assistance it gave to fugitive slaves, the local Vigilance Committee sponsored adult-education courses. At the time of the 1860 census she is listed as being able to do so, and further proof of her literacy appears in letters Nell wrote Passmore Williamson in 1856. In one, he said Jane had asked for his address, evidently so that she could write him herself. In another letter, Nell indicated that she and Passmore had corresponded directly: "Jane Johnson called in this morning and expressed much pleasure on hearing from you," Nell wrote. He passed along her latest address and remarked that she was "quite well. Her Boys are progressing finely at School, for all these advantages of freedom she feels heartfelt gratitude for your exertions."[3]

Sometime during the Civil War, Jane and Passmore met. Details of their seeing each other—the first and only time since her rescue in 1855—are unknown. Passmore was quoted making a brief reference to their meeting in an obituary about him that a newspaper printed nearly forty years after the event. The article included Passmore's account of the rescue. He explained that after Jane was whisked away in a carriage from the Walnut Street wharf, "I never saw the woman from that time until Boston, during the war."[4] Unfortunately, nothing further is known about their meeting. If Passmore wrote his wife or one of his cousins about it, the letter does not exist. If he talked about it to a friend, the friend made no record of what he said. The meeting remains a mystery. So many questions remain unanswered: the reason that Passmore was in Boston, when and where the two got together, what the circumstances of their meeting were, what they said. It must have been an emotional moment for both of them.

Jane suffered through a two-week bout with dysentery during an epidemic in Boston and died on August 2, 1872—coincidentally on what was John Hill Wheeler's sixty-sixth birthday. She was buried in Woodlawn Cemetery in Everett, five miles north of Boston, in a double plot denoted only by a metal marker with the number 74. Her age then was given as fifty-nine, which would mean that she was about forty-two years old at the time that she and her boys were rescued in Philadelphia in 1855.[5]

A controversy has developed in recent years over whether Jane is the author of an unprecedented original, handwritten nineteenth-century manuscript, *The Bondwoman's Narrative*. The author's name on the covering page is given as Hannah Crafts, "A Fugitive Slave Recently Escaped from North Carolina." The slave woman whose story is recounted in the novel is owned by a family named Wheeler, and there are scenes in it that take place in North Carolina and Washington. Although there are discrepancies in dates, and the escape of the heroine of the novel in no way resembles the rescue of Jane Johnson, the question arises: could Hannah Crafts be a pseudonym that Jane Johnson adopted?

The manuscript came into the possession of Henry Louis Gates, Jr., chairperson of Harvard's Afro-American Studies Department, who was able to have it published in 2002 along with his research into who might have written it. He could not trace any person named Hannah Crafts who had been a slave. After extensive research, Gates concluded that it was possible that Hannah Crafts might have been a slave once owned by John Hill Wheeler, but she was not Jane Johnson. However, Katherine E. Flynn, a scientist by profession whose hobby is genealogy, researched in depth what little is known about Jane Johnson—she found her name in municipal records in Boston—and came to believe that Jane and Hannah Crafts may likely indeed be one and the same person. The controversy has spawned a cottage industry of academic researchers, whose essays have been published in *In Search of Hannah*

Crafts: Critical Essays on The Bondwoman's Narrative, which Gates and Hollis Robbins edited. The more than twenty essays in the volume include studies into the novel's allusions to authors such as Charles Dickens, Walter Scott, and Charlotte Brontë. Some of the contributing scholars have gleaned its connection to other slave accounts as well as popular contemporary novels. One, calling the work a hybrid, compares the book's happy ending to sentimental women's novels. Still another ponders the reason that publishers might not have been interested in publishing the manuscript in the nineteenth century. Others debate who did write the book. Gates and Robbins believe that whoever Hannah Crafts was, she and Jane Johnson must have known one another. However, the question of the authorship of *The Bondwoman's Narrative* remains unresolved.

Jane's son Daniel went to sea, though whether he worked as a sailor or in a stewarding capacity is not known. He was listed as residing in Boston in 1865, but disappears from available records after that. More is known about her younger boy, Isaiah. He was only fifteen years old but lied about his age and said he was eighteen so that he could enlist in 1863 in a black unit, the 55th Massachusetts Volunteer Infantry. He was a drummer boy with Company K—"a little dark complex'd boy, nothing more than a boy . . . the Captain's pet," according to the recollection of one of the unit's soldiers many years later.[6] The 55th served in operations in South Carolina and Georgia. At the Battle of Honey Hill on November 30, 1864, the regiment suffered the highest casualties, losing 144 men.[7] Isaiah returned to Boston after being mustered out, but there is no record of his whereabouts after 1872.[8]

Jane Johnson's former master, John Hill Wheeler, returned from Nicaragua in disgrace. He made the mistake of supporting William Walker, the so-called filibusterer, or insurgent, who seized control of the country. Walker's plan was to unite Central America into one military empire and to reintroduce slavery in it as a way of developing the region's agricultural resources. Without authorization, Wheeler, who sympathized with Walker's scheme, provided him with legitimacy by recognizing his regime in the name of the United States. It was a premature and ill-advised act. Great Britain viewed American recognition of Walker as reason to become embroiled once again in the area, and, subsequently, when Costa Rica invaded Nicaragua, it was with British complicity.

Wheeler's action enraged Secretary of State William Marcy, who requested his recall. Franklin Pierce refused to do so. However, on

March 2, 1857, a few days before Pierce's term of office came to an end, Wheeler met with the president. "He resolved to have no diplomatic relations with Nica[ragua]," Wheeler noted in his diary, forcing him to realize that Pierce had "of course no use for me." He resigned "on this ground alone," Wheeler insisted, though afterwards most persons believed he was forced to resign, and his reputation ever since suffered. Wheeler never acknowledged that he had acted unwisely. When Walker was captured by the British navy, turned over to Honduran authorities and executed by them in the fall of 1860, Wheeler described him as "a victim to the cruelties of Spanish American character, and English perfidy."[9]

Wheeler had returned to Washington in January 1857 with a severely infected finger on his right hand. He went to Philadelphia to have it amputated. In the fall of that year, Secretary of the Interior Jacob Thompson appointed him his department's superintendent of documents.[10] His position apparently did not last long, because a few days before Christmas, Wheeler found a position as the clerk of the Committee for Foreign Affairs.[11] In all that time, he never abandoned his quest for restitution for the loss of Jane Johnson and her children. Entries in his diary in the succeeding years include several references to his pursuit of a lawsuit against Passmore Williamson. Obviously unsuccessful, he began preparing a "memorial" to the Pennsylvania legislature in January 1860 regarding "the forcible taking away of my negroes . . . by a mob for which I hope to be indemnified by the State."[12] Nothing, however, ever came of any of his efforts.

Wheeler and his family were residing at 444 H Street North when the Civil War broke out in April 1861. He had seen the war coming as early as four months earlier, commenting in his diary, "This question (Slavery) is shaking this Union to the center."[13] Despite his being a proponent of slavery, he was against the war, and, when hostilities broke out, he remarked, "God knows where it is to end."[14] Wheeler returned to North Carolina during the war but did not remain there. He traveled to England in 1863 to do research for another edition of his history of the state. In London that December, he was among five thousand persons who attended Sunday services to hear the sermon of a well-known minister named Spurgeon. The cleric spoke on the humanity of Christ "with great eloquence." But, Wheeler wrote, "I was however much chagrined to hear him refer to Eva in *Uncle Tom's Cabin,* and holding her and Christ together as exemplary of that simplicity and purity which we ought to imitate. Had he lived among darkies he could better appreciate their characters."[15]

Portions of Wheeler's diary are missing, but those entries that survive are surprisingly devoid of critical remarks about the war and the North. Perhaps he purposely excised them. Wheeler does comment at times about the war's progress. He summed up the situation at the end of 1863, well after the Battle of Gettysburg and the fall of Vicksburg that July, saying, "Doubtless in the South the war has borne on the land with a fearful distress; much suffering and privation; but it is endured with patience and a fixed purpose to be free or to cease to exist."[16] His son Levi Woodbury Wheeler, who served in a number of North Carolina artillery regiments, was captured during the Battle of New Bern in March 1862. Woodbury was confined at first in New York City, then removed to the notorious Johnson's Island prison camp in Lake Erie off Sandusky, Ohio. Wheeler noted in his diary that, after several months' confinement, Woodbury was exchanged.[17] But he makes no mention of his older son, Charles Sully Wheeler, who served in the federal navy. Nor does he mention his stepbrother Junius Brutus Wheeler, who taught mathematics at West Point before joining the Union engineer corps in March 1863 as a captain; Junius's service included actions in Arkansas and Missouri.

Wheeler returned to Washington after the war, but he always claimed his legal residence was North Carolina. The nameplate affixed to his front door on H Street coupled his name and the state's, and North Carolina was engraved on the lid of his coffin when he died. A contemporary biographer said that he "labored cheerfully till the end," working on books, though "during his closing years he suffered much."[18] Wheeler was seventy-six years old when he passed away on December 7, 1882. The house in Murfreesboro, North Carolina, which his father had purchased in 1814 and which was the family home until 1867, is now a museum.

Until the beginning of the Civil War, William Still continued his work as clerk of the Pennsylvania Anti-Slavery Society and as chairman of the Acting Committee of the General Vigilance Committee. He had the satisfaction of witnessing his older brother, Peter Friedman's, reunion in 1855 with his family. Guided by an abolitionist named Seth Concklin, Friedman's wife and three children had fled Alabama by boat in 1851. However, they were recaptured in Indiana, where Concklin lost his life under mysterious circumstances. Friedman was finally able to garner the five thousand dollars necessary to buy their freedom by appealing for donations at abolitionist meetings, where he spoke of his family's enslavement and Concklin's death. Once his wife and children were freed, Friedman changed the family name to Still and resettled in New Jersey.

Throughout the 1850s and into the new decade, William Still continued to chronicle the accounts of runaway slaves, though several times he had to hide his records in a cemetery building to prevent detection. Particularly dangerous were the days, weeks and months following John Brown's raid on Harper's Ferry in the fall of 1859. Frederick Douglass had approached Still with plans for the raid many months before it occurred, but Still thought the idea unwise and bound to fail. Like Douglass, he declined to join in the plot. However, after the raid took place and Brown was captured, Still's name was linked to one of the participants, and despite the notoriety that it engendered, he took into his home the widow and daughter of John Brown while they were en route to visit Brown before his execution.

Although he had resigned from the Anti-Slavery Society at the outbreak of the war and started what turned out to be a prosperous stove and coal business, Still was instrumental during the war in the organization of a series of lectures in Philadelphia dealing with race relations, human rights, and citizenship. Among its speakers were Frederick Douglass, William Lloyd Garrison and William D. Kelley, the judge who had presided at Still's trial in 1855 and later became a Republican congressman.[19]

In the latter part of the war, another of Lucretia Mott's sons-in-law, Edward M. Davis, approached Still. Davis was a member of a supervisory committee seeking a post sutler to serve soldiers at Camp William Penn outside of Philadelphia. Sutlers were often unscrupulous merchants who took advantage of troops, selling them provisions and sometimes shoddy supplies at exorbitant prices. Davis told Still he had to take the position because the committee had confidence in his "ability and integrity." Still accepted.[20]

After the war, on the very day that the Pennsylvania Anti-Slavery Society, its mission accomplished, disbanded in 1871, its members first unanimously passed a resolution urging Still to publish "his personal reminiscences and experiences" related to his and the society's work in helping escaped slaves to freedom.[21] The book, entitled *The Underground Railroad*, came out the following year. Running almost eight hundred pages, it was subtitled "a record of facts, authentic narratives, letters, &c., narrating the hardships, hair-breadth escapes and death struggles of the slaves in their efforts for freedom, as related by themselves and others, or witnessed by the author; together with sketches of some of the largest stockholders, and most liberal aiders and advisers of the road." Until Still's book, the "aiders and advisers" had become identified almost exclusively as whites, most of them Quaker to boot, and the stories they told stressed their deeds and heroism. Still's book focused on the fugitives themselves. It was their stories he told and their courage he underlined. And it underscored the role of the blacks who had helped them. The book has become one of the primary sources for the stories of fugitive slaves and the assistance they received. It sold reasonably well at the time—between five and ten thousand copies by the late 1870s[22]—and attracted revived interest almost a century later, when a reprint was issued during the civil rights movement of the 1960s. It is the classic account of the blacks' own struggle against slavery.

A successful businessman throughout the remainder of his life, Still nevertheless remained unwavering in his dedication to improving the lot of black people. He became intricately active in the Pennsylvania Abolition Society, which renewed its efforts to help educate once-enslaved blacks and offer them work training. He was the society's vice president in 1888 and became its president in 1896, a post he held until his death.[23] And almost single-handedly, Still began in 1859 a campaign to compel the city's streetcar lines to end their discrimination against black passengers, who were compelled to ride on the outside platforms of the cars. He was motivated to do so, he said, when, returning from Camp William Penn on a "bitter cold day" that was "almost intolerable," he had to ride on the platform of a streetcar even though he had paid "the same as those who enjoy comfortable seats inside by a good fire."[24] As he noted at the time, both slaves and free blacks were allowed in cars and omnibuses in New Orleans; black women were permitted on omnibuses in Cincinnati; both men and women were allowed inside public-transportation vehicles in Chicago as well as (with minor exceptions) on omnibuses in New York City. However, it was a different story in Philadelphia. One-time slave William Wells Brown recalled returning to Philadelphia after extensive travels in England and Europe and being barred from a Chestnut Street streetcar on his first day home. "The omnibuses of Paris, Edinburgh, Glasgow, and Liverpool, had stopped to take me, but what mattered that? My face was not white, my hair was not straight; and, therefore I must be excluded from a seat in a third-rate American omnibus."[25]

As Still put it, "However long the distance they may have to go, or great their hurry—however unwell or aged, genteel or neatly attired—however hot, cold or stormy the weather—however few in the cars, as the masses of the colored people now understand it, they are unceremoniously excluded."[26] Despite personal attacks on his reputation and threats against his life, Still persisted, and the state legislature finally prohibited such discrimination in 1867, eight years after he began his campaign.

The list of Still's other achievements is equally astounding. He served on the Freedmen's Aid Commission, founded in 1880 the first black Young Men's Christian Association. (His daughter Caroline would establish its counterpart for black women.) He helped manage homes for aged blacks and for destitute black children, as well as an orphan asylum for the children of black soldiers and sailors. Yet, because Still was outspoken, he ran into criticism from Philadelphia blacks when he supported a Democratic candidate for mayor in 1874 and again when he came out against the establishment of a separate colored men's bank, believing that it was premature. And for all his accomplishments, by the time of his death as the result of a heart attack on July 14, 1902, when he was eighty years old, Still was a forgotten hero. In recent years, descendants have organized the William Still Underground Railroad Foundation in an effort to restore the memory of his life and his accomplishments.

In the years leading up to the Civil War, Still and Passmore Williamson remained more than just fellow members of the General Vigilance Committee's Acting Committee. When Still took probably one of the most serious risks of his life by sheltering a participant in the Harper's Ferry raid—in flagrant defiance of the federal government—he confided what he had done to only two persons outside his family whom he felt he could trust, J. Miller McKim and Passmore.[27]

The relationship between Still and Williamson continued after the Civil War as well. Soon after peace had been restored in 1865, Still hosted an "entertainment" at his home in honor of William Lloyd Garrison. Passmore and his wife, Mercie, attended the celebration.

When Still's daughter Caroline married on January 4, 1870, Passmore and Mercie were among the more than sixty persons who were invited to attend the wedding. Caroline Still married Edward A. Wiley, a former slave who had joined the Union army after it penetrated Alabama. Other invitees included Dillwyn Parrish, J. Miller McKim, Mary Grew, and Sarah Pugh. Lucretia Mott spoke at the ceremony.[28] "Carrie," as she was called, was a graduate of Oberlin College, which in the early 1830s was the first school in the country to admit both women and blacks. Wiley later attended Oberlin College but did not graduate. She went on to become a doctor, and, among other things, was active in the temperance movement. It is not clear why or when the marriage ended. Caroline subsequently married Matthew Anderson, pastor of the Berean Presbyterian Church.

Four years later, in 1874, Still and Passmore were together on the platform of Concert Hall when Still spoke, urging blacks to vote for principles rather than for political parties or individual candidates.[29] They served together as well on the committee that arranged the celebration of the one hundredth anniversary of the Pennsylvania Abolition Society in 1875.[30]

In many ways, however, Passmore shied away from public attention after his release from Moyamensing. On November 17, 1855, two weeks after he returned home, an anti-slavery meeting in honor of Mary Ann Shadd Cary, publisher of the *Provincial Freeman,* was held in Philadelphia. Still was on the committee that arranged the rally and invited Passmore to attend. But Passmore said he did not want to be "lionized, or take part in any meeting got up for that purpose." And although he promised to attend when he was told that blacks were desirous of seeing him, he did not show up for the event.[31] Similarly, at a Republican rally a few months later in Pittsburg, Passmore was introduced to the assemblage to a rousing half-dozen cheers, but he remarked that he did not feel the ability to address the convention at any length, nor indeed did he have the disposition to do so. He attributed their spontaneous greeting solely to the circumstances of his case, "which had lifted his humble name into notice."[32]

Although he was outwardly reticent to take advantage of the notoriety he had gained, Passmore, like William Still, never abandoned the abolitionist cause or the struggle for black rights. Fittingly it seems, at a rally held in April 1859 for the purpose of taking a stand against the removal of any escaped slave from Philadelphia, it was Passmore who averted a violent confrontation with a horde of anti-abolitionist hecklers. The rally, held at the Sansom Street Hall, drew what Lucretia Mott's sister Martha Wright described as "a disorderly multitude of sympathisers [sic] with the South" whose "constant cheers and groans drowned the voice of speakers." The "mob," she said, "repeatedly resolved that they wd. [sic] not associate with niggers, and there were many present, so designated, from Robt. Purvis & family, to the deepest shades, & some were much terrified." The mob started up the aisles toward the speakers' platform. "The tumult" became great, and some women in the audience, including one who had been present when anti-abolitionists burned Pennsylvania Hall in 1838, became "alarmed & excited." Sensing the mob's explosive nature, Passmore took it upon himself to summon a force of police officers. They arrived just as the rioters reached the platform and quickly arrested "the disorderly ones." J. Miller McKim said that "it was the first time that the mob had ever been obliged to yield."[33]

That December, Passmore was elected again to the Acting Committee of the General Vigilance Committee.[34] In the summer before the Civil War broke out, he became involved in another slave case, though this one ended differently from Jane Johnson's. Passmore obtained a writ of habeas corpus to bring into court a slave woman, the servant of a Virginian named Conquest who was then residing in Philadelphia. "That moral sleuthhound . . . Williamson seems to have indoctrinated her with the principles of the Constitution," *The New York Times* reported. But the slave master had outwitted him. Before the day of the court appearance, according to *The Times*, Conquest took the woman on a tour of the city that included streets that were "the haunts of the free colored population." What she saw, the newspaper continued, was "poverty and suffering; rags insufficient for decent shelter to the limbs; eager hunger in hollow eyes and cheeks; sloth, vice and misery, on all sides." Despite Williamson's persuasiveness, it pointed out, freedom "has no better equivalents to offer for a lifelong home and comfortable subsistence." "The truth is," the newspaper said, "it's not the Southern household servant who feels the pinch of servitude. Comfortably housed, lavishly fed, indulged, and very often spoiled, their lives are easily indolent. . . . The Abolitionist offers no substitute for these comforts." So it was not surprising that the woman declared that "she did not think it would be honorable to leave" her master.[35]

Passmore remained an active member of the Anti-Slavery Society while it existed and of the Abolition Society throughout his life, continuing to battle against slavery before the Civil War and then promoting the education of blacks after it. And he always intended, he said, to write a report on what he called the *"Wheeler vs. Williamson"* case, "giving a full account of the purgation." Or so he wrote his cousin George Pyle. "It might properly be called, if I had sought a fancy & descriptive title 'How I got in & how I got out.'"[36] If, indeed, Passmore did write his version of the rescue, its existence is unknown. Perhaps more frustrating is the lack of any remarks Passmore made regarding how he felt about the Civil War. One would expect that, even though as an abolitionist he had abandoned pacifism, the violence of the conflict, the loss of so many lives, would have appalled him. On the other hand, the emancipation of the slaves that resulted would certainly have provided a great deal of satisfaction. It is unfortunate that there is no record of his reaction.

When war did come, Passmore traveled for health reasons to Cuba. Mercie accompanied him. Ironically, the trip was efficacious for him, but not for her. The couple now had four children—Mercie had given birth to their second son, Charles Sumner, on November 1, 1857—but they left all their youngsters behind so that Passmore could take full advantage of the rest and recuperation. He had never fully recovered from the physical ordeal of the hundred days he had spent in prison. He experienced what he called "Lumbago or Rheumatism of the muscles of the back." The stiffness had become severe at times for more than a year, so much so that by the fall of 1861 he was at first lame, and "eventually," he wrote cousin George Pyle, his condition almost "destroyed the motive power of the whole machine." Totally incapacitated, he lay in bed for eight weeks. Finally, his doctor recommended "a warm climate & salt bathing."

The couple embarked from New York City on February 20, 1862, landing in Havana five days later. It had been the dead of winter when they left, but the temperature on their arrival in Cuba, Passmore noted, was ninety degrees. They stayed in Havana for a week, then traveled to Matangas. There Mercie became "violently ill of Bilious dysentery & from the disease & the violent treatment." She was "entirely broken down" when they left Matangas to return home in the last week of March, so much so that she was bedridden for almost a month after their return.[37]

There is a puzzling mystery about certain events following the death of Passmore's father, Thomas, particularly so because of Passmore's public reputation for integrity. Thomas Williamson had always supported his son's involvement in the rescue of Jane Johnson as well as his son's other activities for the Vigilance Committee. Thomas was even active himself in helping blacks. He took in a family of manumitted slaves from Virginia before Christmas of 1857, and when a group of Oberlin, Ohio, townspeople as well as college professors and students were imprisoned for helping a runaway slave named John Price in 1858, he donated one hundred dollars to help them fight charges of violating the Fugitive Slave Law.[38]

In the middle of August 1871, Thomas fell ill on an evidently blistering afternoon while attending the funeral of a friend in Bristol, Pennsylvania, north of Philadelphia. He suffered a stroke in the graveyard, losing the use of his left hand and foot. Thomas was too ill to be removed to his home in Philadelphia, and he soon suffered attacks of paralysis and what Passmore called "a softening of the brain," which was probably hastened by "his exertion and exposure to the action of the sun."[39] The elder Williamson died in Bristol on August 26 at the age of seventy-six.

Thomas bequeathed a number of personal items to Passmore—his gold Swiss chronometer, his eight-day clock, his books and his office furniture. He also named Passmore executor of his estate,[40] which was worth more than $163,000[41]—a hefty sum in those days. Proceeds from the trust Passmore supervised were to be divided equally between Thomas's second wife, Deborah, and his children—his son, Passmore, and his two daughters, Ann and Mary.

Passmore soon discovered that he would have to convert some of his father's securities to settle Thomas's financial commitments and "to meet engagements alre[a]dy made."[42] Four years later, the worth of the estate was down to under $50,000, and his siblings sued him. The money, Passmore acknowledged, had been lost in stock speculation and investments in unauthorized securities that a court decided were not allowable.[43] In addition, his father's role as executor of an estate of a relative devolved upon Passmore after Thomas's death. Passmore was accused of mixing these securities, stocks, and investments with those of Thomas's estate and then selling them.[44]

One of the investments Passmore had made was in the Schuylkill Navigation Company, which had subsequently leased its canal works to the Philadelphia and Reading Railroad. In all, the trust held one hundred shares of preferred stock, more than $6,500 in loan certificates and a so-called boat-and-car loan of $3,000. The railroad declared bankruptcy. Passmore sued the railroad, but what he hoped to accomplish is unclear, for the railroad had already declared its insolvency.[45] The suit, it appears, should have made against the canal company, which had suspended payments of its debts and obligations.

It is difficult to explain Passmore's behavior in these matters. He most certainly had the experience to handle business affairs. Perhaps he merely made some unwise financial decisions, investing in speculative stocks, for example, in the hope of increasing the value of his father's trust. As far as it is known, the issue was never resolved legally. Was it a matter of poor judgment? Or, as his relations believed, financial chicanery?

To the public, which was undoubtedly unaware of his familial financial problems, Passmore continued to embrace noble, worthwhile causes. He remained active in the Abolition Society after the war, was involved in the Home for Destitute Colored Children and the Nurses' Home of Philadelphia. He also joined Mary Grew on the executive committee of the Pennsylvania Woman Suffrage Association. Together they worked on a petition calling for the enfranchisement of women that was submitted to a state constitutional convention held in 1873. The convention rejected the appeal to grant women voting rights but did provide a provision in a new state constitution that women over twenty-one years old were eligible for any office in, or management of, public schools.[46]

Mercie died on October 29, 1878. She was fifty-four years old. She and Passmore had been married thirty years. Of their four children, the youngest, Charles Sumner Williamson, a mechanical engineer by training, became noted in an avocation that he followed, entomology. In addition, his studies and interest in botany—he kept his own herbarium—led to the discovery of a new species of *Marshallia*, which he found on a field trip to Wilmington, North Carolina. It was named in his honor, *Marshallia Williamsonii*.[47]

It is uncertain whether it was before or after Mercie's death that Passmore cultivated the beard that he wore in his later years. Its generous hirsute character made it difficult to recognize him as the same thirty-something abolitionist agitator whose photograph, taken in prison, had been widely disseminated. Somehow or other, a reporter for the *Philadelphia Times* recognized Passmore—or maybe he was pointed out by an acquaintance—as Passmore was walking along Chestnut Street one autumn day in 1884, on the eve of that year's national elections. The reporter introduced himself and began asking questions.

The reporter's interview ran under the headline, "An Old Republican's Lament." Sixty-two years old at the time, Passmore complained to him about the "ravages of rheumatism" he was suffering and that he was terribly upset by the scandals that had rocked the Grant administration.[48] Passmore had remained loyal to the Republican Party, serving, for example, eight months after his release from Moyamensing as a delegate to the state convention in June 1856, which nominated John C. Fremont for president.[49] The party, however, had changed dramatically over the past thirty years. The Civil War had settled the issue of slavery, but Reconstruction had failed, leaving blacks with no voting privileges and little political power. On top of which, conservatives had taken control of the party. All of this bothered Passmore, but what was especially troubling to him was the corruption that colored the administration of Ulysses S. Grant. After Grant's second term, he switched his allegiance to the Democratic Party.[50] In what was for him a loquacious comment, Passmore told the reporter:

"Yes, I was at the cradle of the Republican Party, and I firmly believe in its principles, but the safety of business and of industry demands a change. The Republican Party that I helped to create amid much obloquy has fulfilled its mission and has degenerated into a mere spoilsmen's camp. It has centralized political power and wasted hundreds of millions to maintain authority. It has centralized wealth, making a few millionaires and many tramps. It has made our government the creature of great monopolies which have seized the lands of the homeless, and it has corrupted our political system until a thoroughly honest presidential candidate is not desired by those who nominate for the party. Note the fall from Lincoln, Chase, Seward, and others. . . . Cleveland is too honest for dishonest Democrats, and that is why tens of thousands of honest Republicans will vote for him, and that is why, I hope and believe, that Cleveland will be elected. Good day, sir."

And with that, the reporter added, "the veteran Republican of early days passed leisurely on his way."[51]

At one time, in 1860, Passmore owned real estate valued at $18,500 and personal property worth $12,000.[52] However, at the time of his death, on Thursday, February 28, 1895, five days after his seventy-third birthday, he was virtually penniless. He had been in failing health for several years, but his condition took a turn for the worse before Christmas. He had, however, been able on a few occasions to attend to business at his office on Arch Street, where cousin Edward Williamson had for some time joined him as a conveyancer. Passmore told his family that he was "almost worn out," but he insisted a few days before his death that he should not be considered "a sick man."

His unmarried daughter Mary Elizabeth, who had been born when he was in Moyamensing Prison, lived with him on Buttonwood Street. When he needed assistance, he would summon her to his upstairs bedroom by ringing a bell. On the morning of the twenty-eighth, he rang. She ran up the staircase. He had spent a good part of the night pacing back and forth. Mary helped him to return to his bed. Within a few minutes he passed away quietly, conscious to the last.[53]

When Passmore's will was admitted to probate several weeks later, its value consisted entirely of personal effects, amounting in value to virtually nothing.[54]

Even though he had renounced participation in Quaker religious services and observances, Passmore was permitted to be buried with his wife, Mercie, in a plot that his father, Thomas, had purchased in the Friends' South-Western Burial Ground, just across the Schuylkill River from Philadelphia in Upper Darby. It is a quiet, tree-shaded cemetery, with large, open, grassy spaces. The family plot, Lot 150 in Section B,[55] is on the west side of the cemetery's Central Avenue, close to where the narrow asphalt road turns into a dirt path. A red maple tree grows nearby. Buried together with the bodies of Passmore, Mercie and Thomas are the ashes of his daughter Sarah Emma Williamson Powell, who died in 1924 at the age of seventy. As is customary in Quaker cemeteries, the headstones are simple, low granite markers that sit barely six inches above the ground. The markers give an individual's name, date of birth and date of death. Thomas's marker is intact, but portions of Mercie's marker have eroded. The markers for Passmore and Sarah have disappeared entirely.

Few parts of the neighborhoods of Philadelphia where much of the action that took place in the story of the rescue of Jane Johnson resemble the way the city looked then. There are still the narrow streets below Independence Hall that run toward the Delaware River, and the abutting homes that line them existed then. But the site of the Anti-Slavery Society's office where William Still worked is now part of Independence Mall. The ornate district court courtroom on the second floor of Independence Hall that John Kintzing Kane had furnished no longer exists. The southwest corner of Seventh and Arch streets, where Passmore, Thomas and later Edward Williamson worked as conveyancers, now houses the imposing Federal Detention Center. Just across from it on Arch Street is the product of a new awareness about civil rights, the African American Museum. The section of Buttonwood Street where Passmore and Mercie resided became part of a small industrial park. A supermarket and its parking lot now occupy the land where Moyamensing Prison stood; only the barest traces of one of its walls remains behind an adjoining senior citizens' center. A high-rise commercial hotel now overlooks the Delaware River where Bloodgood's Hotel and the Walnut Street wharf—the site of Jane Johnson's rescue a century and a half ago—once rested.

At his death, Passmore Williamson was president of the Pennsylvania Abolition Society. Fittingly, its vice president, William Still, drafted the society's testimonial to him:

> [Passmore] was a faithful member of the Pennsylvania Society
> for promoting the Abolition of Slavery, the Relief of Free Negroes
> unlawfully held in Bondage, and the Improvement of the Con-
> dition of the African Race for nearly half a century. He had
> reached the age of 73 years and was President of the Society
> at the time of his death. . . .
>
> He found himself unpopular with the oppressor, but beloved
> by the oppressed.
>
> He stood between slavery and liberty in rescuing a mother
> and her child[ren] from a United States Minister and a slave-
> holder, though he suffered thereby privations and imprisonment.
>
> He practically illustrated that slaves can not breathe where
> Penn bequeathed civil and religious liberty. . . .
>
> No wavering, no weakness, almost uncompromising, all knew
> where to find him when it came to a question of right, of truth,
> of justice, and of freedom and humanity.[56]

Epilogue

That voice shall roll on, 'mong the hills of the North,
In murmurs more loud till its thunders break forth . . .
'Twill cry, in God's name, "Go break every yoke,"—
Like the tempests of Heaven, shaking mountain and sea,
Shall the North tell the South, "Let the bondman go free."

"I'll be free, I'll be free!" *Anti-Slavery Harp*, 20
(to be sung to the air "Sweet Afton")

Some two weeks after Passmore Williamson's release from Moyamensing Prison, Lucretia Mott wrote her sister Martha, "We talked over Passmore, wh. like everythg else is becoming an old story."[1]

An old story? Like everything else? Mott completely misjudged the impact that the case against Passmore Williamson represented. Like other dramas involving slavery—escapes, recaptures, the personal courage of blacks and whites who helped those in bondage—the rescue of Jane Johnson and the ordeal that Passmore Williamson experienced in prison turned the words of abolitionists into human images. Like the effect that Harriet Beecher Stowe's *Uncle Tom's Cabin* enjoyed, the consequences were enormous. Slavery was not an abstract institution. It involved human beings, people—young, old, even those still unborn—who lived or would be born into a world without a future. Their stories compelled northerners to face their complicity with slavery and, at the same time, underscored the ruling Democratic administration's lack of moral justification for the institution. Describing abolitionists as vicious fanatics was counter-productive, making it seem that the men and women who helped runaways were more principled, honest, and even law-abiding than the Democratic officials who attacked them. If anything, the overreaction of southerners and their prime Democrat supporters in the North to these events proved self-defeating.

The conflict that broke out in 1861 was ostensibly about states' rights, about who governs whom, but its genesis was in the compromise over human bondage reflected in the federal constitution. War finally settled the question of slavery, outlawing it forever. Unfortunately, however, the memory of slavery—the scores of years that it was tolerated, the trauma and indignities that generations of blacks suffered as forced laborers, the strained, psychologically damaging relationship between blacks and whites that it promoted—left America with a legacy of racial bias that, a century and a half after the Civil War, remains unresolved in our own time. It is reflected in segregation, whether in housing or schools; in discrimination, whether in job opportunities or in financial assistance; and in the persistent belief among too many Americans that blacks are inherently inferior. In that sense, slavery survives, omnipresent, the subtext of today's racism.

NOTES

There's a good time coming boys,
A good time coming;
The pen shall supersede the sword,
And right, not might shall be the lord,
In the good time coming.

"There's a Good Time Coming,"
Anti-Slavery Harp, 39

There are a number of discrepancies in the spelling of names in accounts of the rescue of Jane Johnson and the legal battles that occurred as a result. For example, Friedman, the last name of William Still's brother, is sometimes spelled Freedman; Custis, the black dock worker who helped rescue Jane, sometimes becomes Custiss or Curtis. The most common error occurs with regard to Passmore Williamson's wife, Mercie. Her name often appears as Mercy, an understandable mistake. When Kane is spelled Cain, it is intentional.

There are also errors with regard to dates. For example, John Hill Wheeler's birth date, as given in Joseph S. Fowler's biographical sketch introducing Wheeler's own "Reminiscences and Memoirs," is incorrectly given as August 2, 1806, not August 6, 1806. The birth date of Williamson's daughter Mary Elizabeth is similarly given as August 2, 1855, in the genealogical form made out by a family descendant in the 1950s. She was born on August 29 of that year. Some newspapers of 1855 incorrectly gave the date of Jane Johnson's appearance at the trial in Philadelphia as August 29. She testified on August 30.

Several of the significant individuals involved in the rescue wrote or testified differently when it came to details. For example, in his affidavit requesting a writ of habeas corpus to be served on Williamson, Wheeler gives Jane Johnson's age as thirty-five, the age of her son Daniel as twelve, and Isaiah's as seven. To confuse matters, during her surprise appearance at the trial of those who had helped rescue her, Jane Johnson identified Isaiah as being a year younger than Daniel, who was ten years old. Yet in the petition she had made out on July 31, she says Isaiah is between six and seven years old. Similarly, at the trial she said Williamson beckoned to her on board the ferryboat, but in her petition she said it was William Still who beckoned to her. It is possible, of course, that at the trial she was trying to protect Still by mentioning Williamson as the instigator. It is also possible that with the passage of time, the recollection of participants and witnesses became a bit clouded.

The most flagrant error was the identity, in *The New York Times* of August 30, 1855, of Williamson's attorney, Charles Gilpin. The newspaper identifies him as Attorney General of the United States under President Martin Van Buren in 1840. That was Henry D. Gilpin.

The following abbreviations are used in the notes:

ALBUM—Album, plus newspaper clippings, *Case of Passmore Williamson vs. John K. Kane,* Historical Society of Pennsylvania

ATWOOD—Williamson family papers and memorabilia, Shirley Atwood, Virginia Beach, Virginia

CASE—*Case of Passmore Williamson; Report of the Proceedings on the Writ of Habeas Corpus, Issued by the Hon. John K. Kane, in the Case of the United States of America ex rel. John H. Wheeler vs. Passmore Williamson, Including the Several Opinions Delivered, and the Arguments of Counsel, Reported by Arthur Cannon* (Philadelphia: Uriah Hunt & Son, 1856). http://memory.loc .gov. Search: Passmore Williamson

CENTRAL—Central Philadelphia Monthly Meeting of Friends

CHESTER—Chester County Historical Society, West Chester, Pennsylvania

DIARY—Papers of John Hill Wheeler (ms62-4529, Microfilm reels 1 and 2), Library of Congress

FLYNN—Katherine E. Flynn, "Jane Johnson, Found! But Is She 'Hannah Crafts'? The Search for the Author of *The Bondwoman's Narrative,*" *National Genealogical Quarterly* 90 (September 2003): 35–55

FRIENDS—Friends Historical Library, Swarthmore College

HARP—William Wells Brown, *Anti-Slavery Harp: A Collection of Songs for Anti-Slavery Meetings* (Boston: Bela Marsh, 1849)

HISTORY—Historical Society of Pennsylvania, Philadelphia

KANE—John Kintzing Kane and Robert Patterson Kane Legal Papers, American Philosophical Society, Philadelphia

LETTERS—Letters, Passmore Williamson, Chester County Historical Society

MOTT—Beverly Wilson Palmer, *Selected Letters of Lucretia Coffin Mott* (Urbana: University of Illinois Press, 2002)

NARRATIVE—[Mary Grew] *Narrative of Facts in the Case of Passmore Williamson* (Philadelphia: Pennsylvania Anti-Slavery Society, 1855)

SMITH—Robert Houston Smith, *The Passmores in America: A Quaker Family through Six Generations* (Lewiston, N.Y.: E. Mellen Press, 1992)

STILL—William Still, *Still's Underground Rail Road Records: Revised Edition with a Life of the Author* (Philadelphia: William Still, 1886)

WHEELER—John H. Wheeler, *Reminiscences and Memoirs of North Carolina and Eminent North Carolinians* (Baltimore: Genealogical Publishing Company, 1966)

Preface

1. Richard S. Newman, *The Transformation of American Abolitionism: Fighting Slavery in the Early Republic* (Chapel Hill: University of North Carolina Press, 2002), 179.

2. John Stauffer, *The Black Hearts of Men: Radical Abolitionists and the Transformation of Race* (Cambridge, Mass.: Harvard University Press, 2002), 1.

Chapter 1—The Chronicler

1. STILL, 87, 90. The description of what Still was wearing is based on the illustration of the rescue of Jane Johnson aboard the ferryboat *Washington*.

2. R. C. Smedley, *History of the Underground Railroad in Chester and the Neighboring Counties of Pennsylvania* (New York: Negro Universities Press, 1968), 218.

3. William Wells Brown, *The Black Man: His Antecedents, His Genius, and His Achievements* (New York: T. Hamilton, 1863), 213.

4. STILL, 86–87.

5. George and Willene Hendrick, eds. *Fleeing for Freedom: Stories of the Underground Railroad, as Told by Levi Coffin and William Still* (Chicago: Ivan R. Dee, 2004), 10, 6.

6. Fergus M. Bordewich, *Bound for Canaan: The Underground Railroad and the War for the Soul of America* (New York: Amistad, 2005), 5.

7. *Statistical View of the United States . . . Compendium of the Seventh Census* (Washington: Beverley Tucker, 1854), 82.

8. Robert W. Johannsen, *To the Halls of the Montezumas: The Mexican War in the American Imagination* (New York: Oxford University Press, 1985), 215, 217.

9. Julie Winch, "Philadelphia and the Other Underground Railroad," *Pennsylvania Magazine of History and Biography* 111, no. 1 (January 1987): 3.

10. Thomas P. Slaughter, *Bloody Dawn: The Christiana Riot and Racial Violence in the Antebellum North* (New York: Oxford University Press, 1991), xi.

11. William J. Switala, *Underground Railroad in Pennsylvania* (Mechanicsburg, Pa.: Stackpole Books, 2001), 151.

12. Judith Bentley, *Dear Friend: Thomas Garrett & William Still, Collaborators on the Underground Railroad* (New York: Cobblehill Books, 1997), 29. The widow's name was Mrs. E. Langdon Elwyn, whose home was on West Penn Square.

13. William C. Kashatus, "Two Stationmasters on the Underground Railroad: A Tale of Black and White," *Pennsylvania Heritage* (Fall 2001): 7.

14. STILL, xviii.

15. Ronaldson's Row is also described as being between Ninth and Tenth streets above Shippen Street, which is today's Bainbridge Street.

16. STILL, xxiv.

17. Ibid., ii. The biographer was James P. Boyd.

18. Ibid., 659.

19. Joseph A. Borome, "The Vigilant Committee of Philadelphia," *Pennsylvania Magazine of History and Biography* 92, no. 2 (April 1968): 329.

20. Benjamin Quarles, *Black Abolitionists* (New York: Oxford University Press, 1969), 156.

21. STILL, xxviii.

22. *Provincial Freeman,* July 8, 1854.

23. Larry Gara, "Friends and the Underground Railroad," *Quaker History* 51, no. 1 (Spring 1962): 12.

24. Bentley, *Dear Friend,* 35.

Chapter 2—The Quaker

1. Passmore Williamson, in a letter to an aunt on August 6, 1846, wrote that his mother was ill and that "it became very evident to her Drs and others attending about her that the last struggle was rapidly approaching . . . she breathed her last between 12 and 1 o'clock this morning," LETTERS. Thomas Williamson subsequently married Deborah M. Garrigues, who was born in 1801 and was in her mid-forties when his first wife died. Deborah died July 2, 1876, in Haverford, Pa. (See SMITH, 198.)

2. *McElroy's Philadelphia Directory* (Philadelphia: Edward C. and John Biddle, 1855).

3. *National Anti-Slavery Standard,* October 13, 1855.

4. CASE, 20.

5. *National Anti-Slavery Standard,* September 29, 1855. Thomas Williamson is quoted in answer to an editorial critical of his son's action and of abolitionists in general that appeared in the *North American and U.S. Gazette.* He describes in detail Passmore's reaction to the note that William Still bore. According to SMITH, 198, the elder Williamson had been a bookkeeper at the Westtown Boarding School in Chester County and subsequently taught school.

6. STILL, 87. Still is quoting from a letter he wrote on July 30, 1855, to the *New York Tribune.*

7. *National Anti-Slavery Standard,* September 29, 1855.

8. "Slavery in the Courts," Association of the Bar of the City of New York City, 2005. http://www.nycbar.org/Library/FeaturedExhibitions2.htm.

9. *National Anti-Slavery Standard,* September 29, 1855.

10. Ibid.

11. Ibid., October 13, 1855.

12. STILL, xxxiv.

13. The physical description of Passmore Williamson is based on photographs of him.

14. Uncited, undated newspaper clipping of letter of August 4, 1855, originally published in the *New York Tribune,* ALBUM.

15. *National Anti-Slavery Standard,* October 13, 1855.

16. Mercie Williamson to Passmore Williamson, February 22, 1850, LETTERS.

17. SMITH, 198n.

18. Ibid., 22, 26.

19. Ibid., 9n.

20. Ibid., 195, 197.

21. Ibid., 198. Passmore had two brothers—Rest Cope, who was born May 8, 1832, and died on August 18 of that year, and Isaac, who was born April 13, 1826. There is no record of what happened to Isaac, but he evidently did not survive childhood. Passmore's sister Ann married Amos Stackhouse, his sister Mary wed Paschal Coggins.

22. Ibid.

23. *Friends' Weekly Intelligencer,* October 5, 1850.

24. SMITH, 120.

25. NARRATIVE, 35.

26. Elizabeth M. Geffen, "Industrial Development and Social Crisis 1841–1854," in Russell F. Weigley, *Philadelphia: A 300-Year History* (New York: W. W. Norton, 1982), 355.

27. *Philadelphia Public Ledger,* March 1, 1895, ATWOOD.

28. Margaret Hope Bacon, *History of the Pennsylvania Society for Promoting the Abolition of Slavery; Relief of Negroes Unlawfully Held in Bondage; and for Improving the Condition of the African Race* (Philadelphia: Pennsylvania Abolition Society, 1959), appendix iv.

29. Newman, *Transformation of American Abolitionism,* 130.

30. Margaret Hope Bacon, *History of the Pennsylvania Society,* 10.

31. Stauffer, *Black Hearts of Men,* 1.

32. Julie Winch, *A Gentleman of Color: The Life of James Forten* (New York: Oxford University Press, 2002), 257.

33. Henry Mayer, *All on Fire: William Lloyd Garrison and the Abolition of Slavery* (New York: St. Martin's Press, 1998), 438–39.

34. Philadelphia Monthly Meeting Minutes, 1845–1857: Minutes of January 27, 1848; Minutes of February 24, 1848; Minutes of March 25, 1848; Minutes of April 27, 1848; Minutes of May 30, 1848, FRIENDS.

35. *Philadelphia Public Ledger,* March 1, 1895, ATWOOD.

36. August 8, 1848, is the marriage date given on the Gilbert Cope Foundation form filled out by a Williamson descendant in the 1950s. However, there are discrepancies between the dates on the form and those on earlier sources.

37. Spring Street Monthly Meeting, Minutes, December 22, 1848, FRIENDS.

38. Passmore and Mercie Williamson lived at 720 Buttonwood Street. Apparently the number was changed when there was a general renaming of the streets in the city. He was subsequently listed as residing at 72 Buttonwood.

39. Pennsylvania Abolition Society Minute Book, vol. 4, 1847–1916 (reel 2), HISTORY. Passmore Williamson's name appears on February 10, 1851 (p. 66), an undated entry (p. 72), March 25, 1852 (p. 75), and another undated entry (p. 84).

40. Theodore Hershberg, "Free Blacks in Antebellum Philadelphia: A Study of Ex-Slaves, Freeborn, and Socioeconomic Decline," in *African Americans in Pennsylvania: Shifting Historical Perspectives,* ed. Joe William Turner and Eric Ledell Smith (University Park: Pennsylvania Historical and Museum Commission and Pennsylvania State University Press, 1997), 216.

41. STILL, 611–12.

42. *National Anti-Slavery Standard,* September 29, 1855. Thomas Williamson wrote, "Within, I think, three minutes afterward, Passmore again threw down his pen."

43. Unless otherwise noted, the description of the encounters at Bloodgood's Hotel and on boarding the ferryboat are a combination of CASE, 9, and STILL, 87.

Chapter 3—The Slave Woman

1. FLYNN, 190.

2. Unless otherwise noted, the accounts relating to Jane Johnson's arrival in Philadelphia, the actions and quotes of her and Wheeler, are an amalgam of STILL, 94–95; NARRATIVE, 14–15; and the petition she endorsed, CASE, 164.

3. FLYNN, 184.

4. The conflict with regard to Jane Johnson's birthplace and age are from NARRATIVE, 14, and FLYNN, 175.

5. STILL, 91.

6. NARRATIVE, 3.

7. Dorothy Porter Wesley and Constance Porter Uzelac, ed., *William Cooper Nell: Selected Writing 1832–1874* (Baltimore: Black Classic Press, 2002), 420.

8. *National Anti-Slavery Standard,* September 8, 1855.

9. DIARY. Wheeler in his entries for both July 10, 1855, and July 31, 1855, says it took him six hours to reach Washington from Philadelphia. The return trip on August 2, 1855, took seven and a half hours. In his diary for August

11, 1855, Wheeler says it took him five hours to reach New York from Philadelphia.

10. STILL, 92.

11. Thomas J. Scharf and Thompson Westcott, *History of Philadelphia, 1609–1884* (Philadelphia: L. H. Everts, 1884), 3:2183.

12. STILL, 92.

13. *Philadelphia Public Ledger,* March 1, 1895.

Chapter 4—The Rescue

1. The rescue of Jane Johnson and her two sons was recounted by no less than six participants and four eyewitnesses. The participants' accounts include court testimony, affidavits, or petitions as well as later descriptions of the incident. William Still recorded one recollection, and there are four accounts by Passmore Williamson, one by Thomas Williamson, three by Jane Johnson, and three by John Hill Wheeler. The sixth participant was the hack driver who drove Jane Johnson and the children from Dock Street. The events of the rescue happened so quickly that participants as well as eyewitnesses differed in some details when describing what occurred, but they all agreed on the nature of what was said and the general outline of the event.

The chief sources for the rescue are CASE, NARRATIVE, and the *Philadelphia City Bulletin,* July 28, 1855. Other major sources are ALBUM, *Case of Passmore Williamson vs. John K. Kane* plus newspaper clippings, Historical Society of Pennsylvania; *National Anti-Slavery Standard,* September 29, 1855, quoting a letter by Thomas Williamson in answer to an editorial in the *North American and U.S. Gazette;* various entries in DIARY; SMITH, 198–99, and STILL, 87–92.

Additional sources are: *Annual Report presented to the American Anti-Slavery Society* (New York: American Anti-Slavery Society, 1856), 24–44, FRIENDS; Ralph Lowell Eckert, "Antislavery Martyrdom: The Ordeal of Passmore Williamson," *Pennsylvania Magazine of History and Biography* 100 (1976): 521–38; Phil Lapsansky, *The Liberation of Jane Johnson* (Philadelphia: Library Company, 2003); *National Era,* September 27, 1855; Pamela C. Powell, "The Case of Passmore Williamson," in *The Daguerreian Annual 2000* (N.p.: Daguerreian Society, 2000), 124–35.

2. There are minor inconsistencies in some of the reports. For example, it is clear from all the initial accounts that Jane Johnson and the children were seated beside Wheeler on the hurricane deck of the ferryboat, out in the open. But in a description of the event forty years later, Passmore Williamson said he came upon the group "in the cabin" and that she was seated "on the floor." In retelling the story, I have tried to reconcile such differences, noting the inconsistencies in footnotes.

3. Passmore Williamson to "Dear Uncle," August 6, 1855, LETTERS. This letter as well as others cited that are addressed to "Dear Sir" were all apparently written to Williamson's uncle, William Williamson. Similarly, letters

from Passmore's cousin, Edward Williamson, to "Dear Sir" are also apparently addressed to William Williamson, who was Edward's father.

4. James McIlhone identifies Custis as having the scar on his neck. From affidavit he made out in Wheeler's behalf and attested to by Alderman Freeman on August 6, 1855, as recounted in uncited newspaper clipping dated August 7, in Album.

5. *Philadelphia Public Ledger,* July 21, 1855, Album.

6. Ibid., see also Case, 7–8

7. *Philadelphia Public Ledger,* July 21, 1855, Album.

8. Uncited newspaper clipping dated August 7, in Album.

9. Minute Book, Pennsylvania Abolition Society, vol. 4, 1847–1916 (reel 30, p. 368) History.

10. Philadelphia Public Ledger, July 21, 1855, Album.

11. *Laws of the Commonwealth of Pennsylvania, 1847* (Harrisburg, Pa.: J. M. G. Lescure, 1847), 208.

Chapter 5—The City

1. Richard F. Engs and Randall M. Miller, *The Birth of the Grand Old Party: The Republicans' First Generation* (Philadelphia: University of Pennsylvania Press, 2002), 34.

2. "Historical Information for Philadelphia," USGS, http://mcmcweb.er .usgs.gov/de_river_basin/phil/modeling.html. September 6. 2006. Go to study area. Go to geography.

3. Ibid., 6.

4. Scharf and Westcott, *History of Philadelphia,* 1:719.

5. Benjamin C. Bacon, *Statistics of the Colored People of Philadelphia* (Philadelphia: T. Ellwood Chapman, 1856), 13–14.

6. *Statistical View,* 296–97.

7. Benjamin C. Bacon, *Statistics,* 13–15. The Abolition Society study was undertaken in 1853.

8. Bentley, *Dear Friend,* 29.

9. Russell F. Weigley, "The Border City in Civil War 1854–1865," in Weigley, *Philadelphia: A 300-Year History,* 383.

10. Julie Winch, *The Elite of Our People: Joseph Willson's Sketches of Black Upper-Class Life in Antebellum Philadelphia* (University Park: Pennsylvania State University Press, 2000), 122.

11. Switala, *Underground Railroad,* 149.

12. Weigley, "Border City," 386.

13. Gary B. Nash, *First City: Philadelphia and the Forging of Historical Memory* (Philadelphia: University of Pennsylvania Press, 2002), 192. Joseph Sturge, who visited in 1841, is quoted.

14. Slaughter, *Bloody Dawn,* 24.

15. Anna Coxe Toogood, "Underground Railroad and Anti-Slavery Movement," National Register Amendment, Independence National Historical

Park, September 2000. http://www.nps.gov/inde/archeology/nramend.htm. September 6, 2006.

16. Ibid., 3.

17. Winch, *A Gentleman of Color,* 285, 296.

18. *Constitution of Pennsylvania 1838,* Duquesne University Law School, http://www.swarthmore.edu/humanities/kjohnsol/pennsylvaniaconstitution .htm. September 6, 2006.

19. Ira V. Brown, *Mary Grew, Abolitionist and Feminist, 1813–1896* (Selinsgrove, Pa.: Susquehanna University Press, 1991), 255.

20. Nilgun Anadolu Okur, "Underground Railroad in Philadelphia, 1830–1860," *Journal of Black Studies* 25, no. 5 (May 1995): 548.

21. Nash, *First City,* 169.

22. Benjamin C. Bacon, *Statistics,* 11.

23. Weigley, "Border City," 386.

24. Geffen, "Industrial Development," 354.

25. Benjamin C. Bacon, *Statistics,* 9.

26. Geffen, "Industrial Development," 307.

27. Weigley, "Border City," op cit, 374–75. The visitor was Charles Godfrey Leland.

28. Scharf and Westcott, *History of Philadelphia,* 1:693–94.

Chapter 6—The Slave Master

1. DIARY, July 17, 1855. Wheeler identifies the other guests as Gov. Gregory of Virginia, Judge Blair Huntingdon, and a judge of the Court of Claims whose name he apparently hoped to enter in his diary, but the space for it remains blank.

2. A Compilation of the Messages and Papers of the Presidents (Washington, D.C.: Bureau of National Literature, 11:675–76.

3. Mayer, *All on Fire,* 441.

4. Hannah Crafts, *The Bondwoman's Narrative,* ed. Henry Louis Gates Jr. (New York: Warner Books, 2002), li–lii.

5. Unless otherwise noted, the description of Wheeler that follows as well as details of his life are from the biographical sketch by Joseph S. Fowler that introduces WHEELER, i–x. Fowler, a former senator from Tennessee, obviously knew and felt favorably toward Wheeler. His sketch, entitled "Memoir of the Author," is rampant with hyperbole.

6. *Frederick Douglass' Paper,* August 31, 1855.

7. FLYNN, 185.

8. Crafts, *Bondwoman's Narrative,* xlvi.

9. Dumas Malone, ed., *Dictionary of American Biography* X:2 (New York: Charles Scribner's Sons, 1936), 50.

10. Crafts, *Bondwoman's Narrative,* xlvi.

11. DIARY, August 13, 1855.

12. The details of Wheeler's trip to Nicaragua are covered in DIARY, entries October 19 through December 19, 1854.

13. DIARY, December 21, 1854.

14. Ibid., June 20, 1855.

15. The description of Wheeler's voyage home and his illness is taken from DIARY, entries June 23, 1855, through July 12, 1855.

16. The description of Wheeler's return visits to New York, Philadelphia, and Washington is taken from DIARY, entries July 8, 1855, through July 17, 1855.

17. STILL, 90.

18. Crafts, *Bondwoman's Narrative*, li.

19. Brenda E. Stevenson, *Life in Black and White: Family and Community in the Slave South* (New York: Oxford University Press, 1996), 180.

20. Robert William Fogel and Stanley L. Engerman, *Time on the Cross: The Economics of American Negro Slavery* (New York: W. W. Norton, 1974), 76 (fig. 18, graph).

21. One would expect Wynkoop, who would have been in his early forties when the Civil War broke out, to have played a role in the war. But he died on December 13, 1857, while hunting birds for his wife's supper. He was accidently shot and succumbed in half an hour.

Chapter 7—The Judge

1. John K. Kane to Geo. M. Justice, September 22, 1855, KANE.

2. W. U. Hensel, *The Christiana Riot and the Treason Trials of 1851* (Lancaster, Pa.: New Era Printing Company, 1911), 57.

3. Opinion of the Court, by Judge Kane, U.S. vs. Samuel Allen, May 9, 1854. Records of the U.S. Circuit Court, Eastern District of Pennsylvania Habeas Corpus 1848–1862. Group 21, National Archives, Mid-Atlantic Region, Philadelphia.

4. Nicholas B. Wainwright, ed., *A Philadelphia Perspective: The Diary of Sidney George Fisher Covering the Years 1834–1871* (Philadelphia: Historical Society of Pennsylvania, 1967), 390.

5. John Kintzing Kane, *Autobiography of the Honorable John K. Kane* (Philadelphia: Privately printed [College Offset Press], 1949), 1.

6. Ibid., 5.

7. George Washington Corner, *Doctor Kane of the Arctic Seas* (Philadelphia: Temple University Press, 1972), 9.

8. Kane, *Autobiography*, 19.

9. Corner, *Doctor Kane*, 11, 13.

10. Ibid., 12.

11. Hensel, *Christiana Riot*, 52.

12. Kane, *Autobiography*, 22.

13. Ibid., iv.

14. Henry Simpson, *Lives of Eminent Philadelphians, Now Deceased* (Philadelphia: William Brotherhead, 1859), 617.

15. Stanley W. Campbell, *The Slave Catchers: Enforcement of the Fugitive Slave Law, 1850–1860* (Chapel Hill: University of North Carolina Press, 1970), 98.

16. Annual Report, Pennsylvania Anti-Slavery Society, 19, FRIENDS.

17. Hensel, *Christiana Riot,* 57.

18. Kane, *Autobiography,* 79–80.

19. Annual Report, Pennsylvania Anti-Slavery Society, 23–24, FRIENDS.

20. Passmore Williamson to "Dear Uncle," August 6, 1855, LETTERS.

21. *Philadelphia Public Ledger,* March 1, 1895, ATWOOD.

22. STILL, xxi.

23. Slaughter, *Bloody Dawn,* ix–x.

24. Campbell, *Slave Catchers,* 153.

25. Hensel, *Christiana Riot,* 52.

26. Minute Book, Pennsylvania Abolition Society, vol. 4, 1847–1916 (reel 2), 72, HISTORY.

27. Hensel, *Christiana Riot,* 79.

28. Robert J. Brent, *Report of Attorney General Brent, to His Excellency, Gov. Lowe, in Relation to the Christiana Treason Trials, in the Circuit Court of the United States, Held at Philadelphia* (Annapolis, Md.: T. E. Martin, 1852), 8, 16.

29. *Provincial Freeman,* December 4, 1851.

30. Hensel, *Christiana Riot,* 85–86.

31. Slaughter, *Bloody Dawn,* 136.

32. Gara, "Friends," 16.

33. Samuel Joseph May, *The Fugitive Slave Law and Its Victims* (New York: American Anti-Slavery Society, 1861), 29–30.

34. Oscar Jewell Harvey and Ernest Gray Smith, *A History of Wilkes-Barre, Luzerne County, Pennsylvania* (Wilkes-Barre, Pa.: Wilkes-Barre *Times-Leader,* 1929), 4:1944–45.

35. True Bill, January Session 1854, January 4, 1854, Records of U.S. Circuit Court, Eastern District of Pennsylvania, Habeas Corpus 1848–1862. Record Group 21, National Archives, Mid-Atlantic Region, Philadelphia.

36. *National Era,* November 24, 1853.

37. Samuel Joseph May, *The Fugitive Slave Law and Its Victims* (New York: American Anti-Slavery Society, 1861), 31.

38. NARRATIVE, 8.

Chapter 8—Consequences

1. Unless otherwise noted, details of Passmore Williamson's return after the rescue of Jane Johnson, his departure from his office, and the visit of the deputy marshals with the writ of habeas corpus are from Thomas Williamson's account in the *National Anti-Slavery Standard,* September 29, 1855.

2. Switala, *Underground Railroad,* 146.

3. STILL, 92.

4. Unless otherwise noted, the legal proceedings of July 19 and 20, 1855, are from CASE, 4–11.

5. *National Anti-Slavery Standard,* September 29, 1855.

6. STILL, 92.

7. DIARY, July 19, 1855. This appears to be a misdating by Wheeler. Passmore Williamson did not appear in court until the next day, July 20. There is also a discrepancy in Mary Grew's NARRATIVE, when she writes that the first court session took place on July 18. That is not possible: that was the date of the rescue of Jane Johnson.

8. *Philadelphia Public Ledger,* July 21, 1855, ALBUM.

9. NARRATIVE, 9.

10. Uncited newspaper clipping dated August 7, ALBUM.

11. *National Era,* July 26, 1855, quoting the *Philadelphia Bulletin* of July 20, 1855.

12. Wheeler's activities are from DIARY, July 19–27, 1855.

13. *National Anti-Slavery Standard,* August 4, 1855.

14. *Philadelphia Sunday Dispatch,* September 9, 1855.

15. *Philadelphia Bulletin,* July 28, 1855.

16. NARRATIVE, 12–13.

17. DIARY, July 19, 1855. Again, this should probably be July 20. Had Wheeler written the entry at a later date and thus misremembered the sequence of events?

18. Wheeler's activities the week of July 20–26, 1855 are from DIARY for those entries.

19. Details of the court proceeding on July 27, 1855 are from CASE, 12–15.

20. Edward Williamson to "Dear Sir," August 13, 1855, LETTERS.

21. *Frederick Douglass' Paper,* August 3, 1855.

22. Margaret Hope Bacon, *History of the Pennsylvania Society,* appendix iii.

23. STILL, 755–56.

24. Passmore Williamson's version of Francis Wynkoop's offer on the ride to Moyamensing is from a clipping of the *Evening Argus,* August 24, 1855, Visitors Book, CHESTER.

25. John K. Kane to "Hon. Mr. Mason," August 5, 1855, KANE.

26. John K. Kane to George M. Justice, Esq., September 22, 1855, KANE.

27. Passmore Williamson to "Dear Uncle," August 6, 1855, LETTERS.

Chapter 9—Pandora's Box

1. Richard Peters, *Report of the Case of Edward Prigg against the Commonwealth of Pennsylvania: Argued and Adjudged in the Supreme Court of the United States, at January Term, 1842* (Philadelphia: L. Johnson, 1842), 5.

2. Ibid., 92.

3. Jane H. Pease and William H. Pease. "Confrontation and Abolition in the 1850s," *Journal of American History* 58, no. 4 (March, 1972): 931.

4. CASE, 14.

5. Eric Longley, "'States' Rights': Do We Have It All Wrong?" http://www.civilwarinteractive.com/ArticleStatesRights.htm. September 6, 2006.

6. Annual Report, American Anti-Slavery Society, FRIENDS, 24.

7. *New York Times*, August 30, 1855.

8. *National Era*, November 22, 1855. The letter is dated November 5.

9. Anonymous letter, n.d., Visitors Book, CHESTER.

10. *Daily Pennsylvanian*, July 20, 1855.

11. Ibid., September 8, 1855.

12. *National Anti-Slavery Standard*, August 18, 1855. The *New York Evening Mirror* is quoted.

13. Malone, *Dictionary of American Biography*, III: 558.

14. Pease and Pease, "Confrontation and Abolition," 932.

15. Uncited newspaper clipping, ALBUM.

16. Mahlon K. Anderson to John K. Kane, November 2, 1855, KANE.

17. "A friend" to "Judge Cane," August 2, 1855, KANE.

18. *New York Times*, August 7, 1855.

19. *Frederick Douglass' Paper*, August 3, 1855.

20. *National Anti-Slavery Standard*, August 18, 1855.

21. Ibid., July 28, 1855.

22. *National Era*, August 30, 1855.

23. Randall O. Hudson and James C. Duram, "The *New York Daily Tribune* and Passmore Williamson's Case: A Study in the Use of Northern States' Rights," *Wichita State University Bulletin* 50, no. 4 (November 1974): 4–5.

24. Uncited, undated newspaper clipping, KANE.

25. Uncited, undated clipping of poem, KANE.

26. *Frederick Douglass' Paper*, August 3, 1855.

27. *Provincial Freeman*, September 22, 1855. The *Free Presbyterian* is quoted.

28. "A friend to Humanity" to "Judge Kane," August 18, 1855, KANE.

29. "A Wife & Mother" to "Judge Kane," September 8, 1855, KANE.

30. Rev. William W. Patton, *Thoughts for Christians, Suggested by the Case of Passmore Williamson* (Hartford, Conn.: Montague & Co., 1855), 15–16.

31. *Frederick Douglass' Paper*, August 24, 1855.

32. Albany, New York, *Evening Journal*, March 9, 1857.

33. *Provincial Freeman*, August 22, 1855. The *New York Tribune* is quoted.

Chapter 10—Moyamensing

1. Henry Schenck Tanner, *New Picture of Philadelphia or the Stranger's Guide to the City and Adjoining Districts* (New York: T. R. Tranner, 1844), 94.

2. Winch, *Elite of Our People*, 24–25.

3. Theodore Dreiser, *The Financier* (New York: Harper & Brothers, 1912), 596.

4. Tanner, *New Picture of Philadelphia,* 94–95.

5. Ibid., 242.

6. "Philadelphia Neighborhoods and Place Names, L–P." http://www.phila .gov/phils/docs/otherinfo/pname2.htm. September 6, 2006.

7. Scharf & Wescott, *History of Philadelphia,* 1:717.

8. *History of the Trial of Castner Hanway and Others for Treason at Philadelphia in November, 1851* (Philadelphia: Uriah Hunt & Sons, 1852), 48. The two escapees were Peter Washington and John Clark.

9. The gibbet was transferred to the Atwater Kent Museum in Philadelphia in the 1940s. It had been intended for Thomas Wilkinson, who was to be hung on Windmill Island in the Delaware River off Market Street, but a number of citizens signed a petition for his release. The gibbet was originally hung in the Walnut Street Prison.

10. Ralph Lowell Eckert, "Antislavery Martyrdom: The Ordeal of Passmore Williamson," *Pennsylvania Magazine of History and Biography* 100 (1976): 532. The previous occupant of Cell 71 was Andrew Heller (Record Group 38, Ledger, p. 560, Philadelphia City Archives). The only reference to Passmore Williamson is in Record Group 38, Prison Daily Occurrences, July 21, 1854, to September 11, 1855. On page 501, a notation for July 27 reads: "Passmore Williamson-Contempt-U.S. Marshal." It is evidently a record of his being brought to Moyamensing by Francis Wynkoop. The City Archives are in dreadful shape and ill-managed. As a result, one cannot find Williamson's name in the Index of Prisoners Ledger or the Receiving Description Ledger. The Sentence Docket Ledger skips from June 30 to August 7, 1855. The Medical Journal, Discharge Index and Discharge Docket for the period that he was in Moyamensing are missing.

11. *National Anti-Slavery Standard,* August 11, 1855.

12. Passmore Williamson to "Dear Uncle," August 6, 1855, LETTERS.

13. *National Anti-Slavery Standard,* August 18, 1855.

14. Passmore Williamson to "Dear Uncle," August 6, 1855, LETTERS.

15. Passmore Williamson to "Dear Wife" (Mercie Williamson), undated but apparently written on August 15, 1855, because of his reference to the Supreme Court meeting the next day, LETTERS. Mercie visited her husband on Saturday, August 4, according to Edward Williamson's letter of August 6, 1855, to "Dear Sir," LETTERS. Other visits took place on Saturday, August 11, according to an uncited August 14 newspaper clipping, ALBUM, as well as on Sunday, August 12, according to another of Edward Williamson's letters to "Dear Sir," August 13, 1855, LETTERS.

16. Passmore Williamson to "Dear Wife," undated, LETTERS.

17. Edward Williamson to "Dear Sir,"August 6, 1855, LETTERS.

18. *National Anti-Slavery Standard,* August 25, 1855.

19. Passmore Williamson to "Dear Cousin," August 3, 1855, LETTERS. This and subsequent letters to "Dear Cousin" that are hereafter cited were evidently written to George Pyle, a cousin on his mother's side.

20. Lucretia Mott to Martha Wright, September 7, 1855, Lucretia Mott Mss, FRIENDS.

21. David Grimsted, *American Mobbing, 1828–1861: Toward Civil War* (New York: Oxford University Press, 1998), 56. James Thome of Hanover, Ohio, is quoted.

22. Lucretia Mott to Maria Mott Davis and Edward M. Davis, August 7, 1855, MOTT.

23. Visitors Book, CHESTER.

24. *Frederick Douglass' Paper,* August 31, 1855. Sumner's letter, dated August 11, while he was aboard the vessel *North Star* on Lake Superior, is quoted.

25. *National Era,* November 8, 1855. The poem, written by N. W. Campbell and entitled "To Passmore Williamson in Moyamensing Jail," is dated September 19, 1855.

26. *National Anti-Slavery Standard,* August 11, 1855.

27. William Cooper Nell Papers, Beinecke Rare Book and Manuscript Library, Yale University.

28. William Cooper Nell to Passmore Williamson, December 3, 1855, LETTERS.

29. Edward Williamson to "Dear Sir," August 27, 1855, LETTERS.

30. *National Anti-Slavery Standard,* August 11, 1855. The *Philadelphia Times* is quoted.

31. Passmore Williamson to "Dear Cousin," August 6, 1855, LETTERS.

32. Passmore Williamson to "Dear Uncle," August 6, 1855, LETTERS.

33. Passmore Williamson to "Dear Cousin," August 3, 1855, LETTERS.

34. Uncited newspaper clipping dated August 14, ALBUM.

35. Edward Williamson to "Dear Sir," August 9, 1855, LETTERS.

36. Passmore Williamson to "Dear Wife," undated, LETTERS.

37. *National Anti-Slavery Standard,* September 1, 1855.

38. Edward Williamson to "Dear Sir," August 25, 1855, LETTERS.

39. *National Anti-Slavery Standard,* August 11, 1855.

40. Ibid., September 1, 1855.

41. Ibid.

Chapter 11—Votes For and Against

1. Margaret Hope Bacon, *Quiet Rebels: The Story of the Quakers in America* (New York: Basic Books, 1969), 19.

2. Passmore Williamson to "Dear Cousin" July 26, 1848, LETTERS.

3. *Provincial Freeman,* September 22, 1855.

4. Edward Williamson to "Dear Sir," September 7, 1855, LETTERS.

5. Samuel P. Bates, *History of Erie County, Pennsylvania* (Chicago: Warner, Beers & Co., 1884), 7.

6. *Frederick Douglass' Paper,* August 10, 1855. The *Philadelphia Bulletin* of August 1 is quoted.

7. *Provincial Freeman,* August 22, 1857. An article in the *North American Report* is quoted.

8. *New York Times,* August 4, 1855. The *Washington Union* is quoted.

9. Frank M. Eastman, *Courts and Lawyers of Pennsylvania: A History* (New York: American Historical Society, 1922), 3:149.

10. *National Anti-Slavery Standard,* August 25, 1855.

11. *McElroy's Philadelphia Directory* (1854).

12. Edward Williamson to "Dear Sir," August 30, 1855, LETTERS.

13. *Philadelphia City Bulletin,* September 8, 1855.

14. Ibid.

15. *Provincial Freeman,* December 1, 1855.

16. STILL, 287–92.

17. Edward Williamson to "Dear Sir," September 15, 1855, LETTERS.

18. *National Anti-Slavery Standard,* September 22, 1855.

19. *Frederick Douglass' Paper,* September 21, 1855.

20. Ibid., October 12, 1855.

Chapter 12—Stranded

1. Unless otherwise noted, the story of the arraignment of the five black rescuers is from the *Philadelphia Evening Bulletin* of July 28, 1855.

2. STILL, 95–96.

3. *National Anti-Slavery Standard,* August 11, 1855.

4. Details of John Hill Wheeler's activities during the latter part of July and into late August are from DIARY, July 28 through August 28, 1855.

5. *Frederick Douglass' Paper,* August 10, 1855, quoting the *New York Tribune.*

6. Crafts, *Bondwoman's Narrative,* liii.

7. Edward Williamson to "Dear Sir," August 29, 1855, LETTERS.

Chapter 13—Two Surprise Witnesses

1. DIARY, August 29, 1855.

2. Ibid., December 28, 1854.

3. The only documents still existing in the Philadelphia City Archives regarding the rescue of Jane Johnson are two deal dealing with Docket 44. One is the bill of indictment against Passmore Williamson, John Ballard, William Still, William Custis, James S. Braddock, James Martin, and Isaiah Moore. The other is a report on the verdict, sentence, and fines.

4. *National Anti-Slavery Standard,* September 8, 1855. The *Evening Post* is quoted.

5. *National Era*, September 6, 1855.

6. *National Anti-Slavery Standard*, September 8, 1855. The *Evening Post* is quoted.

7. Edward Williamson to "Dear Sir," August 29, 1855. LETTERS.

8. Ibid.

9. *Provincial Freeman*, September 15, 1855. The *Philadelphia Public Ledger* is quoted.

10. J. D. Brown, *Arcade Hotel Guide* (Philadelphia: Inquirer Printing Office, 1856), 30.

11. Edward Williamson to "Dear Sir," August 30, 1855. LETTERS.

12. *National Anti-Slavery Standard*, September 8, 1855. The *Philadelphia Evening Post* is quoted.

13. STILL, 94.

14. Twenty-second Annual Report, Philadelphia Female Anti-Slavery Society, 9, FRIENDS.

15. STILL, 94.

16. *National Anti-Slavery Standard*, September 8, 1855. The *New York Tribune* is quoted.

17. Ibid., September 8, 1855. The *Philadelphia Evening Post* is quoted.

18. *National Anti-Slavery Standard*, September 8, 1855. The *New York Tribune* is quoted.

19. Ibid., September 8, 1855. The *Philadelphia Evening Post* is quoted.

20. Twenty-second Annual Report, Philadelphia Female Anti-Slavery Society, 9. FRIENDS.

21. ibid.

22. *National Anti-Slavery Standard*, September 8, 1855. The *Philadelphia Evening Post* is quoted.

23. Edward Williamson to "Dear Sir," September 1, 1855, LETTERS.

24. *National Anti-Slavery Standard*, September 8, 1855.

25. *National Era*, September 6, 1855.

26. STILL, 96. The *New York Tribune* is quoted.

27. *National Anti-Slavery Standard*, September 8, 1855. The *Philadelphia Evening Post* is quoted.

28. Ibid.

29. Edward Williamson to Passmore Williamson, September 1, 1855, CHESTER.

30. STILL, 96.

31. Lucretia Mott to Martha Wright, September 4, 1855, Lucretia Mott Mss, FRIENDS.

32. Twenty-second Annual Report, Philadelphia Female Anti-Slavery Society, 11, FRIENDS.

33. *Provincial Freeman*, September 8, 1855.

34. DIARY, September 1, 1855.

35. Ibid., September 3–4, 1855.

36. Ibid., September 5, 1855.

37. Ibid., August 30, 1855.

Chapter 14—Legalistics

1. Edward Williamson to "Dear Sir," September 26, 1855, LETTERS.

2. *Daily Pennsylvanian,* August 30, 1855.

3. Edward Williamson to "Dear Sir," September 26, LETTERS.

4. *Frederick Douglass' Paper,* October 5, 1855.

5. Edward Williamson to "Dear Sir," September 22, 1855.

6. *National Anti-Slavery Standard,* October 6, 1855.

7. Ibid., September 29, 1855.

8. *Frederick Douglass' Paper,* December 14, 1855.

9. The petitions are noted in the *Journal of the House of Representatives* for the following dates in 1856: February 19, February 27, March 5, March 18, March 20, April 21, May 6. *A Century of Lawmaking for a New Nation: U.S. Congressional Documents and Debates, 1774–1875.* http://memory.loc.gov. Go to journal of the House of Representatives. Go to specific date.

10. Visitors Book, CHESTER.

11. Edward Williamson to "Dear Sir," September 26, 1855.

12. Wainwright, *Philadelphia Perspective,* 250.

13. Ibid., 251.

14. Ibid.

15. Edward Williamson to "Dear Sir," September 20, 1855.

16. Ibid., September 22, 1855.

17. Ibid., September 20, 1855.

18. Albert J. Wahl, "The Pennsylvania Yearly Meeting of Progressive Friends," *Pennsylvania History* 25, no. 2 (Spring 1958): 133.

19. The events surrounding Jane Johnson's petition are taken from an appendix to CASE, 164–91.

20. "Proceedings upon the Petition of Jane Johnson. United States District Court, Eastern District of Pennsylvania.," 2. http://memory.loc.gov. Search: Case of Passmore Williamson. Go to Appendix.

21. Ibid., 3–8.

22. Ibid., 8–18. Kane's ruling is also available in "Opinion of Judge Kane, *United States of America, ex Relatione Wheeler, vs. Williamson,*" (reprint of *American Law Register* IV: November, 1855), 1–19.

23. NARRATIVE, 8.

24. Wainwright, *Philadelphia Perspective,* 251.

25. *National Era,* October 18, 1855.

26. Edward Williamson to "Dear Sir," October 22, 1855.

27. The courtroom battle and final resolution of Passmore Williamson's case are taken from CASE, 98–163.

28. *Frederick Douglass' Paper,* November 16, 1855.

29. Edward Williamson to "Dear Sir," October 31, 1855.

30. *Provincial Freeman,* November 15, 1855.

31. *New York Times,* November 3, 1855.

Chapter 15—Revenge

1. Summons Case, *Passmore Williamson vs. John K. Kane,* November Term 1855, Delaware County Government Archives.

2. *Provincial Freeman,* December 22, 1855. The *Chester County Republican* is quoted.

3. *National Era,* November 15, 1855. The *Daily Wisconsin* is quoted.

4. *Daily Pennsylvanian,* November 8, 1855.

5. Uncited, undated newspaper clipping, ATWOOD.

6. *Journal of the House of Representatives of the Commonwealth of Pennsylvania of the Session begun at Harrisburg on the first of January,* A.D., *1856* (Harrisburg: A. Boyd Hamilton, 1856), 120, 122, and *Journal of the Senate of the Commonwealth of Pennsylvania of the Session begun at Harrisburg on the first day of January,* A.D., *1856* (Harrisburg: A. Boyd Hamilton, 1856), 184–85.

7. Passmore Williamson to "Dear Cousin," February 9, 1856, LETTERS.

8. Passmore Williamson to "Dear Cousin," June 15, 1856, LETTERS.

9. Legal Page Lawsuit, KANE.

10. Demurrer Book and Paper Book, KANE.

11. Richard Hildreth, ed., *Atrocious Judges: Lives of Judges Infamous as Tools of Tyrants and Instruments of Oppression Compiled from the Judicial Biographies of John Lord Campbell . . . with an Appendix Containing the Case of Passmore Williamson* (New York: Miller, Orton & Mulligan, 1856).

12. John K. Kane to "Honor. Judge Grier," February 14, 1857, KANE.

13. John K. Kane to "Hon. Mr. McClelland," February 16, 1857, KANE.

14. Ibid., June 6, 1857, KANE.

15. R. McClelland to "Hon. Judge J. K. Kane," June 8, 1857, KANE.

16. John K. Kane to "My dear Sir" (James Buchanan), July 16, 1857, KANE.

17. Moses Kelly to "Sir" (James Buchanan), August 24, 1857, KANE.

18. John K. Kane to "President of the United States" (James Buchanan), November 13, 1857, KANE.

19. James Buchanan's endorsement of Moses Kelly's report of August 24, 1857, dated August 25, 1857, KANE.

20. Continuance Docket "F," Court of Common Pleas, Delaware County Government Archives.

21. J. Miller McKim to Elijah F. Pennypacker, Elijah F. Pennypacker Mss., FRIENDS.

22. *Philadelphia Public Ledger,* March 1, 1895, ATWOOD.

23. Wainwright, *Philadelphia Perspective,* 292–93, 390.

Chapter 16—Aftermath

1. FLYNN, 170.
2. Ibid., 172.
3. Ibid., 175–76.
4. *Philadelphia Public Ledger,* March 1, 1895, ATWOOD.
5. FLYNN, 174–75.
6. Ibid., 173.
7. Mark Mayo Boatner III, *The Civil War Dictionary* (New York: David McKay, 1959), 585.
8. FLYNN, 173.
9. DIARY, April 7, 1861.
10. Ibid., January 18, 1857, summary of life's events
11. Ibid., December 22, 1857.
12. Ibid., January 11, 1860.
13. Ibid., December 13, 1859.
14. Ibid., September 12, 1861. This entry is obviously misdated and should read April 12, 1861, when Fort Sumter was fired upon in Charleston. Also, Wheeler dated the entry a Friday. September 12 was a Thursday.
15. Ibid., December 20, 1863.
16. Ibid., December 31, 1863.
17. Ibid., March 14, 1862, summary.
18. WHEELER, vi, ix.
19. STILL, lvii.
20. Ibid., xlix.
21. Ibid., xxxv.
22. Stephen G. Hall, "To Render the Private Public: William Still and the Selling of *The Underground Railroad,*" *Pennsylvania Magazine of History and Biography* 127, no. 1 (January 2003): 53.
23. Margaret Hope Bacon, *History of the Pennsylvania Society,* appendix iii.
24. STILL, liii.
25. John R. McKivigan, ed. *Abolitionism and American Reform* (New York: Garland, 1999), 15.
26. William Still, *A Brief Narrative of the Struggle for the Rights of the Colored People of Philadelphia in the City Railway Cars* (Philadelphia: Merrihew & Son, 1867), 3.
27. STILL, xxii–xxiii. Still's name was mentioned in a memorandum found on John Henry Kagi. He sheltered Osborne Anderson.
28. *Christian Recorder,* January 8, 1870.
29. Ibid., March 12, 1874.
30. Ibid., March 25, 1875.
31. *Provincial Freeman,* December 1, 1855.
32. *National Era,* February 28, 1856. Passmore Williamson was introduced at a morning session on Friday, February 22.

33. Martha Coffin Wright to Eliza Osborne, April 9, 1859. Garrison Family Papers, Sophia Smith Collection, Smith College. www.binghamton.edu/womhist/mcw/doc4.htm. September 6, 2006.

34. *National Era,* March 8, 1860.

35. *New York Times,* August 30, 1860.

36. Passmore Williamson to "Dear Cousin," April 2, 1856, LETTERS.

37. Passmore Williamson to "Dear Cousin," June 6, 1862, LETTERS.

38. *New York Times,* July 20, 1859.

39. Passmore Williamson to "Dear Cousin," August 27, 1871, LETTERS. Thomas's second wife, Deborah, died on July 2, 1876, in Haverford, Pennsylvania. She was in her mid-seventies. She had outlived Thomas by five years.

40. Appeal of Mary W. Coggins and Anna W. Stackhouse, Estate of Thos. Williamson, ATWOOD.

41. Uncited, undated newspaper clipping, ALBUM.

42. Passmore Williamson to William Darlington, December 8, 1871, LETTERS.

43. Uncited, undated newspaper clipping, ALBUM.

44. Response of Anna M. Stackhouse, executrix of estate of Anna W. Stackhouse, decreased, et al, Court of Common Pleas, No. 1, County of Philadelphia, December Term 1911, ATWOOD.

45. *Passmore Williamson vs. Philadelphia and Reading Railroad Company,* February 11, 1888, Common Pleas Court No. 3, County of Philadelphia," HISTORY.

46. NARRATIVE, 149–51.

47. Witmer Stone, "Charles Sumner Williamson," reprint from *Bartonia* for 1914, 3, CHESTER.

48. *New York Times,* October 5, 1884. The *Philadelphia Times* of October 4 is quoted.

49. Scharf and Westcott, *History of Philadelphia,* 1:722. Among the eleven delegates from Philadelphia to the convention were William S. Pierce and Charles D. Cleveland.

50. *Philadelphia Public Ledger,* March 1, 1895, ATWOOD.

51. *New York Times,* October 5, 1884. The *Philadelphia Times* of October 4 is quoted.

52. SMITH, 199.

53. *Philadelphia Public Ledger,* March 1, 1895, ATWOOD.

54. Ibid., March 22, 1895, ATWOOD. The newspaper clipping is headed "Passmore Williamson's Will." It is labeled "L 3, 22, 1895"—indicating, it would seem, that it was taken from the issue of March 22, 1895, some three weeks after Williamson's death. The exact amount of the estate's value is unclear. A slight tear in the clipping occurs where the amount is given. The size of the missing space indicates that the amount quoted was minimal, no more than three or four figures at best. An attempt to trace this clipping in

the *Ledger* proved unsuccessful. It is quite possible that this news item, less than two inches of a newspaper column, did not run in all editions of the newspapers or that it was misdated by the family member who preserved it.

55. CENTRAL has interment records that include Williamson family entries in both its Register of Interments, Book 1418, Register-Lots (from 1862 to 1952), and Orders for Interment, 1865–1883. The Register of Interments from 1863 has the record of the interments of both Passmore and Mercie Williamson. Order for Interment Book 1703, Orders for Interment, Book A, notes that Passmore's burial is in a lot granted to his father Thomas. Book 420, Record of Interments, Book B 1864, records the interment of Sarah E. Williamson Powell at the age of seventy. The whereabouts of the burial of either Thomas's first wife, Elizabeth, or his second wife, Deborah, are unknown. The latter died in Haverford, Pennsylvania.

56. Visitors Book, CHESTER. The society adopted the testimonial on April 4, 1895. It had been drafted on March 29, with William Still signing it as vice president.

Epilogue

1. Lucretia Mott to Martha Wright, November 16, 1855, FRIENDS.

BIBLIOGRAPHY

Then arouse ye, brave hearts, to the rescue come on!
The man-stealing army we'll surely put down;
They are crushing their millions, but soon they must yield,
For freemen have risen and taken the field.

"We're Coming! We're Coming!" *Anti-Slavery Harp,* 31
(to be sung to the air "Kinloch of Kinloch")

Archives and Manuscript Sources

American Philosophical Society, Philadelphia
    John Kintzing Kane and Robert Patterson Kane Legal Papers
Shirley Atwood, Virginia Beach, Virginia
    Williamson Family documents, related newspaper clippings, and photo-
        graph of Passmore Williamson
Beinecke Rare Book and Manuscript Library, Yale University
    William Cooper Nell Papers
Central Philadelphia Monthly Meeting of Friends
    Interment Records and map, Friends' South-Western Burial Ground
    Map of Friends' South Western Burial Ground
Chester County Historical Society, West Chester, Pennsylvania
    Letters, Passmore Williamson
    List of Visitors, Passmore Williamson Visitor Book, Moyamensing Prison
    Witmer Stone, *Charles Sumner Williamson,* 1914
Delaware County Government Archives, Lima, Pennsylvania
    Continuance Docket "F," Court of Common Pleas
    Summons Case, Passmore Williamson vs. John K. Kane, November Term
        1855
Friends Historical Library, Swarthmore College
    Annual Report, American Anti-Slavery Society, 1856
    Twenty-second Annual Report, Philadelphia Female Anti-Slavery Society,
        1856

Lucretia Mott Mss
Elijah F. Pennypacker Mss
Minutes, Philadelphia Female Anti-Slavery Society, 1833–1870
Minutes, Philadelphia Monthly Meeting (Arch Street), 1845–1857
Passmore Williamson vs. John K. Kane. Argument for Defendant
Genealogical Society of Pennsylvania
Passmore Williamson family record, George Cope Files
Historical Society of Pennsylvania
Album, plus newspaper clippings, *Case of Passmore Williamson vs. John K. Kane*
Passmore Williamson vs. Philadelphia and Reading Railroad
Map of the City of Philadelphia as Consolidated in 1854
Pennsylvania Abolition Society Records
Library Company of Philadelphia
Newspaper files
Samuel Joseph May, Anti-Slavery Tract No. 15 new series, "The Fugitive Slave Law and Its Victims." New York: American Anti-Slavery Society, 1861.
Library of Congress
Papers of John Hill Wheeler (ms62–4529, microfilm reels 1 and 2)
National Archives, Mid-Atlantic Region, Philadelphia
Record Group 21, Records of U.S. Circuit Court and U.S. District Court, Eastern District of Pennsylvania
New York Public Library, Schomburg Center for Research in Black Culture
Fourteenth Annual Report, Pennsylvania Anti-Slavery Society, 1851
New-York Historical Society
"Proceedings of a meeting to form the Broadway Tabernacle Anti-Slavery Society"
Pennsylvania Historical and Museum Commission Library, Harrisburg
Laws of the General Assembly of the Commonwealth of Pennsylvania, 1847
Philadelphia City Archives
Docket, Quarter Sessions Court, August term, 1855
Record Group 38, Prison Daily Occurrences, Moyamensing Prison
Smith College, Northampton, Massachusetts
Garrison Family Papers, Sophia Smith Collection Library of Congress
Wheeler, John Hill. Papers (ms62–4529, microfilm reels 1 and 2).

Books

Ashmead, Henry Graham. *History of Delaware County, Pennsylvania*. Philadelphia: L.H. Everts & Co., 1884
Bacon, Benjamin C. *Statistics of the Colored People of Philadelphia*. Philadelphia: T. Ellwood Chapman, 1856.
Bacon, Margaret Hope. *History of the Pennsylvania Society for Promoting the Abolition of Slavery; the Relief of Negroes Unlawfully Held in Bondage; and*

for Improving the Condition of the African Race. Philadelphia: Pennsylvania Abolition Society, 1959.

———. *In the Shadow of William Penn.* Philadelphia: Central Philadelphia Monthly Meeting, 2001.

———. *The Quiet Rebels: The Story of the Quakers in America.* New York: Basic Books, 1969.

Barbour, Hugh, and J. William Frost. *The Quakers.* New York: Greenwood Press, 1988.

Bates, Samuel P. *History of Erie County, Pennsylvania.* Chicago: Warner, Beers & Co., 1884.

Bentley, Judith. *Dear Friend: Thomas Garrett & William Still, Collaborators on the Underground Railroad.* New York: Cobblehill Books, 1997.

Biographical Encyclopaedia of Pennsylvania of the Nineteenth Century. Philadelphia: Galaxy, 1874.

Black, Henry Campbell. *A Law Dictionary.* St. Paul, Minn.: West Publishing, 1910.

Black, Jeremiah S. *Essays and Speeches of Jeremiah S. Black, With a Biographical Sketch by Chauncey F. Black.* New York: D. Appleton, 1885.

Blockson, Charles L. *African Americans in Pennsylvania: Above Ground and Underground: An Illustrated Guide.* Harrisburg, Pa.: RB Books, 2001.

Boatner, Mark Mayo III. *The Civil War Dictionary.* New York: David McKay, 1959.

Bordewich, Fergus M. *Bound for Canaan: The Underground Railroad and the War for the Soul of America.* New York: Amistad, 2005.

Brandt, Nat. *The Town That Started the Civil War.* Syracuse, N.Y.: Syracuse University Press, 1990.

Brent, Robert J. *Report of Attorney General Brent, to His Excellency, Gov. Lowe, in Relation to the Christiana Treason Trials, in the Circuit Court of the United States, Held at Philadelphia.* Annapolis, Md.: T. E. Martin, 1852.

Brown, Ira V. *Mary Grew, Abolitionist and Feminist, 1813–1896.* Selinsgrove, Pa.: Susquehanna University Press, 1991.

Brown, J. D. *Arcade Hotel Guide.* Philadelphia: Inquirer Printing Office, 1856.

Brown, William Wells, ed. *Anti-Slavery Harp: A Collection of Songs for Anti-Slavery Meetings.* Boston: Bela Marsh, 1849.

———. *The Black Man: His Antecedents, His Genius, and His Achievements.* New York: T. Hamilton, 1863.

Campbell, Stanley W. *The Slave Catchers: Enforcement of the Fugitive Slave Law, 1850–1860.* Chapel Hill: University of North Carolina Press, 1968.

Case of Passmore Williamson; report of the proceedings on the writ of habeas corpus, issued by the Hon. John K. Kane, in the case of the United States of America ex rel. John H. Wheeler vs. Passmore Williamson, including the several opinions delivered, and the arguments of counsel, reported by Arthur Cannon. Philadelphia: Uriah Hunt & Son, 1856.

A Century of Lawmaking for a New Nation: U.S. Congressional Documents and Debates, 1774–1875. http://memory.loc.gov.

Cohen, S. E. *Philadelphia Shopping Guide and House Keeper's Companion.* Philadelphia: King & Baird, 1858.

A Compilation of the Messages and Papers of the Presidents. Washington, D.C.: Bureau of National Literature, 1912.

Constitution of Pennsylvania 1838. Duquesne University Law School. http://www.swarthmore.edu/humanities/kjohnsol/pennsylvaniaconstitution.htm.

Corner, George Washington. *Doctor Kane of the Arctic Seas.* Philadelphia: Temple University Press, 1972.

Crafts, Hannah. *The Bondwoman's Narrative.* Edited by Henry Louis Gates Jr. New York: Warner Books, 2002.

Downs, Winfield Scott, ed. *Encyclopedia of American Biography.* New York: American Historical Society, 1934.

Dreiser, Theodore. *The Financier.* New York: Harper & Brothers, 1912.

Eastman, Frank M. *Courts and Lawyers of Pennsylvania: A History.* Vol. 3. New York: American Historical Society, 1922.

Engs, Richard F., and Randall M. Miller. *The Birth of the Grand Old Party: The Republicans' First Generation.* Philadelphia: University of Pennsylvania Press, 2002.

Feldberg, Michael. *The Philadelphia Riots of 1844: A Study in Ethnic Conflict.* Westport, Conn.: Greenwood Press, 1975.

Fogel, Robert William, and Stanley L. Engerman. *Time on the Cross: The Economics of American Negro Slavery.* New York: W. W. Norton, 1974.

Gara, Larry. *The Liberty Line: The Legend of the Underground Railroad.* Lexington: University of Kentucky Press, 1961.

———. *The Presidency of Franklin Pierce.* Lawrence: University of Kansas Press, 1991.

Garraty, John, and Mark C. Carnes, eds. *American National Biography.* New York: Oxford University Press, 1999.

Gates, Henry Louis, Jr., and Hollis Robbins, eds. *In Search of Hannah Crafts: Critical Essays on The Bondwoman's Narrative.* New York: Basic Civitas, 2004.

Gienapp, William E. *The Origins of the Republican Party 1852–1856.* New York: Oxford University Press, 1987.

Gopsill's Philadelphia City Directory 1895. Philadelphia: James Gospill's Sons, 1895.

[Grew, Mary.] *Narrative of Facts in the Case of Passmore Williamson.* Philadelphia: Pennsylvania Anti-Slavery Society, 1855.

Grimsted, David. *American Mobbing, 1828–1861: Toward Civil War.* New York: Oxford University Press, 1998.

Guide to Philadelphia: Its Public Buildings, Places of Amusement, Churches, Hotels, &c. Philadelphia: John Dainty, 1868.

Hamm, Thomas D. *The Quakers in America.* New York: Columbia University Press, 2003.

————. *The Transformation of American Quakerism: Orthodox Friends, 1800–1907.* Bloomington: Indiana University Press, 1988.

Harvey, Oscar Jewell, and Ernest Gray Smith. *A History of Wilkes-Barre, Luzerne County, Pennsylvania.* Vol. 4. Wilkes-Barre: Wilkes-Barre Times-Leader, 1929.

Hendrick, George, and Hendrick, Willene. *Fleeing for Freedom: Stories of the Underground Railroad as Told by Levi Coffin and William Still.* Chicago: Ivan R. Dee, 2004.

Hensel, W. U. *The Christiana Riot and the Treason Trials of 1851.* Lancaster, Pa.: New Era Printing Company, 1911.

Hildreth, Richard, ed. *Atrocious Judges: Lives of Judges Infamous as Tools of Tyrants and Instruments of Oppression Compiled from the Judicial Biographies of John Lord Campbell . . . with an Appendix Containing the Case of Passmore Williamson.* New York: Miller, Orton & Mulligan, 1856.

Hinshaw, William Wade, and Thomas Worth Marshall. *Encyclopedia of American Quaker Genealogy.* Philadelphia: Genealogical Publishing Co., 1938.

History of the Trial of Castner Hanway and Others for Treason at Philadelphia in November, 1851. Philadelphia: Uriah Hunt & Sons, 1852.

Ingle, H. Larry. *Quakers in Conflict: The Hicksite Reformation.* Knoxville: University of Tennessee Press, 1986.

Johannsen, Robert W. *To the Halls of the Montezumas: The Mexican War in the American Imagination.* New York: Oxford University Press, 1985.

Johnson, Allen, and Dumas Malone, eds. *Dictionary of American Biography.* New York: Charles Scribner's Sons, 1959–60.

Journal of the House of Representatives of the Commonwealth of Pennsylvania of the Session Begun at Harrisburg on the First of January, A.D., 1856. Harrisburg: A. Boyd Hamilton, 1856.

Journal of the Senate of the Commonwealth of Pennsylvania of the Session Begun at Harrisburg on the First day of January, A.D., 1856. Harrisburg: A. Boyd Hamilton, 1856.

Kane, John Kintzing. *Autobiography of the Honorable John K. Kane.* Philadelphia: Privately printed [College Offset Press], 1949.

Kashatus, William C. *Just Over the Line: Chester County and the Underground Railroad.* West Chester, Pa.: Chester County Historical Society, 2002.

Khan, Lurey. *One Day, Levin . . . He Be Free; William Still and the Underground Railroad.* New York: E. P. Dutton, 1972.

Konkle, Burton Alva. *The Life of Chief Justice Ellis Lewis, 1798–1871.* Philadelphia: Campion, 1907.

Lapsansky, Phil. *The Liberation of Jane Johnson.* Philadelphia: Library Company, 2003.

Lewis, Joseph J. *Passmore Williamson vs. John K. Kane: Action for False Imprisonment, before the Court of Common Pleas of Delaware County/Argument of Joseph J. Lewis, Esq. of Westchester, on the Part of the Plaintiff, Delivered at Media, December 17th and 18th, 1856.*

Litwack, Leon. *North of Slavery.* Chicago: University of Chicago Press, 1961.

Malone, Dumas, ed. *Dictionary of American Biography.* Vol. 10, part 2. New York: Scribner's Sons, 1936.

Mannix, Daniel P., and Malcolm Cowley. *Black Cargoes: A History of the Atlantic Slave Trade 1518–1865.* New York: Viking Press, 1962.

Martin, John Hill. *Martin's Bench and Bar of Philadelphia.* Philadelphia: Rees Welsh & Co., 1883.

May, Samuel Joseph. *The Fugitive Slave Law and Its Victims.* New York: American Anti-Slavery Society, 1861.

Mayer, Henry. *All on Fire: William Lloyd Garrison and the Abolition of Slavery.* New York: St. Martin's Press, 1998.

McElroy's Philadelphia Directory. Editions of 1849, 1854, 1859, 1860, 1864. Philadelphia: Edward C. and John Biddle, 1849–64.

McKivigan, John R., ed. *Abolitionism and American Reform.* New York: Garland, 1999.

Mires, Charlene. *Independence Hall in American Memory.* Philadelphia: University of Pennsylvania Press, 2002.

Nash, Gary B. *First City: Philadelphia and the Forging of Historical Memory.* Philadelphia: University of Pennsylvania Press, 2002.

Nash, Gary B., and Jean R. Soderlund. *Freedom by Degrees: Emancipation in Pennsylvania and Its Aftermath.* New York: Oxford University Press, 1991.

National Cyclopaedia of American Biography. New York: James T. White & Company, 1898.

Needles, Edward. *The Pennsylvania Society for Promoting the Abolition of Slavery.* New York: Arno Press & the New York Times, 1969.

New York City Directory for 1854–55. New York: Charles R. Rode, 1854.

Newman, Richard S. *The Transformation of American Abolitionism: Fighting Slavery in the Early Republic.* Chapel Hill: University of North Carolina Press, 2002.

Niles, Henry C. *Jeremiah Sullivan Black: And His Influence on the Law of Pennsylvania.* N.p., [1903].

Palmer, Beverly Wilson, ed. *Selected Letters of Lucretia Coffin Mott.* Urbana: University of Illinois Press, 2002.

Patton, Rev. William W. *Thoughts for Christians, Suggested by the Case of Passmore Williamson.* Hartford, Conn.: Montague & Co., 1855.

Peters, Richard. *Report of the Case of Edward Prigg against the Commonwealth of Pennsylvania: Argued and Adjudged in the Supreme Court of the United States, at January Term, 1842.* Philadelphia: L. Johnson, 1842.

"Proceedings upon the Petition of Jane Johnson. United States District Court, Eastern District of Pennsylvania." http://memory.loc.gov.

200

Quarles, Benjamin. *Black Abolitionists*. New York: Oxford University Press, 1969.

Ramson, Roger L., and Richard Sutch. *One Kind of Freedom: The Economic Consequences of Emancipation*. Cambridge: Cambridge University Press, 1977.

Scharf, Thomas J., and Thompson Westcott. *History of Philadelphia, 1609–1884*. 3 vols. Philadelphia: L.H. Everts, 1884.

Sexton, John, and Nat Brandt. *How Free Are We? What the Constitution Says We Can and Cannot Do*. New York: M. Evans, 1986.

Siebert, Wilbur H. *The Underground Railroad from Slavery to Freedom*. New York: Macmillan, 1898.

Simpson, Henry. *Lives of Eminent Philadelphians, Now Deceased*. Philadelphia: William Brotherhead, 1859.

Slaughter, Thomas P. *Bloody Dawn: The Christiana Riot and Racial Violence in the Antebellum North*. New York: Oxford University Press, 1991.

Smedley, R. C. *History of the Underground Railroad in Chester and the Neighboring Counties of Pennsylvania*. Reprint of 1883 original. New York: Negro Universities Press, 1968.

Smith, Robert Houston. *The Passmores in America: A Quaker family through Six Generations*. Lewiston, N.Y.: E. Mellen Press, 1992.

Statistical View of the United States . . . Compendium of the Seventh Census. Washington: Beverley Tucker, 1854.

Stevenson, Brenda E. *Life in Black and White: Family and Community in the Slave South*. New York: Oxford University Press, 1996.

Still, William. *A Brief Narrative of the Struggle for the Rights of the Colored People of Philadelphia in the City Railway Cars*. Philadelphia: Merrihew & Son, 1867.

———. *Still's Underground Rail Road Records: Revised Edition with a Life of the Author*. Philadelphia: William Still, 1886.

Stauffer, John. *The Black Hearts of Men: Radical Abolitionists and the Transformation of Race*. Cambridge, Mass.: Harvard University Press, 2002.

Stranger's Guide in Philadelphia. Philadelphia: Lindsay & Blakiston, 1857.

Switala, William J. *Underground Railroad in Pennsylvania*. Mechanicsburg, Pa.: Stackpole Books, 2001.

Tanner, Henry Schenck. *New Picture of Philadelphia or the Stranger's Guide to the City and Adjoining Districts*. New York: T. R. Tanner, 1844.

Trow's New York City Directory for the Year ending May 1, 1856. New York: John F. Trow, 1855.

Turner, Joe William, and Eric Ledell Smith. *African Americans in Pennsylvania: Shifting Historical Perspectives*. University Park: Pennsylvania Historical and Museum Commission and Pennsylvania State University Press, 1997.

Wainwright, Nicholas B., ed. *A Philadelphia Perspective: The Diary of Sidney George Fisher Covering the Years 1834–1871*. Philadelphia: Historical Society of Pennsylvania, 1967.

Walther, Eric H. *The Shattering of the Union: America in the 1850s.* Wilmington, Del.: Scholarly Resources, 2004.

Waugh, John C. *On the Brink of the Civil War: The Compromise of 1850 and How It Changed the Course of American History.* Wilmington, Del.: Scholarly Resources, 2003.

Weigley, Russell F., ed. *Philadelphia: A 300-year History.* New York: W. W. Norton, 1982.

Wesley, Dorothy Porter, and Constance Porter Uzelac. *William Cooper Nell: Selected Writings 1832–1874.* Baltimore: Black Classic Press, 2002.

Westcott, Thompson. *Guide Book to Philadelphia.* Philadelphia: Porter and Coates, 1875.

Wheeler, John H. *Reminiscences and Memoirs of North Carolina and Eminent North Carolinians.* Baltimore: Genealogical Publishing Company, 1966.

Who's Who in British History: Beginnings to 1901. London: Fitzroy Dearborn, 1998.

Wilson, Henry. *History of the Rise and Fall of the Slave Power in America.* Vol. 2. Boston: James R. Osgood, 1874.

Wilson, James Grant, and John Fiske. *Appleton's Cyclopedia of American Biography.* 6 vols. New York: D. Appleton, 1887–89.

Winch, Julie, ed. *The Elite of Our People: Joseph Willson's Sketches of Black Upper-Class Life in Antebellum Philadelphia.* University Park: Pennsylvania State University Press, 2000.

———. *A Gentleman of Color: The Life of James Forten.* New York: Oxford University Press, 2002.

———. *Philadelphia's Black Elite: Activism, Accommodation, and the Struggle for Autonomy, 1787–1848.* Philadelphia: Temple University Press, 1988.

Articles

Berlin, Ira. "American Slavery in History and Memory and the Search for Social Justice." *Journal of American History* 90, no. 4 (March 2004): 1251–68.

Borome, Joseph A. "The Vigilant Committee of Philadelphia." *Pennsylvania Magazine of History and Biography* 92, no. 2 (April 1968): 320–51.

Cary, Lorene. "I Want My Freedom: Jane Johnson's Escape with the Philadelphia Vigilance Committee, 1855." Taken from *The Underground Railroad* by William Still (Porter & Coates: Philadelphia, 1872). Philadelphia: Free Library of Philadelphia, 2003.

Eckert, Ralph Lowell. "Antislavery Martyrdom: The Ordeal of Passmore Williamson." *Pennsylvania Magazine of History and Biography* 100 (1976): 521–38.

Flynn, Katherine E. "Jane Johnson, Found! But Is She 'Hannah Crafts'? The Search for the Author of *The Bondwoman's Narrative.*" *National Genealogical Society Quarterly* 90 (September 2002): 165–90.

Bibliography

Gara, Larry. "Friends and the Underground Railroad." *Quaker History* 51, no. 1 (Spring 1962): 3–19.

Hall, Stephen G. "To Render the Private Public: William Still and the Selling of *The Underground Rail Road*." *Pennsylvania Magazine of History and Biography* 127, no. 1 (January 2003): 35–55.

Harriger, Katy J. "The Federalism Debate in the Transformation of Federal Habeas Corpus Law." *Publius* 27, no. 3 (Summer 1997): 1–22.

"Historical Information for Philadelphia." USGS, http://mcmcweb.er.usgs .gov/de_river_basin/phil/modeling.html.

Horton, James Oliver. "Flight to Freedom: One Family and the Story of the Underground Railroad." *Magazine of History* 15, no. 4 (Summer 2001): 42–45.

———. "William Still: From Slave to Conductor." *Footsteps* 5, no. 1 (Jan–Feb 2003): 32–35.

Hudson, Randall O., and James C. Duram. "The *New York Daily Tribune* and Passmore Williamson's Case: A Study in the Use of Northern States' Rights." *Wichita State University Bulletin* 50, no. 4 (November 1974): 3–15.

Kashatus, William C. "Two Stationmasters on the Underground Railroad: A Tale of Black and White." *Pennsylvania Heritage* (Fall 2001): 5–11.

"Letters of Negroes, Largely Personal and Private [Part 6]." *Journal of Negro History* 11, no. 1 (January 1926): 186–214.

Longley, Eric. "'States' Rights': Do We Have It All Wrong?" http://www.civil warinteractive.com/ArticleStatesRights.htm

Mires, Charlene. "Slavery, Nativism, and the Forgotten History of Independence Hall." *Pennsylvania History* 67, no. 4 (Autumn 2000): 481–502.

Okur, Nilgun Anadolu. "Underground Railroad in Philadelphia, 1830–1860." *Journal of Black Studies* 25, no. 5 (May 1995): 537–57.

"Opinion of Judge Kane, United States of America, ex Relatione Wheeler, vs. Williamson." Reprint of *American Law Register* IV, November, 1855, 1–19.

Pease, Jane H., and William H. Pease. "Confrontation and Abolition in the 1850s." *Journal of American History* 58, no. 4 (March 1972): 923–37.

Pease, William H., and Jane H. Pease. "Antislavery Ambivalence: Immediatism, Expediency, Race." *American Quarterly* 17 (Winter 1965): 682–95.

"Philadelphia Neighborhoods and Place Names, L–P. http://www.phila.gov/ phils/docs/otherinfo/pname2.htm. September 6, 2006.

Powell, Pamela C. "The Case of Passmore Williamson." *The Daguerreian Annual 2000*, 124–35.

Schnell, Kempes. "Anti-Slavery Influence on the Status of Slaves in a Free State." *Journal of Negro History* 50, no. 4 (October 1965): 257–73.

"Slavery in the Courts." Association of the Bar of the City of New York City, 2005. http://www.nycbar.org/Library/FeaturedExhibitions2.htm March 13, 2006.

Stone, Witmer. "Charles Sumner Williamson." Uncredited reprint from *Bartonia* for 1914, 1–4.

Tate, Gayle T. "Free Black Resistance in the Antebellum Era, 1830 to 1860." *Journal of Black Studies* 28, no. 6 (July 1998): 764–82.

Toogood, Anna Coxe. "Underground Railroad and Anti-Slavery Movement," National Register Amendment, Independence National Historic Park, September 2000. http://www.nps.gov/inde/archeology/nramend.htm. September 6, 2006.

Turner, Edward Raymond. "The Underground Railroad in Pennsylvania." *Pennsylvania Magazine of History and Biography* 36 (1912): 309–18.

Wahl, Albert J. "The Pennsylvania Yearly Meeting of Progressive Friends." *Pennsylvania History* 25, no. 2 (Spring 1958): 128–38.

Washington, Linn, Jr. "The Chronicle of an American First Family." William Still Underground RR Foundation, Inc., n.d.

Winch, Julie. "Philadelphia and the Other Underground Railroad." *Pennsylvania Magazine of History and Biography* 111, no. 1 (January 1987): 3–25.

Newspapers and Periodicals

Christian Recorder
Daily Pennsylvanian
Delaware County Republican
Evening Journal (Albany, N.Y.)
Frederick Douglass' Paper
Friends' Intelligencer and Journal
National Anti-Slavery Standard
National Era
New York Daily Times
New York Tribune
Philadelphia City Bulletin
Philadelphia Public Ledger
Philadelphia Sunday Dispatch
Provincial Freeman

Dissertations

Sawin, Mark Horst. "Raising Kane: The Making of a Hero, the Marketing of a Celebrity. " Master's thesis, University of Texas at Austin, 1997.

Williams, Carolyn Luverne. "Religion, Race, and Gender in Antebellum American Radicalism: The Philadelphia Female Anti-Slavery Society, 1833–1870." PhD diss., University of California, Los Angeles, 1991.

Lectures

Densmore, Christopher. "Be Ye Perfect: Anti-Slavery and the Progressive Friends of Chester County, Pennsylvania." Friends Historical Association, Philadelphia, November 11, 2002.

Pinsker, Matthew, "William Still and the History of the Underground Railroad." Central Pennsylvania Consortium Conference, Dickinson College, February 24, 2003.

INDEX